The Violence Formula

The Violence Formula

*Why People Lend Sympathy and
Support to Terrorism*

by

TERRELL E. ARNOLD

Lexington Books

D.C. Heath and Company • Lexington, Massachusetts • Toronto

Library of Congress Cataloging-in-Publication Data

Arnold, Terrell E.
The violence formula.

Includes index.
1. Terrorism. 2. Violence. 3. Asylum, Right of. I. Title.
HV6431.A763   1988   322.4'2   86-45292
ISBN 0-669-13153-9 (alk. paper)

Published simultaneously in Canada
Printed in the United States of America
International Standard Book Number: 0-669-13153-9
Library of Congress Catalog Card Number: 86-45292

The paper used in this publication meets
the minimum requirements of American National Standard
for Information Sciences—Permanence of Paper
for Printed Library Materials, ANSI Z39.48-1984.

ISBN 0-669-13153-9

88 89 90 91 92 8 7 6 5 4 3 2 1

To
YVONNE:
patient supporter,
critic, and editor, but most of
all beloved wife.

Contents

Introduction

I BECAME deeply interested in the issues that form this book on the campus at the University of California, Berkeley, in 1964–65. Lyndon Johnson and Barry Goldwater were contending for the presidency. Ronald Reagan was making the Goldwater campaign speeches that brought him into national prominence as a conservative spokesman. The Vietnam War was heating up. And brewing out of a not yet articulate discontent with that war was Berkeley's Free Speech movement. The movement's pattern of protest against U.S. military involvement in Indochina would be put in every living room by electronic media, and it would be mirrored across the nation and abroad on university campuses. In the afternoons and evenings, when my heavy graduate study program in economics permitted, I visited around the campus and watched.

Also roaming the campus at that time was a remarkable intellect, a self-educated philosopher-longshoreman named Eric Hoffer. He, much earlier than I, had become interested in the dynamics and the psychology as well as the substance of activist movements, and he had summed up his thoughts in a book called *The True Believer*. That book provided the most penetrating assessment I have yet read on the chemistry of activism and protest. As I read Hoffer I gained insights into the events unfolding before my eyes at Berkeley, insights that have helped shape the themes of this book.

My own firsthand experiences with protest at that stage included two years in Egypt as a U.S. embassy officer during Gamal Abdel Nasser's romance with the Congo and Patrice Lumumba's regime in Stanleyville. In Cairo, my wife and I lived in an apartment on the island of Zamalik in the Nile, and our building also contained the Cuban embassy. Not long after we moved in we learned that Egyptian students looking for a politically safe place to sound off had discovered that it was not only okay but encouraged by Nasser for them to meet in front of the Cuban embassy and protest U.S. policy toward Cuba, the Congo, and the Middle East. Looking down from a neighbor's apartment on a swirling sea of heads, as I did several times, I saw just how quickly the mood of such a crowd could turn from civil disobedience to violence. In those watches, maintained to support the U.S. embassy's political reporting, I also came to appreciate just how easily such a crowd, once formed for whatever purpose, could be manipulated by someone with very different objectives from those the organizers may have had in mind.

That experience in Egypt was followed by two years in Calcutta during the first major postindependence resurgence of Hindu-Muslim communal violence. The lesson of that experience was that the people who lived in grinding poverty and existed under subhuman living conditions and who, on the face of things, seemed to have the best reasons for taking their grievances to the streets were not usually the ones who threw the Molotov cocktails. Rather, the choice of violence seemed to come out of a higher, more affluent stratum. That tour at the U.S. consulate general, Calcutta, also provided a continuing exposure to protest activities of the University of Calcutta, a campus bred of the volatile intellectual traditions of the Bengalis, and there the way patterns of campus protest were spreading like a global fad became very apparent. An assignment to Berkeley, ironically, was meant to provide a quiet retreat from all that ferment, but what it provided instead was an intense exposure to the birth pangs of a growing decision-making procedure: coercive bargaining by protest and confrontation.

The immense attractiveness of the protest habits that had spread on American campuses was brought home further by the activities of Ceylonese students during a tour in Colombo in 1969–70. This was the period of Sirimavo Bandaranaike's surprisingly successful effort to win the premiership from the conservative party of Dudley Senannayake, who by most analysts, including myself, was considered a shoo-in. Campus unrest played a significant role in driving Sri Lanka toward the radical left, a trend that Mrs. Bandaranaike, whatever her intentions, was ultimately unable to control. The backlash overturned her government.

By the time we arrived in Manila in the summer of 1971, those now familiar protest habits had become well established in the Philippines, and we were just in time for a year of intense protest and political party warfare that set the stage for Ferdinand Marcos's declaration of martial law. In Manila it became clear to me that the Philippines, even with more than a generation of experience with a democratic political system, was not equipped to achieve a broader political consensus than it had. The political consensus procedure in effect at the time was described to me as "rudimentary pork barrel enforced by private armies," but a young generation of technocrats was learning and for their ages and numbers having tremendous impact on decisions. Today some of those men are seasoned cabinet officers in Corazon Aquino's government, but at the time Philippine politics was a game gone amok. All the protest strategies, from mass rallies and marches by students to hand grenade attacks on the opposition by unknown perpetrators, were tried in a few short months. The outcome was martial law and at least a decade more of government by Marcos than more moderate approaches would ever have delivered. The fact that Marcos's opponents went outside the system to try to bring him down made it seem justifiable for him to go outside the system to respond.

After almost five years as an observer in the Philippines, I was assigned by the State Department in early 1976 as a senior foreign service inspector. At that time we did so-called conduct of relations inspections, which meant that the teams I led were expected to look at U.S. policy toward each country as well as to evaluate the performance of the U.S. embassies. Thus, during the next three years I was able to test all my emergent theories about political protest and the consequences of this procedure on the staffs and leadership of twenty-six U.S. diplomatic missions in such diverse areas as Britain, Ireland, Japan, Brazil, Argentina, and sixteen sub-Saharan African countries, including Nigeria, Ghana, Ethiopia, Kenya, Tanzania, and Zambia.

This exposure led me deeper into examining the violent end of protest: terrorism and insurgency. Looking at Uruguay, where the Tupamaros had virtually destroyed a democracy, and at Argentina, where the clash with the Montaneros had cut deep rifts in political consensus, I could see very clearly the price a society can pay for dissent and official responses when both go out of control. The burned-out war machines that I saw scattered across the Ibo tribal (Biafran) region of Nigeria starkly symbolized that reality.

The spread of terrorism and insurgency in the early 1980s said that something was woefully sour about the way many societies were making decisions. There were other danger signals as well. In the U.S. government, all national policy decisions appeared to be growing harder and harder to make. The greatest and most continuous democratic experiment in the world was in trouble because it could not make lasting decisions. The useful life of major decisions, especially on controversial issues, was becoming shorter. And the reason to me was clear: protest strategies were emerging as an alternative to institutional decision making.

Protest strategies begin with lobbying by groups and individuals of the institutional decision forums, the Congress, and state or local legislative bodies and executive authorities. If the decision favors those groups and individuals, fine. If not, they increasingly take their causes to the streets. A side step can also occur here. Dealing with bureaucrats is often frustrating; they are not always prepared or necessarily empowered to do what people want done, and since taking the case to the media and the street is more exciting, people often bypass the institutional approaches.

The two-part strategy is one I encountered in the doctrine of revolutionaries abroad. The New People's Army in the Philippines provided a good example of it in late 1986 when it informed Corazon Aquino's government in effect that its members would seek to participate in the political process as a way of achieving power but would not renounce the right to armed struggle. In short, they have announced their intent to turn the Philippine government into a Marxist regime by fair means or foul, and anyone who is concerned about the political future of that country has been duly warned.

Protest and civil disobedience are conventionally seen as powers reserved to the people. In the separation of governing functions within American society, those powers became a Fifth Estate, after the executive, legislative, and judicial branches of government, and the media. They act as a hedge against the failure of institutions and leadership. They provide a way, in short, of correcting the course when the ship of state wanders. In the past few decades, however, those powers have become the central outlets for a growing urge of the people to participate. In that context, the question posed by the increasing diversity of American society, in which practically every individual group is a minority, is how much protest and civil disobedience can the system handle? What are the issues on which resort to these powers is reasonable? What are the ground rules?

Setting limits on protest becomes terribly important in light of the visible merging of the strategies of peaceful protest, civil disobedience, terrorism, and insurgency. This is the violence formula, and use of it is growing. I have already seen signs that peace groups in Europe, more out of naiveté than design, have made common cause with terrorists in an effort to defeat the deployment of Pershing II and cruise missiles as part of the Western European NATO defense commitment. Such evidence as the use of a common vocabulary has suggested a linkup between the Red Army Faction and the Greens. In this case, even from across the Atlantic one could see that the desire of the Greens and other peace groups to defeat deployment of intermediate nuclear forces was leading them to avoid questioning the motives of others who chose to join in the movement. The desire for help in a cause that looked noble generated a blinding expediency.

In the United States a near miss on such a linkup occurred in the 1970s, when the SDS (Students for a Democratic Society) tore itself apart on the issue of foreign involvement and the uses of violence. Unfortunately, the breakup of SDS left East and West Coast fragments of the Weather Underground, a terrorist organization, in its wake.

The convergence of protest decision strategies became increasingly apparent to me during 1981–85 while I worked first as chairman of the Department of International Studies at the National War College and then as deputy director of the Office of Counterterrorism in the State Department. In the latter job, intelligence on terrorist and insurgent activities and threats was provided in a daily briefing. Protest in Europe, observed through the combined lenses of media and intelligence, provided a case model for the pattern of convergence.

Protest in Europe also provided insights into another important source of linkages, the concern of many people about global issues. The global issues (poverty, hunger, human crowding, human rights, and the environment) provide a natural set of rallying points for people seriously concerned about trends in the human condition. People who try to make constructive contributions in dealing with any of these issues are on the side of the angels almost anywhere in the West. One has to listen very carefully to the rhetoric people use, however, because the language used by terrorists has often been crafted around the terms we use to describe our best motives. What is said in self-justification by an IRA gunman who kneecaps a juror in Belfast or by a Hezballah terrorist who kidnaps the American University librarian in Beirut may sound very like what is said by a peace marcher in Washington.

As the language of protest has developed and spread, it has assumed the country-to-country sameness of an international patois. A troublesome aspect of that sameness is that it becomes easy to slip from one plane of protest to another without noticing exactly where you are. The media, particularly electronic, have helped to encourage this condition by adopting a "looks the same, sounds the same, is the same" kind of equalizer in the language they use to cover the news. In part this impression is created by the very summary coverage of most news stories; short words, short sentences, and brief reports do not give the reporter much room for nuance. That sort of blandness about violence leaves an impression that everybody does it, therefore there must be some justification for it.

There is an echo of that cynicism and lack of nuance in the attitudes of many protesters. Almost any organizer of a protest rally or a march will tell you that you should keep the propositions and the signs simple. If the ideas are too complicated they will not have appeal, either to the protesters or to the media. Unfortunately, that simplicity breeds a set of ideas that is intolerant, that closes the mind, and tends to move the holder of the ideas toward extreme positions. The natural push of this mindset is toward confrontation, and if the boundary marking the resort to violence is unclear, the choice of violence becomes relatively easy to make.

The claim that "everybody does it" has a frightening ring when we look at the extremist groups in the United States. Rightist groups, notably the KKK White Patriots Party, the Aryan Nations, the Order, and others, have adopted an aggressive-defensive posture on use of terrorist violence to avoid change or intrusion in their life-styles. Leftist and special interest groups, including the Weather Underground, the Puerto Rican nationalists, and ethnic terrorists such as the Armenian Secret Army for the Liberation of Armenia, use violence in immediately destructive ways that do not appear to serve any very clear future goals. Since the United States now has about the largest cluster of ethnic groups and subcultures on earth, permitting any groups to maintain or train private armies can create a potentially explosive situation. Moreover, the extremist models encourage other ethnic or cultural groups to adopt violence to defend their own boundaries.

As I began the preparations for writing this book, I also became aware of the increasing use of political violence as the centerpiece of prime-time television. As terrorist attacks grew in number and intensity through the early 1980s, it became fashionable for even the soap operas to play on the theme of terrorist attacks. The regular violence programs, such as "Magnum P.I.," "MacGyver," "The Equalizer," and "Spenser for Hire," gave political violence about equal billing with ordinary crime. Playing right to the heart of this trend, during a major terrorist incident one terrorist is reported to have said, "Don't shoot now. We're not on prime time."

All of these currents in the flow of information and the development of attitudes about violence are causing a steady erosion of the boundary between violent and nonviolent means for promoting change. Adoption of the concept of liberation theology by elements of the Roman Catholic clergy in Latin America and elsewhere has only hastened that erosion; the idea has gained substantial following as well among Protestant groups, particularly those affiliated with the so-called Sanctuary movement. Moral and legal restraints on the resort to violence, therefore, are being loosened by persistent assault from many directions.

I have set out in this book to map the dynamics and some of the consequences of the socializing of violent methodologies. The trend should scare us, because it has immense capacity for setting aside and then unraveling our most sacred institutions, and by those I mean very specifically the ones that protect our right to be ourselves.

To prevent that, we must learn to make and to defend critical distinctions. There are material differences, and we know it, between what a democracy does to defend itself and what democracy's enemies do to overturn it. It is foolish genorosity to act as if the two sets of responses are the same and thereby to legitimate the ambitions of large and small tyrannies in many parts of the world. Democracies must operate within the law, to be sure, and for that we need clear definitions. In particular we need definitions of crime that do not shift with the identities and the motives of the doers; we need definitions of terrorism that do not change because we either like or dislike the cause of the user. In a society of extreme plurality, we must distinguish among issues that represent genuine matters of human and civil liberty and issues that represent mere preferences of individuals and groups.

I know that before this book ever gets out of my computer there will be enormous resistance to the idea that the liberties we enjoy in the late twentieth century must be surrounded by norms and personal disciplines or we will destroy them and probably ourselves. There have been great books written to deliver dire warnings about the tyranny of the state. Aldous Huxley's *Brave New World* painted one picture of overorganization that may have a budding modern counterpart only in the People's Republic of China. George Orwell painted another, supposed to mature in 1984, that would represent the ultimate refinement of state control.

Neither of those visions, in my judgment, portrays the most serious threat to human liberty on our crowded planet. That threat lies with our increasing inability to live with one another at close range, specifically, the decline in our ability to agree on stable, working relationships. Such agreements are essential for us to enjoy the maximum possible liberty while assuring that others enjoy an equal share. That takes understanding; it takes restraint; it takes discipline; and it takes continuing processes of adjustment and compromise. This book ends up placing the highest priority on promoting those attitudes and skills, because achieving and sustaining them is the alternative to the violence formula.

1

Terrorism:
The War of Definitions

O N September 5, 1986, four hijackers took over Pan Am Flight 073 in Karachi, Pakistan, and on September 6, 1986, a group of young Palestinians attacked a synagogue in Istanbul, Turkey. These attacks provoked Pope John Paul II to say "It is necessary, without delay, to do everything possible to put an end to the incessant escalation of hatred and terrorism." Addressing a worldwide audience in a satellite-relayed telecast, the pope seems to have felt that he could speak with confidence that people everywhere would understand his use of the word *terrorism*.

In a not entirely facetious effort to define the word, Brian Jenkins, the eminent terrorism expert of the Rand Corporation, once said to me and others in a conference, "Terrorism is what the bad guys do." That judgmental definition imparts a warm, cozy feeling because it suggests that the people we like are not terrorists, even though they may be blowing up somebody's neighborhood. But we cannot dismiss the problem so easily and leave the meaning of the word entirely at the mercy of the user. Defining terrorism is essential to determining who is a terrorist. Only after defining the term can we make or defend policies concerning what to do about terrorism and about terrorists.[1] So, since the purpose of this book is to challenge people on sensitive values, beliefs, and causes they support, I feel an obligation to define up front the subject I intend to talk about throughout the book.

A Working Definition

In the September 1986 issue of *Harper's*, Christopher Hitchens calls me a nice guy for admitting that I do not have a universally accepted definition of terrorism. He then deplores at length the notion that many people, particularly in the Reagan administration, use the term as if they know what it means, but no one, he complains, really has a working definition.[2] As he said, I admit that I cannot give a universally acceptable definition, but I do have a working definition. Judging from my talks with business, professional, religious, and academic audiences throughout the United States, most people have a working definition. So does practically every journalist who comments on the subject when a terrorist incident dominates television prime time and the headlines.

Terrorism, the generic term, was defined decades ago in *Webster's New Collegiate Dictionary* as "a mode of governing, or of opposing government, by intimidation." The origins of this usage, says the dictionary, lie in the tactics of supporters of the revolutionary tribunal during the 1793–94 Reign of Terror in France, and in the methods of opponents of the czarist rulers of Russia.[3] Implicit in both historic instances is the fact that the motives for terrorism were normally political.

Terrorism, as it has evolved during the past two decades, has developed more specific meaning. During 1984 congressional hearings on terrorism legislation, building on dictionary efforts, I read a definition for the record in an attempt to recognize the changing content of the term:

> Terrorism is the use or threatened use of violence for a political purpose to create a state of fear which will aid in extorting, coercing, intimidating or causing individuals and groups to alter their behavior.[4]

To flesh out this definition, I went on to explain that

> A terrorist group does not need a defined territorial base or specific organizational structure. Its goals need not relate to any one country. It does not require nor necessarily seek a popular basis of support. Its operations, organization and movements are secret. Its activities do not conform to the rules of law or warfare. Its targets are civilians, non-combatants, bystanders, or symbolic persons and places. Its victims generally have no role in either causing or correcting the grievance of the terrorists. Its methods are hostage-taking, aircraft piracy or sabotage, assassination, threats, hoaxes, and indiscriminate bombings or shootings.

Then, to highlight the international aspects of the problem, I added,

> Terrorism is international when the victims, the actors, the location of a terrorist incident, or the means used to carry out the act involve more than one country.[5]

I quickly found that people had a problem with my definition; they thought it was too long. People like short, crisp, unambiguous terms for something that bothers them as much as terrorism does. To meet that demand, I reduced my definition to two sentences:

> Terrorism is the use or threatened use of violence for a political purpose to create a state of fear that will aid in extorting, coercing, intimidating, or causing individuals and groups to alter their behavior. Its methods are hostage taking, piracy or sabotage, assassination, threats, hoaxes, and indiscriminate bombings or shootings.

"Better," people said, "but still not short enough."

As a consultant to the vice president's Task Force on Combating Terrorism, in late 1985 I helped tackle the definition problem again. Large parts of the definition I had used in statements before both House and Senate committees made it into the vice president's public report on the work of the task force, but the result was still not a short, handy definition. "Terrorism," states the report, "is a phenomenon that is easier to describe than define."[6] That was a good start, but the Task Force could not find a neat, short phrase that embraced all aspects of this complex subject.

Years ago, when I was a student in a high school science course, my teacher defined electricity by saying, "Electricity is what it does!" That evening I used the definition sagely on my father, a self-taught technician in radio and electrical systems, and he retorted, "I know a great deal about what electricity does, but I still don't know what it is, and neither does your teacher." It was clear that my teacher's effort to define behaviorally was not very persuasive, even with someone who had a lot of examples already in his head.

In the case of terrorism, nonetheless, the subject actually lends itself readily to definition by example; the best path to a working definition appears to be through behavior; and a good place to start is with what people as a rule think terrorists do. There has been no debate, for instance, on media use of the term *terrorism* to describe the following cases:

> The 1978 kidnapping and murder of former Italian premier Aldo Moro by members of the Italian Red Brigades

> The January 1982 assassination of a Turkish consul in Los Angeles by a member of the Armenian group JCAG, the Justice Commandos of the Armenian Genocide

The April 1983 bombing of the U.S. embassy in Beirut by members of the group called Islamic Jihad, or the Islamic holy war

The October 1983 bombing of the Martyr's Shrine in Rangoon, Burma, by members of the North Korean armed forces

The December 1983 bombing of Harrod's department store by members of the Irish Republican Army, (IRA)

The 1984–87 series of kidnappings of more than a dozen Americans and others by members of Islamic Jihad calling themselves Hezballah, or Party of Allah

The June 1985 hijacking of TWA Flight 847 by Hezballah

The August 1985 kidnapping of an American businessman in Bogotá, Colombia, by the 19th of April movement

The October 1985 hijacking of the Italian cruise ship *Achille Lauro* by members of the Palestine Liberation Front

The December 1985 grenade and machine gun attacks at the Rome and Vienna airports by members of the Libya-based Abu Nidal group

The 1986 in-flight sabotage of TWA Flight 840 by members of the Palestinian extremist group called 15 May.

I have cited a large number of cases here to show that it is possible to build a cluster of examples around an unequivocal central concept of terrorism. The American media have reported these and countless other politically motivated violent crimes as acts of terrorism, and their use of the term has not been challenged by the public; nor should it be. The cases are clear-cut.

The Conflict of Values

The problem Christopher Hitchins and many other people are struggling with is not a lack of definition. It is a question of values. In the past few years I have made many speeches to audiences in widely scattered parts of the United States and abroad, and I have responded to questions on all aspects of terrorism. Hardly anybody in my audiences ever asks me to tell them what terrorism is. The people who ask me to define my terms as a rule are not quibbling with me about what terrorism is; they are prepared to argue with me about what it means.

The conflict of values arises over what such incidents mean and what should be done with, to, or about the perpetrators. As an Italian judge said in rendering his first verdict against the *Achille Lauro* hijackers, they had "a just cause," but it was "flawed by bad means." President Zia-al-Haq of Pakistan made similar comments about the young Palestinians who hijacked Pan Am Flight 073 on September 5, 1986. In the *Achille Lauro* case, the clear judicial distinction between means and ends obviously carried over into the court's final judgment, wherein the hijackers were found guilty but received comparatively mild sentences, given that one of their crimes was the murder of a passenger, an American, Leon Klinghoffer.

The distinction between means and ends drawn by the Italian judge is the crux of the problem of defining terrorism. Failure to recognize that terrorism is a means, a violent tool, of political extremists causes the term to carry a lot of unnecessary freight. And people bring a lot of their own freight to the word. For example, when I read the definition of terrorism into the record of Sen. Jeremy Denton's subcommittee of the Senate Judiciary Committee, the senator very graciously referred to my statement as "brilliant." Senator Denton's statements on this and other occasions have shown clearly that he is concerned about terrorism as a means. However, when I read the same definition into the record of the House Foreign Affairs Committee, Subcommittee on Government Operations, Congressman Stephen Solarz suggested, in effect, that I had misplaced some of my marbles. His questions and those of other members of the committee about the use of the term *terrorists* to describe members of the African National Congress or the Irish Republican Army made it clear that they were more interested in the ends being pursued by these groups.[7]

Those objecting to my definition generally are more interested in ends than in means, and their arguments suggest that they do not want any label attached to the means being used by groups they favor or support which would interfere with the activities of those groups.

Keeping the label from interfering with what they want to do or what they support is a driving urge among the people who seem to have most trouble with the definition of terrorism. They try to avoid the label because they know very well that the word *terrorism* sends out strong negative signals.

Those negative signals are reliable and easy to use. The Sandinista regime in Nicaragua, for example, has spent millions of dollars on propaganda in the United States to argue that (1) their repressive actions against their own Nicaraguan people do not constitute terrorism, and that (2) the insurgent activities of anti-Sandinista Nicaraguans, the so-called contras, do constitute terrorism. The reason Sandinista leaders find the financial costs of this strategy palatable is that they know they can rely on the average person's definition of terrorism to do most of the work for them; if they can pin the label *terrorist* on their opponents, Sandinista propaganda strategists think that they will not need to explain what the term means. And they are right.

The arguments can continue regarding particular groups and whether they are legitimate, or over given causes and whether they are just. Indeed, this is the ground on which much of the debate arises about the legitimacy of U.S. support for the Afghan rebels, the contras, and Jonas Savimbi's National Union for the Total Independence of Angola (UNITA), or on the other hand about U.S. official opposition to the activities of the African National Congress and other groups such as the Faribundo Martí National Liberation Front in El Salvador. But what kept Americans off airplanes going to Europe in the summer of 1986 was not a debate about terrorist motives; it was a clear recognition of their means. The roster of cases I cited earlier has become part of the average person's meaning for the word. As a result, to borrow a phrase from the English classical economist, Alfred Marshall, a basic understanding of what terrorism is has become part of "the common property of all sensible people."[8]

Knowing what terrorism is, we may yet be far from knowing what to do about it. At least we can stop pretending, however, that the definition of the deed is in any sense elusive. It is not.

Terrorist Motivations

Defining terrorism as a means confronts us squarely with the problem of terrorist motives. It is very easy to attribute all terrorist activity to some "root cause." However, we must be careful not to impute our own motives to the terrorists, because in our efforts to define we tend to simplify greatly. In a good deal of the verbal milling around over definitions that occurs in both the print and electronic media, one gets the impression that all terrorists are interested in overthrowing the government. Some are, but people who set out to overthrow a government forcibly are usually called either insurgents or revolutionaries. They may use terrorism as a means. Whether they are terrorists, mostly terrorists, mostly insurgents, or insurgents depends on what they do, not on what they want, nor on what they say.

In any case, there is no simple way to make that judgment, because terrorists' reasons for doing what they do make up a varied list of immediate, intermediate, and long-term objectives. Some of the common goals appear in the following list; particular groups or individuals pursuing a specific goal are shown in parentheses:

Money (narcoterrorists or insurgent groups FARC and M-19 in Colombia)

Power (terrorism-sponsoring states and active insurgencies)

Suppressing political opposition (Botha, Castro, Marcos, Ortega, Pinochet, Qaddafi)

Achieving political or social change (the Weather Underground)

Avoiding political or social change (the Aryan Nations)

Settling a political grievance (the Armenian groups JCAG and ASALA)

Promoting a way of life (the sheriff's Posse Comitatus)

Supporting a cause (abortion clinic bombers)

Getting another terrorist out of jail (Hezballah, or Islamic Jihad)

Staying out of jail (Georges Ibraham Abdallah and brothers)

Helping a friend or client on any of the above (Action Directe, Abu Nidal)

Terrorist motives change from time to time, of course, because terrorist groups are living structures for which a dominant motive is survival. That requires money, some power and influence, safe haven, weapons, and life support arrangements, the desire for any of which can spur a terrorist group to plan and carry out an attack.

Not surprisingly, the varied motivations of terrorists cause people to try to distinguish among acts, and there are important distinctions to be drawn. As an illustration, during 1983–84 there was a spate of hijackings to Cuba. These cases normally involved one or more members of the group known as the Marielitos, the term widely used to describe Cubans who escaped the country by boat during 1979. Individual boat people grew homesick and chose aircraft hijacking as their means for returning to Cuba. As the number of such hijackings increased, a debate developed among the State Department, Central Intelligence Agency, Federal Aviation Administration, Federal Bureau of Investigation, and other federal agency members of the Interdepartmental Group on Terrorism over how to treat data on the Marielito hijackings. Arguing against counting these attacks as terrorism, CIA representatives made the point that the actions of a homesick Cuban who seeks to return home or of a disaffected Pole who seeks asylum in the West are not motivationally like such hijackings as the 1985 takeover of TWA Flight 847 or more recently of Pan Am Flight 073. FAA representatives argued, with support from others, that the cases must be dealt with in much the same way, regardless of any distinctions one may draw respecting motivations. While recognizing that the distinction drawn by the CIA was not unimportant, government strategists had to work with the broader definition, because it is their responsibility to protect passengers, crews, aircraft, and bystanders from hijackings, irrespective of the motives of the hijackers. CIA representatives in this discussion were not quibbling over the definition of the acts involved; they were arguing about the weight that should be attached to motives.

In looking at the reasons for terrorist actions we encounter some rather broad assumptions. For example, "individuals and groups have the right to fight, if necessary, for their freedom," states Charles William Maynes, the editor of *Foreign Policy* magazine,[9] but does that hold true no matter what is the grievance and regardless of the nature or the track record of the government being attacked? It obviously does not, but the definitional confusion about who is a terrorist starts with this kind of generalization. Maynes lists some criteria in this article, however, that are essential to keeping one's values straight about what is terrorism and what is not:

"Acts of violence in a struggle for freedom should be directed against agents of the oppressive government, not against innocent civilians"

"The struggle should be confined to the territory" [of the actor and the offending government]

"Means should be appropriate to ends"[10]

Insurgency versus Terrorism

By applying the criteria supplied by Maynes, we can distinguish between terrorist crime and legitimate warfare. To help that process along, during the congressional committee hearings mentioned earlier I read a definition of insurgency into the record. It began with another dictionary approach:

Insurgency is a state of revolt against an established government. An insurgent group has a defined organization, leadership and location. Its members wear a uniform. Its objectives are acquisition of political power, achievement of participation in economic or political opportunity and national leadership or, ultimately, taking power from existing leadership. Its primary interests relate to one country. Its methods are military and paramilitary. Its targets are military, both tactical and strategic, and its legitimate operations are governed by the international rules of armed conflict. It operates in the open, and it actively seeks a basis of popular support.[11]

This definition of insurgency rules out practically everything that terrorists routinely do. Most conflicts of values arise when insurgents start using terrorist tactics because they are losing, they are in a hurry, or they think no one will notice that they have suddenly stopped behaving like revolutionaries and have become criminals. A widespread failure to distinguish between categories of violence is of immense help to the terrorists; it permits them to use the cover of an insurgency to commit acts of terrorism without having their legitimacy stripped away.

Well-established views on the role of violence in modern society are far from helpful in enforcing the distinction between terrorism and insurgency. Many people accept the notion that all sorts of grievances accumulate in this life, and if one cannot find some nonviolent form of redress, the path of violence is always open. Prime-time television uses this reasoning as a standard plot device, and to be sure, as revealed in half-hour episodes, the distinctions among declared war, guerrilla warfare, ordinary crime, coercive business practices, physical cruelty within the household, and terrorism are sometimes glossed over and left very unclear.

Television, the movies, old-time radio shows, and the detective story have all more or less cultivated a philosophy of violence that has as its central premise, if the bad guys do it it's bad, but if the good guys do it you must wait to see how things turn out before condemning them. Just maybe, in the end, the hero who did something that is recognized by all to be horribly criminal will prove to have done so for such a good reason that the crime is seen to be forgivable.

Through countless scenarios of this type the judgment is elaborated and reinforced that only people we dislike use terrorism. The other version of that is the much-roasted old chestnut, "One man's terrorist is another man's freedom fighter." Both of these statements are efforts to rationalize or apologize for the terrorists, and they have, to me, a remarkable capacity for turning off the mind, for stopping people from thinking about the implications of terrorist violence by attributing to such attacks a superficial kind of normalcy.

The idea that such violent outbursts are normal leads far too easily into the notion that all forms of political violence are the same. They are not. One should be able to distinguish between, for example, the insurgent attacks of the Afghan people against the Soviet troops who occupy their country, and an attack by those same rebels on shoppers in a Kabul market, or the explosion of a bomb in Harrod's department store in London, which is explained by the IRA as part of its effort to expunge Protestantism along with the British from Northern Ireland.

Terrorism Carries Weight Anyway

Despite the apparent impediments to general agreement on a definition of terrorism, the term carries great weight. In heated argument on particular cases, I have heard individuals come close to saying, "I really don't want to admit that the act you speak of is terrorism, because if I do admit that, I will have to condemn the act." The individual saying that recognizes clearly that keeping the terrorism label off actions is essential to avoid being caught supporting a dubious cause. On the other hand, pinning the terrorism label on what someone else does is a potent propaganda weapon. It goes without saying that such a game is very difficult to play if one does not know what terrorism is. If you are going to play, you must have a working definition of *terrorism* that runs up the old antenna whenever necessary and lets you know that you are about to come out on the wrong side.

Hostage Reactions to Terrorist Motives

The way some former hostages describe their reactions to former captors often reveals a deep emotional dimension to the conflict of values. Why terrorists do what they do and how they got that way are questions that engage a great deal of the emotional energy of former hostages and members of their families. Former Iran hostage Moorhead Kennedy developed an elaborate conception of his captors and their thought processes during his 444 days of captivity, and he interprets the terrorist to the public in his speeches and writings.[12] Jeremy Levin came back home in February 1985, after having escaped from Hezballah, to say that he harbored no ill will toward his former captors; the Reverend Benjamin Weir made a similar statement on his return, and Fr. Lawrence Martin Jenco was reported by family members to have said a number of times that he forgave his captors. We have heard this reaction described as the "Stockholm syndrome," but there is more to it than that.

Strong values obviously drive such charitable impulses. Jerry Levin and his wife, Lucille (called "Sis"), are both deeply religious people. Jerry came out of captivity saying that he, until then of Jewish faith, had become a Christian as a result of studying the New Testament closely during his long confinement. The Levins were drawn to the Middle East, to Beirut, by a nearly missionary urge to be helpful. The Reverend Weir, who had lived for decades in the region and considered it home, and Father Jenco had both demonstrated a compassionate spirit and a willingness to work with and help the troubled people of Lebanon. Being willing to forgive the people who confined them against their will, for more than a year in each case, would come quite naturally to these three former hostages.

Their acts of forgiveness, however, take as a given the fact that each was the victim of a sustained act of terrorism. The conditions of captivity leave no doubt of this. What each has focused on instead is how he wants to feel about the experience and how he wants others to see it. I am not a psychologist, but I would say that there is a psychic healing process at work here. Forgiving the terrorists seems to be an essential part of it, but there is no argument that the crime was terrorism.

Terrorists and their sponsors count on such emotions to help their causes. Their objective is to get onlookers to see their actions in motivational terms, to look at and be swayed by the merit of their cases, rather than to be turned away by the brutality of their methods.

A Declining Strategy

The chances that an act of terrorism will succeed in meeting the terrorist's objective depend ultimately on the act's being seen by observers as something other than terrorism. In the great majority of incidents in recent years, the terrorists have failed on that score, and the propaganda support of their sponsors has not been sufficient to overcome the imagery of crime. Perhaps recognizing this fact, the hard-core extremists such as Abu Nidal gave up drawn-out events, such as hijackings accompanied by specific demands, in favor of short, sharp attention getters like acts of sabotage and bombing. These deliver a message without getting caught up in negotiating situations that involve a high risk of misinterpretation, failure, capture, and death.

Yasir Arafat and the leadership of the Palestine Liberation Organization (PLO) core organization have had to face the fact, demonstrated by public reactions to attacks in the 1980s, that they have been losing the battle of perceptions. With such attacks as the *Achille Lauro* hijacking, the bombings at Rome and Vienna airports, and the sabotage of TWA Flight 840, Palestinian terrorist activity become counter productive. The new spate of kidnappings launched by Islamic Jihad in late 1986 was nothing but a closed circle of hostage takings and killings for the sole purpose of getting other terrorists out of jail. By focusing attention almost exclusively on the acts of terrorism themselves, these incidents have deflected real attention away from the long-term Palestine issues and the causes Palestinian terrorists profess to support.

The terrorists who try to get billed as freedom fighters still believe that they have a chance to win hearts and minds, to convince people that what they are doing is not terrorism. They therefore stage high-profile media events such as hostage takings and hijackings. The terrorists of the Abu Nidal school have decided to make their point with the incident itself, accepting the probability that it will be seen as terrorism, but apparently proceeding on the theory that short, specific acts have long-term significance in creating pressure for change. The so-called freedom fighter school of terrorists tries to avoid having the terrorist label pinned on them. The Abu Nidal school does not care.

Avoiding a Double Standard

Democratic governments and peoples have to care. They must pay close attention to what has become the natural freight the word *terrorism* carries. The dispute over U.S. policy in Central America illustrates what happens when people do not squarely face that fact. Since 1981 a sporadic propaganda war has been waged over U.S. official support for the Nicaraguan Democratic Resistance, the contra rebels in Nicaragua. It has become completely predictable that whenever any new legislative proposal on contra aid is about to come to a vote, opponents in the United States, the Soviet Union, Cuba, Nicaragua, and elsewhere make full use of the openness of American society to attack any assistance plan. The charge of terrorism is used by all critics against the contras, and cases are cited. Even though hard evidence—the kind the U.S. government has had to present to justify actions such as the April 14, 1986, raid on Libya—is rarely if ever provided, some people tend to believe the charge, and administration officials have not done nearly enough to present facts to overcome it.

The selective vision people use with regard to terrorism has been a constant feature of the debate over policy toward Central America. Church and other groups involved in the sanctuary movement have used the broadside charge of terrorism frequently against the governments of El Salvador, Guatemala, Honduras, and at times even the United States. On the other hand, these critics have been reluctant to admit the terrorist or other repressive acts of the Sandinistas or of the Salvadoran rebel group, the Faribundo Martí National Liberation Front.

The Moral Questions

Since terrorism is usually considered to be criminal behavior, it seems at least possible that Judeo-Christian moral-ethical teachings would shed some light on definitions. The problem, however, is how to look at the issues without taking sides before you start. In an effort to get at this difficulty, Martha Crenshaw of Wesleyan University suggests in her introductory chapter to the edited work, *Terrorism, Legitimacy and Power*, that one should develop a "neutral" definition of terrorism and then seek to judge whether use of the instrument is legitimate or illegitimate.[13]

According to Crenshaw terrorists use "premeditated and purposeful violence" to achieve political power. She then extends this definition by borrowing a definition from political scientist and author Harold Lasswell, who suggested that terrorists attempt to achieve their goals by "arousing acute anxieties." Terrorism defined in this fashion, Crenshaw continues, can be found in regimes of either democratic or authoritarian types, and it can be judged on a moral basis depending on what means are used and what ends are pursued. She then suggests that terrorists can be considered legitimate or illegitimate depending on the ends they serve. If a terrorist carries out an act that perpetuates or creates a regime of "privilege and inequality," that kind of work is obviously not in the same moral class with tearing down such a regime. If a terrorist act is designed to preserve the community, that act obviously has higher moral weight than an act designed to destroy the community. If an act of terrorism creates a condition of social injustice that is greater than the condition being contested by the terrorist, the moral acceptability of that act is questionable, but presumably not if the act creates a less unjust condition.

The means chosen by the terrorist also make a difference to the morality of the act in Crenshaw's model. If you were an IRA terrorist trying to get the attention of British authority, there would be an important moral difference, in Crenshaw's estimate, between blowing up the statue of Winston Churchill on Massachusetts Avenue in Washington, D.C., and blowing up a hotel in Brighton, England, in an attempt to assassinate Prime Minister Margaret Thatcher and members of her cabinet. Crenshaw then suggests that moral distinctions can be drawn about terrorism depending on whether the victims are decision makers and others such as police officers—people who may be sources of harm to the terrorists—or innocent bystanders, either local or foreign. Thus, she concludes, one can develop a "neutral" definition of terrorism that then permits moral judgments to be made. One can decide whether an act of terrorism is justified depending on how effective it appears to be politically.

I find Crenshaw's effort a noble one, but I wonder how far it really takes us. First, it seems to me that, stripped to the bone, what the Crenshaw model says is that people who espouse libertarian and democratic causes can use terrorism if they don't go too far. Under those rules, what you need to get a license to kill are democratic credentials and a sizable grievance that you think the system won't fix for you by peaceful means. We are back to the good guys and the bad guys. The only claims to legitimacy you need to make are that you are on the side of social justice and democracy, and that your methods are no more severe than what is represented by the grievance you say the system won't fix.

Who Owns *Democracy?*

This logic is a key to Pandora's box, and the troublemakers in that box are propagandists. Terrorism in the Crenshaw model would be a legitimate weapon if used in aid of democratic principles and social justice. It would be illegitimate for any other purpose. That sounds good until you look at the way terms like democracy and social justice are being used in the propaganda warfare of the Soviet Union and of anticolonial, anti-Western regimes. Unfortunately, *democracy* and *social justice* are not copyrighted terms. Anybody can use them and put his own spin on them. The Sandinistas did just that, persuading many of us that they were a democratic alternative to Somoza. Castro did the same and created a repressive dynasty in Cuba. The Sandinistas clearly are bent on doing what Fidel did.

If the word *terrorism* becomes neutral, then the propagandists in the terrorism-sponsoring states and in terrorist groups do not have to worry about being called terrorists. They only have to be concerned about being labeled antidemocratic and anti–social justice. Thus, their job becomes a lot easier, and the job of democracy's defenders becomes a lot harder.

Terrorism as Crime

A neutral definition of terrorism really has no role because the terminology of crime covers the entire waterfront. So far as I'm aware, every known type of terrorist attack is a crime under U.S. law. These acts are considered crimes without reference to the reasons for their commission. The political motive is all that distinguishes terrorism from ordinary crime, and if the political motivation is removed, which in effect it is when the term *terrorism* becomes politically neutral, then we don't need the word to define the problem. This fits the position taken for some time by the Department of Justice and the FBI; all they believe is needed to investigate and prosecute in terrorism cases is a statute making the specific acts a crime under federal law. To specify a political motive and try to deal with terrorism as a separate body of crime would greatly complicate the administration of justice, as these agencies see it.

Defending Yourself

The problem Crenshaw was struggling with is terribly important, and I don't mean to push it aside. How do you get to a position from which you can issue a broadside condemnation of terrorism and still retain the right to defend yourself, your values, friends, and institutions? The correct answer to this question in my view is the law enforcement approach taken by Justice and the FBI. All the acts of terrorists that I cited earlier in this chapter are crimes under the U.S. penal code; they are crimes *no matter who commits them, no matter why they are committed, and no matter who the victims are.* I have read and listened to several attempts to define terrorism so that a police constable in Northern Ireland is a legitimate target, a military command in Germany is a legitimate target, government officials in El Salvador are legitimate targets, and so on. At one point in the 1986 Senate consideration of a United States–British extradition treaty[14] the suggestion was made that somehow a distinction should be drawn between attacks on ordinary citizens and on military personnel or police officers. This idea, fortunately, was quickly squelched.

The obvious point of such an effort is to draw a protective circle around groups the definers like, but the attempt is both reckless and hypocritical. The hypocrisy lies with the fact that we do not define crimes within the American legal system in that calculated and selective fashion, and to protect the rule of law we must not subvert American legal principles in the attempt to cope with crime in other countries.

Selective definition is reckless, of course, because everybody can play that game. A permissive attitude toward violence in a good cause—goodness to be defined by the user or the user's friends and sponsors—is the most dangerous weapon democratic societies can unleash against themselves in the climate of low-level warfare that exists today.

A Better Answer

There is a better answer. National Security Decision Directive 138, signed by President Ronald Reagan in June 1984, has taken a lot of flak from critics who believe that it launched the United States on a proactive response to terrorism.[15] This directive nonetheless puts the issue exactly right in its unclassified preamble by saying that "the US Government considers the practice of terrorism by any person or group in any cause a threat to our national security."[16] This means that U.S. interests are best served by the nation's taking every appropriate action to discourage the resort to terrorism. It also means that American approaches to conflict situations must be kept above reproach. The point is that if we in the United States lack the will to restrain ourselves, we don't have the moral authority to restrain anyone else. If the contras, the Faribundo Marti rebels, or any other group seeking official or private U.S. support engages in terrorism, the United States has two choices: persuade them to stop, or back away. Trying to apply a double standard, to have it both ways, is legally and morally wrong, and it is not sustainable policy for a democracy.

By making that choice, democratic societies are not in any sense stripped of remedies, nor are they rendered defenseless. The United States is well equipped within its own territory to deal with acts of terrorism and terrorist groups through normal exercise of police power. Americans are protected in further broad measure by the fact that American society works to deal with the great majority of people's grievances without resort to violence. The problems are how to cope with attacks in places such as Lebanon where political and social controls have collapsed; how to deal with governments whose leaders now use terrorism as an instrument of state; how to deal with elements within democratic societies that increasingly choose violent methods to advance or defend their causes; and how to keep the sympathies of individuals and groups for favored causes and groups from promoting or sustaining the resort to violence.

These problems provide the elements of the violence formula that is the central concern of this book. Many other countries struggle with these challenges, searching for ways to deal with terrorism while protecting their values and institutions. Our values in the end must tell us what to do, because the definition of terrorism as politically motivated crime is all too clear.

2

Some Place to Hide

"THE United States will go up in flames" if it tries to make war on the Muslims, Imam Mohamed Azi asserted to Walter Cronkite on the nationally televised program, "War in the Shadows."[1] These remarks were not the detached assessments of a terrorism analyst; they were the sober predictions of an Islamic fundamentalist. As Cronkite observed, the imam also has close ties to the Ayatollah Khomeini.

Azi made no bones about where he would stand in the event of collision between the United States and Islam, and that seems entirely explicable until you learn that he is an American citizen. He was speaking from a secure, safe haven in the United States, but his threat was that a "sufficient apparatus" of like-minded Islamic fundamentalists exists in the nation and they would attack this safe haven if the United States were to take any action that "substantially offended" an Islamic country. Some form of reprisal, he said, would be "entirely realistic."[2]

In other words, the Imam Mohamed Azi told Walter Cronkite that the members of the Islamic fundamentalist "apparatus" in the United States would violate one of the oldest principles of political asylum and safe haven: they would attack the country that extended protection to them.

The type of threat made by the imam has turned into reality in countries of Western Europe, and it already has caused European governments to reexamine traditional practices of extending asylum to political dissidents from abroad. It is forcing those governments as well as the United States to develop new approaches to screening travelers at border crossings and to revise their management of border controls.

If such moves continue to gather momentum, political asylum will be one of the late twentieth century casualties of terrorism. With it will go an honored tradition and perhaps one of the great pressure valves of both ancient and modern societies.

Why is such an important and humanitarian gesture in jeopardy? What are Western practices in this field, and how serious are the pressures that are causing governments in some instances to change habits that are centuries old? In order to understand how they might come about, you need some history.

I have an old dictionary, and in looking up the word *asylum* I was startled to see that of four definitions given, the first three deal with the idea of sanctuary.[3] Only the fourth defines *asylum* as a place where insane people go; all the other definitions are concerned with extending protection to criminals, debtors, the destitute, and, finally, the afflicted.

The political dissident is not on the list of potential candidates for asylum in my old dictionary! But it was compiled, after all, in 1951. Since that time, much of the world's literature on processes of political change, the spectrum of left and right political philosophies, protest strategies, and the global assessment of pressures on the human condition has been written or revised. Since that time the political dissident has come to occupy center stage in the asylum practices of several countries, while more recently such refugees have become a source of ordinary crime and terrorist activity in their countries of safe haven. The political dissident, therefore, is among the most common recent beneficiaries of political asylum and is the most likely source of trouble for the future extension of such protection.

Safe Haven: A Legal and Moral Concept

The idea of safe haven goes back to very early practices of governments and the Church in Europe. In essence, over several centuries, governments, having control of the territory and the laws of states, developed concepts of political asylum. Meanwhile churches, with control over canon law and Church properties such as cathedrals and monasteries, developed concepts of sanctuary.

The basic principle of asylum, which grew up having both moral and legal content, was that a person could seek it to obtain justice, including a fair trial, but not to avoid punishment for a crime. Both the grant of asylum by the state and of sanctuary by the Church assumed a combination of clean hands on the part of the seeker and some repressive act or intent directed against that person.

As a matter of practice, the authority of the state was essential to make the system work. The state provided the laws and the police the power to protect the beneficiaries of asylum and to assure that the sanctuary of the Church was not violated or wrongfully used.

The evolution of stable governments that were able to guarantee due process of laws and the proliferation of religious denominations caused Church extension of sanctuary to fall into disuse. However, the state practice of granting asylum to refugees has continued in one form or another in many countries.

Grants of asylum have never been unlimited. A practical limitation that evolved was that the recipient of asylum was not allowed to attack or take threatening actions against the country that provided safe haven. Nor was it considered appropriate for the recipient of asylum to mount actions against third parties within the territory of the safe havening country. The expectation was that the recipient of asylum would do nothing either to threaten or to embarrass the host. In sum, the individual granted safe haven was expected to respect the laws of the host country.

Current Practices

Present approaches by governments to grants of asylum or the policing of them are anything but uniform. Take the case of U.S. dealings with Filipino nationals living in the United States. During the last several years of the Marcos regime, Philippine opposition leaders such as Raul Manglapus or Benigno Aquino, who lived in the United States after Ferdinand Marcos released him from prison until shortly before he was assassinated in August 1983, had a fair amount of freedom to campaign for Marcos's overthrow. However, when it appeared in January 1987 that Marcos, who now lives in Hawaii, was preparing to make a forcible return to Manila to assist a coup attempt by military officers against Corazon Aquino, U.S. authorities intervened to show that U.S. tolerance for Filipino exile actions against the Aquino government is limited.

Until quite recently, the French interpreted the rules of safe haven in such a way that terrorist or insurgent activities could not be mounted in France by a safe-havening individual or a group safe-havening in that country. Judging from the behavior of some groups, however, that did not rule out attacks against people or officials of that person's home government as long as the attacks occurred outside of France.

There has always been a certain amount of tension around the offer of safe haven by one government to the citizen of another country. Governments are usually sensitive about it, because the offer of safe haven is at minimum a de facto criticism of conditions in the country of origin. The offer says that the other government is repressive, somehow extremist, insensitive to human rights and dignity, or unable to cope, which is not likely to help that country deal with its own internal politics. Governments dislike having other governments say these things, particularly if they are true, but the real objection is that granting safe haven to a dissident constitutes low-level interference in the internal affairs of another country. If the individuals safe havened are allowed to agitate freely against the government of their country, the tensions can be expected to become acute, because the safe-havening country may be at least passively supporting a rebellion.

Spain's Problems with the Basques

France has had to recognize and deal with mounting tension with Spain over French safe havening of Basque terrorists. Despite objections made by Spain over a period of several years, the most France had been prepared to do was move safe-havening Spanish Basques out of the border regions or, if they were particularly troublesome, expel them from the country; the French were not prepared to send them back to Spain.

In the early 1980s the unwillingness of French authorities to cooperate became a source of growing frustration to Spanish law enforcement officers and to the military, both of whose members and leaders were regular targets of Basque terrorism. Consequently, in 1984 a rightist group suspected of ties to the Spanish police raided the Basque region of France, attacking and killing nine Spanish Basques.[4]

The raid was a blunt sort of message both to Basque terrorists and to French authorities. France thus had a choice: either take action to curb the movements of Spanish Basques in France, or live with the probability that the Spanish would take care of the matter themselves by carrying out further raids in France. Thus, in September 1984 the French Council of State approved the extradition of three Basques who were involved in several attacks that caused the deaths of six people. This ruling has held up so far under the onslaught of criticism from French Basques, but also from socialists who long have defended France's tradition of political asylum.

A series of bombings in France, carried out by Palestinian and Armenian terrorists during mid-1986, appears to have strengthened the French will to curtail the traditional freedom enjoyed by political dissidents in that country. Those bombings were an attempt by members of the family of a Lebanese, Georges Ibrahim Abdallah, to get him out of jail before he went to trial for complicity in the murders of U.S. deputy military attaché Charles Ray and Israeli diplomat Yacov Barsimantov. Despite those bombings and other efforts of Abdallah's terrorist group, the Lebanese Armed Revolutionary Faction, to intimidate French authorities, and apparently despite strong reservations expressed by officials of the French ministries of Justice and Foreign Affairs, in February 1987 a special French court sentenced Abdallah to life imprisonment. That sentence, even more than the extradition of Spanish Basques, sounded the end of traditional French thinking about political asylum. It remains to be seen, however, just how far a country as steeped in this tradition as France will actually go.

As a footnote to the issue of safe-havening Basques, an April 1987 report from Madrid suggests that Spain's problem also extends to Algeria. A secret protocol reportedly exists between Madrid and Algiers to the effect that Algeria would not harbor more than thirty Basque dissidents at any one time, and Algiers would inform Madrid of the entry of known Basque Fatherland and Liberty members. The accidental death in Algeria of a well-known Basque leader whose presence had not been made known to Madrid suggests that the pact is not working.[5] That Spain could not get a number lower than thirty, which appears to give the Basques considerable freedom to protect their members who are most at risk at any one time, is an indicator of how intractable the transborder safe-haven problem really is.

Concerns about Networking: Euroterrorism

Italy has had problems similar to those of France within the past year, but the culprits are a good deal harder to trace. Following the December 27, 1985, attack by the radical Palestinian Abu Nidal group at Rome's Leonardo da Vinci Airport, Italian police concluded that the four terrorists involved had been provided with ammunition and weapons by someone in Italy. The range of suspected sources included the Mafia, members of Italy's Red Brigades, and Palestinians resident in Italy. But whatever the source might be, the fact the Italians had to confront was that a support infrastructure for international terrorist operations existed in Italy. Moreover, available evidence suggested that the infrastructure might include other Europeans as well as Middle Easterners.[6]

Italy has also been concerned about the practice of Red Brigades members' escaping into France for safe haven. One report placed the number of such escapees at 150 in mid-1985. Up to that point the French had refused to extradite,[7] but changes in French thinking since that time may improve Italy's chances, particularly since concern has been growing among European governments about the spread of Euroterrorism, the cooperation of domestic terrorist groups from country to country.

During early 1986, especially following the La Belle Disco bombing in Berlin and the U.S. raid on Libya, Italy and several other European governments became convinced that part of the terrorism support infrastructure was being provided by Libyans through the Libyan People's Bureaus in various European capitals and that some of the assets used by the bureaus were Libyan exiles in those countries. As a result, European governments expelled more than one hundred Libyan "diplomats" and restricted the number and the freedom of action of those permitted to remain. France and Italy began to require visas of travelers with the object of preventing the arrival, engagement in terrorist acts, or possible safe havening of any new terrorists in their territory. Italy was confronted with the need to require visas of travelers from North Africa, thus overturning a well-established practice of open borders, when Italian authorities found that the Rome airport attackers carried Tunisian passports that apparently had been confiscated by Libyan authorities from workers and turned over to the terrorists.

West German authorities were shocked recently to discover a functioning terrorist safe haven in their country. West Germans have been saying regularly that the domestic terrorists in the Red Army Faction and the so-called Revolutionary Cells are under control. But in January 1987, the arrest of Ahmed Hamadei, older brother of one of the accused hijackers of TWA Flight 847, Mohammed Ali Hamadei, helped uncover an in-place infrastructure for terrorist attacks of Middle Eastern origin in West Germany. The elder Hamadei enjoyed safe haven in Germany and used his residency to plan and support terrorist activities.

The United States and the IRA

Since the 1920s, a polite tension has existed between the United States and Great Britain over sources of U.S. support for rebellion in Northern Ireland. British authorities at times have charged that the main source of funds and weapons for the Irish Republican Army and other groups is in the United States, principally people of Irish ancestry in the northeastern part of the country. Their support has been potent sustenance to continuing rebellion in Northern Ireland, even though that support has weakened in recent years, because of public revulsion following such IRA atrocities as the murder of Lord Mountbatten. It should be noted, however, that with rare exception the IRA and other Irish groups have confined their activities in the United States to fund-raising and gunrunning; they have not gone in for terrorism.

In addition to providing money and weapons, the United States in effect has given safe haven to IRA terrorists, and its courts have helped. This has been done through judicial application of a modern departure from the historical rules of safe haven called the "political offense exception" to extradition treaties with other governments. This exception permits a judge to decide that a crime was committed for a political reason and to extend political asylum by refusing to authorize extradition of that individual to stand trial at home. Many treatries still have this provision. In 1986, however, the U.S. Senate consented to ratification of a change in the U.S.-British extradition treaty which was designed to stop safe havening of IRA terrorists in the United States. This treaty action is discussed in detail in chapter 3, but for the purposes of this overview it will suffice to note that the treaty change was designed to prevent the safe havening of people accused of violent crimes.

This change in the treaty actually reinstated the ancient principle of asylum that said that if the person who sought safe haven was found to be guilty of a crime, that person would be sent back to stand trial in the jurisdiction where the crime was committed. In other words, there was a common law version of extradition that governments historically used to discourage abuses of political asylum and sanctuary.

Protection from Abuses

As this discussion shows, the rules of the game on safe haven constitute an important subject of international practice. Observance of the rules matters, possibly a great deal, to the safety or freedom from terrorism and other forms of lawlessness of the safe-havening country, and failing to enforce the rules can seriously disrupt relations between countries.

In an age of easy, rapid movement of people across national boundaries, what does an open, complex society like that of the United States do to maintain the rules of safe haven? Are those rules in reality very different from the rules that apply to any resident alien? In some respects it would not seem so, but American experience on this subject is growing rapidly. In the period since the fall of Saigon, for example, thousands of people from Indochina, many of whom qualify as political refugees, have come to reside in the United States. Within the past few years, patterns of Mafia-like crime, extortion, and intimidation have grown around these new communities. The pattern bears some resemblance to that of the tong wars in Chinatowns of the West Coast of nearly a century ago. It has many of the overtones of the "Cosa Nostra," because like the Sicilian Mafia the criminal leadership draws on its own ethnic community for recruits and the prey too is often its own people.

Terrorism Links to Crime

I bring up this example because of the increasingly apparent linkup of modern crime with political violence. The old and new criminal organizations have created a natural milieu for trade in drugs, black market dealings in arms, terrorism, and more traditional Mafia activity. The traditional underworld in consequence has become ever more dangerous and antisocial. It is sustaining and using a volatile blend of material and political motivations.

The linkups of terrorism, narcotics trafficking, and other crime in countries such as Colombia, Mexico, much of Central America, and elsewhere only add to the problems of making sensible judgments about a grant of safe haven. Border control authorities in many countries have developed practices for screening out known criminals, and those screening devices increasingly have been applied to drug traffickers. Now they must be applied with growing frequency to the potential terrorist, and frequently that person will look like many other political dissidents seeking safe haven. Thus, whether they want to or not, border controllers are having to distinguish between applicants who are not likely to abuse safe haven and applicants who might not only violate the rules of safe haven, but also link up with local groups to commit violent acts.

Making Safe Haven Decisions

The deceptive thing about deciding to give someone political asylum is that the decision looks simple. And some cases are easy. The persecution and murder of Jews in Germany before and during World War II made the United States decide in the late 1940s that providing safe haven to the victims was an essential act of humanity. In the cases of Soviet artists, musicians, physicists, writers, and other political dissidents who have defected, the United States feels itself on firm ground where safe haven is concerned. The steady flow of escapees out of Eastern Europe continues to validate the utility of safe haven.

The picture is not perfect, however. We seem to like some categories of victims better than others. The media and human rights advocates do not view politicians, military personnel, and intelligence officers who defect from the East with anything like the enthusiasm afforded an established dissident, even though the personal adjustments and the real dangers involved in the escape of a government official may be far more harrowing than the mere walk from checkpoint to checkpoint that goes with an arranged departure. Here we learn, perhaps a bit awkwardly, that certain intellectual skills and professions make some escapees more appealing than others.

As we move from the area of the East-West struggle, the picture of asylum becomes less clear. The major international organizations critiquing human rights performance seem far more comfortable making judgments about dissidents of the Left, who are persecuted by the Right, than they are about rightist dissidents who argue that they have no political say in a place like Nicaragua. Yet in its political history the United States has never been very good at either making or enforcing such distinctions. There are issues on which it is difficult to tell Left from Right, and there are occasions when it clearly doesn't matter. The basic fact to keep in mind here, however, is that the criteria for judging who is deserving of political asylum are set in law. That law says in essence that an individual must be fleeing some form of political oppression to qualify as a political refugee. In fact, the U.S. Supreme Court ruled on March 9, 1987, that to qualify as a political refugee one has to show "a well-founded fear" of persecution in one's home country.[8] That ruling is more generous than previous interpretation of the law by the Immigration and Naturalization Service, but not everyone qualifies as a political refugee because people can decide to leave their native land for a host of reasons that are not basically political, including the fact that it may be difficult if not impossible to make a decent living.

Here we get to the volatile core of the modern practice of determining political asylum or refugee status. Historically any decision to offer sanctuary or asylum was likely to be a local matter attracting little attention unless the person was someone of eminence. Now, in many instances, the extension of political safe haven becomes an immediate embarrassment to the refugee's country of origin. Governments and ethnic or other pressure groups use the cases of dissidents to try to bring about political changes or the release of more refugees by recalcitrant governments. The facts get magnified and distorted by the media, by governments, and by pressure groups, and specific cases often take on a life of their own. Such cases, whether or not they represent true instances of repression, become major bones of contention in relations between countries, or between groups within countries.

The relationship between the Reagan administration and the church groups in the Sanctuary movement on the handling of refugees from Central America is a case in point. I discuss the set of issues posed by the Sanctuary movement in chapter 5, but for purposes of discussion here, the confrontation is an outgrowth of the earlier relationship between church and state with regard to the subject of sanctuary, except that the church is ignoring one of the basic rules: in order for the system to work, the church must uphold the laws of the state. The state in turn must maintain its credibility with the church, or groups and individuals will seek ways around its authority, but in the past the system broke down when the church refused to observe the laws of the state.

Safe Haven and the Media

Among the factors that must be considered in relation to modern granting of safe haven is the readiness with which the individual can interact with the country he or she has left. Through media the individual can make a public case against that country, and even if the facts of the case are not true, the story can have immense impact abroad. It can also reinforce or stir up sources of dissent at home. The individual can also conspire with others to develop an insurgency or to mount acts of terrorism against the former country. Both the means to execute such a plan and to deliver an attack are readily to hand in most countries. In many instances, therefore, the modern safe-havening dissident has become a source of immediate concern and possibly danger to the country of origin. This involves the safe-havening country and the country of origin in a much more potentially intense relationship over the individual involved than was historically ever likely to develop.

The instant information environment works also to the advantage of the country of origin. Historically, a safe-havening individual practically speaking disappeared, and considerable effort was often needed to find that person. Now, the leaders of a country of origin can track a dissident by following media reports. Moreover, the "let's pretend he's not here" approach taken by a safe-havening country which was possible in the past is now often canceled by media reports on the individual's whereabouts, particularly if he or she is a well-known dissident. Safe haven thus tends to become an overt matter very quickly, often with immediate impact on bilateral relations.

The Impact of Terrorism

Because of the spread of terrorism, governments are more closely scrutinizing visitors to their countries, first, to satisfy themselves that visitors are not bringing trouble to their own streets, and second, to avoid being in the awkward situation of harboring a terrorist who is wanted by another government. Inadvertent safe havening of a terrorist can cause either problem. Moreover, increasingly troublesome is the fact that in recent years traveling terrorists have linked up with local groups or other traveling groups to carry out attacks. The Lebanese Armed Revolutionary Faction appears, for example, to have joined up with the Armenian Secret Army for the Liberation of Armenia to mount the effort in France to free Georges Ibrahim Abdallah.

Canada, bent on increasing its population through fairly liberal immigration policies, was shocked in 1985 by a Sikh separatist attack mounted probably from Montreal. This group, apparently made up of permanent residents who had been in Canada for some time, planted a bomb on an Air India flight and brought about the deaths of 329 people over the Atlantic. Thus Canada has had no choice but to look more closely at visitors from the Indian subcontinent. As I did final editing on this chapter, deep concern was being expressed by many Canadians over violence in the Sikh community of Vancouver, British Columbia, which is thought to be the largest Sikh enclave in the Western Hemisphere. Sparked by the illegal landing of 170 Sikhs from a boat in that area, the concerns centered on fratricide within the Sikh community, as young militants try to wrest leadership from their elders, and on reported involvement of that community in the financing and conduct of terrorist activity in support of Sikh separatism.

These developments, understandably, are making established ethnic communities in the United States and elsewhere very nervous. They fear, again quite understandably, that concern by other communities and law enforcement officials can lead to restrictions on the immigration or freedom of movement of their members and possibly their exclusion. But the picture is hardly one-sided. The speech that Imam Mohamed Azi made to Walter Cronkite is a chiller in this regard. And FBI reports that members of the Shia community in Michigan are known to be sympathetic to the Lebanese terrorist group Hezballah are not reassuring in the context of Hezballah's continued kidnapping of Americans in Beirut, even though nothing more than sympathy may be extended by this community. Perhaps helping a terrorist in Lebanon to kidnap Americans is not breaking the traditional rules of safe haven, but it is close, and those who do should not be surprised if they become a concern to their host governments because they pose a danger.

Where to from Here?

The modern challenge to traditions of safe haven poses one of the great dilemmas of our times. Many communities contain little colonies of immigrants from a variety of ethnic or cultural groups. A natural characteristic of any such group is loyalty to kith and kin in other places, but these groups have obligations to the other ethnic groups immediately around them and to the community at large. Failure to recognize this is the reason safe haven is in trouble. Hardly any country will experience bombings like those that France did at the hands of Middle Eastern terrorists in the summer of 1986 without changing its habits in some degree, and we are all the losers in that.

The final nail in the coffin of safe haven in the West will come, however, if we fail to see a basic truth: we cannot meddle freely in each other's affairs through the all too convenient mechanism of safe haven without consequences for the stability of Western society. That is not merely because none of us has a corner on truth and morality. It is mainly because the rules and the institutions of law do not work well under the onus of constant tinkering by people who have no responsibility for making them work, and none of the countries regularly involved in providing safe haven either have or necessarily want responsibility for the laws in refugee countries of origin. In any case, the net effects of forays into another country's affairs through importing a dissident or exporting an activist are not necessarily helpful; they are frequently quite destructive, even if they may be satisfying to the actors.

The threats to safe haven, therefore, are in our habits. Some time ago, Western nations adopted safe haven as a quick fix, mostly for the conscience, for repressive, primitive, or ineffective treatment of human rights in other countries. Rather than expend the money, time, and patience needed to help source countries develop or repair ailing institutions, and often giving up on efforts to moderate behavior, Western nations looked around for some kind of a bypass, and they found the concept of safe haven. The bypass in this case is volatile, because what it tells people is that they don't have to stay at home and work out their problems; they can leave. That sounds like a humanitarian gesture, and it frequently is, but the long-term effect of this pattern is that numerous small, weak societies will be regularly drained of their most active and most talented people.

We have talked a lot over the past few decades about the "brain drain," meaning the drift of the educated element from the Third World to the West. We haven't looked at what it means to steal another society's most vigorous people—vigor demonstrated by the will to leave—whether or not they are educated; but the advanced societies regularly do this through the enticement of safe haven.

The second element of volatility in the resort to safe haven is the fact that the West has been importing little slices of everybody's problems. To illustrate: In early 1987 the Federal Bureau of Investigation launched an effort to curtail activities in the United States by the Popular Front for the Liberation of Palestine, a Marxist subgroup of the Palestine Liberation Organization. The PFLP has engaged in many terrorist attacks against Americans and other foreigners as well as against Arabs in the Middle East. According to an FBI report, members and/or supporters of the PFLP in the United States are seeking to join up with "violent and nonviolent" organizations to promote PFLP activities abroad, specifically in Palestine. The FBI charges include conducting underground activities, fund-raising for the PFLP organization abroad, and providing recruits to the PFLP. Accordingly, deportation actions were undertaken against seven Palestinians and one Kenyan.[9]

The deportation effort appears to have failed for procedural reasons, but the PFLP is not an isolated case. In the past decade, Armenian terrorists have assassinated Turkish diplomats in the United States and Canada, and Palestinian terrorists have carried out or assisted in terrorist attacks in France, Germany, Italy, Britain, Spain, and elsewhere. As noted earlier, Sikh separatists have planned and executed bombings from Canada. There are numerous other examples. All of these happen to be acts of terrorism carried out by people who brought their grievances with them when they came seeking safe haven.

Up to now we have not established any rules for individuals or groups who are traveling with grievances in their luggage. There is nothing in the famous invitation on the Statue of Liberty that says you can't live in the United States and plot to go home again and shoot the head of state. Obviously some rules are needed on that, to protect American interests at home as well as to protect the interests of another country. Specifically, we need rules on conspiracy that will severely inhibit, if not altogether prohibit, the planning, support, and execution of terrorist attacks from U.S. territory. Other governments need similar laws to make any real dent in the current pattern of terrorism for export.

Wherever we go from here, democratic societies, including that of the United States, cannot be as generous and openhanded as they have been in the past. We must reach and somehow enforce understandings with safe-havening individuals respecting involvement in political activity abroad, when that activity in any way involves the use of violence against groups or governments in other countries. On this point, neither the United States nor other democratic countries can have it both ways; we cannot give free rein to groups we like and effectively constrain the groups we don't like. Our laws do not make such distinctions, and any attempt to impose them only increases the stresses on our decision processes.

Finally, I think we need to recognize that the extension of safe haven is no mere matter of national or personal preference; the decisions have consequences that are global. Because of its use as a springboard to terrorism, safe haven has come to pose a high risk to the many because of the potential crimes of a few. Those few are destroying the nest for others who may have genuine cause to seek a traditional grant of asylum. The offer of safe haven is meant as a humanitarian gesture, but what happens when the person who receives it subverts its use to lend sympathy or to provide support to terrorists, or to take direct part in acts of terrorism?

3

When Is a Crime
Not a Crime?

O N a shadowy street in Belfast, Northern Ireland, a young man, Kevin
McNulty, is making his way homeward with a bag of groceries in his
arms. He is unarmed and alone, and his dress would not distinguish him from
the thousands of other citizens who daily walk the streets of Belfast. Six months
ago, when he turned twenty-one, Kevin applied to join the police constabulary,
and with many frustrating delays he finally has been accepted as a new recruit.
Still in training, he does not yet have an assigned beat. Suddenly, as he moves
down the poorly lighted street, three dark-clad individuals thrust themselves
in front of him and force him to stop. They don't ask his name; they don't
inquire about his destination. One of the trio levels a silenced automatic pistol
at him and fires two shots. Kevin falls to the street, and without a word,
the three dark figures disappear into the night.

A few days later, one of the three participants in the killing of Kevin McNulty
is captured in an unsuccessful bank robbery attempt, and he is placed in custody
by Belfast police. In his possession at the time of capture are an automatic pistol
and a silencer. On a hunch the police inspector asks for ballistics comparison
of slugs from the body of Kevin McNulty and test bullets from the captured
automatic. The comparison is positive; the slugs have identical markings. Under
questioning the young bank robber fingers his two cohorts, and with arrest
warrants in hand the police go to pick them up, only to discover that one has
left Northern Ireland and is said to be on his way to the United States.

On the basis of an alert from British authorities, U.S. law enforcement officers are able to trace the suspect to Boston, where he is found visiting a
cousin. He is placed under arrest, and the British file a request for his extradition on a charge of deliberate and premeditated murder. In his testimony

before the judge hearing the extradition request, the suspect claims that he is a member of the IRA and that he and the other two people involved in the killing of Kevin McNulty were engaged at the time in "fighting a guerrilla war to oust the British from Northern Ireland."[1] The attack, therefore, says the suspect, was not a crime but an act of war.

That the suspect has taken part in an act of willful murder is not really disputed. In effect, the evidence of the crime is placed before the court. However, the hearing is not on the evidence of the crime but on the motives of the perpetrator. The nature of the suspect's request is that because the killing of Kevin McNulty was politically motivated he should not be sent back to Northern Ireland to stand trial. The judge agrees and denies the British request for extradition.

The McNulty case is a composite of IRA crimes, but it is drawn from fact. At least four IRA criminals have secured safe haven in the United States as a result of court decisions in New York and California. In these cases too the crimes as such were not disputed, but all of the defendants claimed that their crimes were politically motivated, and the judges agreed.

The Political Offense

Many governments apply such a concept of political offense. Almost simultaneously with the arrival of the hijackers of the Italian cruise ship *Achille Lauro* in Sicily, where they were handed over to the Italians for trial, U.S. authorities requested that Italy extradite Abu Abbas, the ringleader of the group involved, to the United States. The United States wanted Abbas, chief of the Palestine Liberation Front hijackers who carried out this attack, to stand trial for the murder of Leon Klinghoffer, the only person killed during the *Achille Lauro* piracy. Italy's Prime Minister Bettino Craxi refused that request, and Abu Abbas was allowed to leave the country; Craxi's decision stirred up a storm of objections from conservative members of his cabinet, which led to the fall of the Italian government. Abu Abbas reappeared in Yugoslavia, where U.S. authorities again filed a request for his extradition. Yugoslavian authorities also denied the request.

In both instances, the Italian and the Yugoslav decisions were based on a finding that the political motive behind the offense charged against Abu Abbas permitted them to invoke the political offense exception. Treaties with Italy and Yugoslavia on this point read about the same way as the U.S.-British treaty. The Italian judge who conducted the trial of the *Achille Lauro* hijackers echoed the Italian and Yugoslav judgments some weeks later, when as was mentioned in chapter 1, he said the hijackers were guilty but expressed sympathy for them by suggesting that the Palestinian cause was just, even though they had used improper means to pursue it.

Extradition brings sharply into focus the differences that exist among governments over the handling of political violence. Those differences, it must be noted right away, arise most vigorously between governments that are parties to extradition agreements, and the most sophisticated of these agreements exist among the democratic governments, mainly between the United States and various governments of Western Europe.

Political violence, some historically local and unique mixture of terrorism and insurgency, was part of the creation of many democratic societies. And remembrance of the violent upheaval that established their present systems causes every one of these violence-born societies to reserve a special place for political violence of its own kind. More than that, the right to resort to political violence to achieve a similar end is enshrined in some way legally and is protected by limits on the authority of law enforcement officers and by constraints on the definitions of crime and on the severity of punishment. Violence is at the root of our culture, therefore, almost in the same linear fashion that volcanic eruptions act as the cause for the existence of many Pacific islands.

That violent kernel of our existence shows up in many facets of our behavior. As Fr. James Burtchaell writes in his chapter of *Fighting Back: Winning the War against Terrorism*, terrorism is "a lineal descendant of traditional warfare," and "Americans must possess a sophistication that is not only political but also historical in order to make a moral response to terrorism."[2]

The Importance of Extradition Treaties

Why does all of this matter? It matters because in extradition law we most often formally declare to the rest of the world our legal position on political violence. A broadly defined political offense exception permits a U.S. court or the court of any participant in such a treaty with the United States to ignore murder, kidnapping, intimidation, and other crimes by saying that they occurred in the course of legitimate acts of political protest. Extradition law thus becomes the broad area where we say what we think terrorism is and what kinds of violence will pass as acceptable behavior in a democracy. The definitions we use in extradition treaties therefore map the permissible latitudes of resort to violence for the criminal, for the political activist, and for authority.

In legal practice this is terribly important because the United States does not use a definition of terrorism in federal criminal statutes, nor do many of the states of the union. Rather, all terrorist acts against persons or property are specific crimes punishable under various sections of federal and state penal codes. Political offense exceptions in extradition treaties cut into that field by saying that any crime is potentially excusable if it is politically motivated. On this basis a crime is not a crime if the person who commits the act somehow manages to escape across a national boundary and, when apprehended, pleads politics as the reason for the crime. As Associate Attorney General Stephen S. Trott once remarked, "One of the most important things a terrorist can possess is an airline ticket to another country."[3] Emphasizing the force of Stephen Trott's point, it is useful to point out that the political offense exception exists in approximately ninety-six treaties between the United States and other countries.

The political offense exception thus sets the tone for definitions of crime in international practice by making possible entirely subjective and localized criteria of what is or is not an acceptable motive, whereas domestic laws on crime normally do not look at the issue of motivation as a determinant of whether an act is a crime. Dealing effectively with the scope and the definitions used in political offense exception language therefore can determine the success of efforts to deal with terrorism or other forms of political violence in the international setting.

Using the law internationally means finding effective ways to bring to bear many different national bodies of law to assure that charges against suspected criminals are properly adjudicated. The accepted instruments for that are extradition treaties. The problem in the international setting, whether the offense is terrorism or other forms of crime, is how to bring an accused individual before a court with appropriate jurisdiction and legal authority to give proper weight both to due process and to law enforcement.

Solving that problem requires that governments work together on some compromise among "competing national policies."[4] Organized groups increasingly are involved in activities that demand some recognition of their status. One class of such groups is insurgents, and if a state happens to subscribe to the aims of an insurgent group, that state probably will lend its support, including such actions as invoking the political offense exception to avoid extraditing a member of the group to another country. The adoption of a political offense exception is an indication that the governments involved may have harbored different views of particular groups or causes and therefore could not reach suitable compromises to make "a more effective agreement."[5]

Creating and maintaining an effective system of extradition is important because if the democracies cannot use police investigative methods and due process in a court of law to deal with terrorists and other criminals who cross national boundaries, then they are severely handicapped in their efforts to combat crime and to lower the level of violence in and around their societies. The true issue, therefore, is whether the democracies are able to use the instruments of law effectively to defend themselves and their citizens. The answer as of now is imperfectly.

Congressional Opinions on Extradition

Conservative and liberal opinions in the U.S. Congress are sharply divided on extradition. This was demonstrated in 1985, when President Reagan sent a revision of the U.S.-British extradition treaty to the Senate for advice and consent. In making the first formal review of extradition issues in many years, the U.S. Senate revealed a startling partisanship on politically motivated crime. Deliberations in the Senate Foreign Relations Committee gave us a look at where American lawmakers stand on the issues for the first time in a hundred years. They also gave us a good current reading on who in the Congress, either by preference or response to constituent pressures, ended up in a position of appearing to support the right of individuals to use political violence, including terrorism. The record of the hearings is worth reading.[6]

The U.S.-British Treaty

The draft U.S.-British treaty sent to the Senate by the executive branch was a revision of an already established extradition treaty between the United States and Britain. The original treaty contains the political offense exception. The new draft treaty retained a political offense exception, but it specified that violent crimes against people would not be covered by the language of that exception. Thus, persons charged with such offenses as murder, kidnapping, maiming, hostage taking, and the like would be extraditable without reference to a defense based on a political motive.

The proposal sounded straightforward enough. Hardly anyone, it seemed, should be able to claim that murdering a private citizen in cold blood was an act of war. Nor could they really argue that shooting an off-duty policeman on his way home was an act sanctioned under the international rules of armed conflict. If the revision of the treaty were approved, therefore, a big hole in extradition law, which permitted known terrorists to commit violent crimes and then seek safe haven in the United States, would be eliminated, while a valuable precedent would be set for reducing the use of this exception by parties to other extradition treaties with the United States.

The clarity of the issue notwithstanding, the U.S. Senate vacillated. For months the draft treaty languished in the Senate Committee on Foreign Relations, where the issue was viewed obviously and almost completely in a partisan way. All of the Democrats on the committee were against the treaty change. In part they were expressing party loyalty; in part they were catering to Irish-American constituents. All the Republicans were in favor except Jesse Helms, who seems to have wanted somehow to legislate a distinction between "terrorists" and "freedom fighters," but judging from the final result, he could not get agreement on definitions.[7]

The Senate approved an amended U.S.-British extradition agreement, but the new treaty language was hedged. The treaty provided for excluding violent crimes from the coverage of the political offense exception, but the Senate provided that humanitarian considerations should be taken into account. If, for example, a U.S. judge were to conclude that a court in Britain would be "prejudiced against an extradition-case defendant because of his political or religious beliefs," the judge could deny extradition.[8]

In my view, what this change in the treaty accomplished was to force judges to look harder at the facts of a case, but the obvious fact that the dispute in Northern Ireland is basically political with religious overtones would seem to give considerable leeway for a defendant to claim prejudice. I note, however, that the revised language has already been used by Britain to obtain the extradition of William Joseph Quinn, one of the four accused IRA terrorists, who is charged with involvement in a bombing campaign in London and with shooting an off-duty constable in the 1970s.[9] Quinn had achieved what appeared to be an enduring safe haven in the United States, but he has been sent back to Britain for trial. Other cases will need to be reviewed in light of renewed British requests. It will take several court decisions to decide whether any real improvement in extradition prospects has resulted from the treaty change. The degree of improvement will depend on how broadly or narrowly the courts interpret the political/religious consideration as a barrier to extradition for violent crimes.

With regard to IRA terrorists, the justification for the political/religious override used by Senate opponents of the treaty revision involved an ironic twist. One of the arguments made in Foreign Relations Committee hearings was that British authorities had adopted a practice of hearing charges against accused IRA terrorists without a jury. Thus, accused terrorists should not be returned to Northern Ireland because they could not be guaranteed a jury trial and if tried by a jury could not count on their political and religious views being given proper weight. However, the reason such trials came to be held without a jury was that IRA terrorists were intimidating jurors, threatening to retaliate in the event of a "bad" verdict and using actual shootings to influence verdicts. Accused IRA members could get a jury trial, therefore, by leaving the jurors alone! Moreover, the system of selecting jurors, involving challenges by counsel such as are commonly used in American courts, often resulted in a jury panel so patently biased toward defendants that justice could not be obtained.[10]

Individual Liberty and Social Need

The debate on treaty language in the Senate drove the issue of extradition squarely into the dilemma that faces societies in the late twentieth century: How do we balance individual liberties against the needs of society as a whole?

In our times, I think that traditional liberalism, existential philosophies, and situational ethical explanations for the legality or morality of behavior have joined together powerfully to create a way of life in which social and institutional values don't count for nearly as much as the individual's right to self-expression. Growing up in a rural setting with ample room to swing my arms without hitting anyone, I have great love for the rights of the individual, and I would go to considerable length to protect individual liberties. But growing up in southern West Virginia during the late 1920s and 1930s was one thing; growing up in a modern city or in the heavily populated Atlantic corridor is another, as we have seen demonstrated in such incidents as the Bernhard Goetz subway encounter. The implications of those changes seem to have been missed in the evolution of many current attitudes toward political action. In the final chapter of this book I will examine those implications in some depth, but for the moment what concerns me in the context of this discussion of extradition is that the ability of society to protect a framework of freedom for the individual is being eroded by adherence to an excessive, almost mystical regard for freedom of political action. That regard in turn provides an expanding area of room for the individual to express himself or herself politically, up to and including the use of the pipe bomb, with little fear of reprisal or punishment from society as a whole. Nor, it seems, need that individual be concerned about the impact of self-expression on the liberty of others. For example, you or I should be able to go to a market or take a plane without fear of a terrorist attack.

It's All Relative!

The confusion in values that has developed in this area is well summed up in reported remarks of Morton H. Halperin, Washington director of the American Civil Liberties Union, during the Senate Foreign Relations Committee hearings on the U.S.-British treaty revision. On the issue of when extradition should be approved, he said that people who "blew up a department store or threw bombs at people on the street" should be extradited "as terrorists," but, he went on, we should deny extradition in the cases of "some violent acts that are part of a traditional rebellion against a government."[11]

One of the things that bothered me about Halperin's remarks is that in the IRA case, the traditional rebels and the department store bombers are the same people. I was also troubled by the notion that a traditional rebellion against a government, any government, would, in his reported formulation, be a safe context for violence, because the idea of rebellion, per se, seems to be enshrined here without any caveats. That thought, to me at least, is every bit as dangerous as it looks, because there are no fixed reference points in it for judging either the legitimacy of grievances or the temper of leadership behavior. The lack of such reference points makes all judgments about cases completely relative.

The blurred picture created by this logic is typified by the approach to defining terrorism that is taken by Conor Cruise O'Brien in a 1982 article.[12] We reserve use of the word terrorism, says O'Brien, "for politically motivated violence of which we disapprove." He admits that that definition is very slippery and makes an effort to tidy up his definitional landscape by saying that he would restrict the term *terrorist* to someone who uses "lethal violence to bring about political change" in a democratic society where "participation" and "consent" are norms. But then, O'Brien says, "democracy is not perfect," and if a minority finds itself being badly served by majority rule, the resort to political violence might be termed "legitimate revolt." This almost comes down to saying that whether or not you should be considered a terrorist depends on what you want and whether you can get that without resort to violence. Since O'Brien's case in point is Northern Ireland, his formulation works perfectly to legitimate the activities of the IRA, if you buy the logic of his argument.

As Martha Crenshaw notes in her own chapter introducing O'Brien's article and others, the central issue is legitimacy.[13] Her argument is that certain uses of terrorist methods—for example, the attacks of the Jewish group Irgun against British troops in Palestine during the late 1940s—are justifiable. And certain reasons for terrorism, she says, can be condoned, such as, for example, attacks by the Jews against their Nazi oppressors. She does not approve, on the other hand, of the attacks of the Red Army Faction against targets in Germany or of the Palestinian movement against airline passengers in Israel. The ultimate judgment of legitimacy, it seems, would have to await a moral reading on the political circumstances of a terrorist act as well as some judgment about the political effectiveness of it.

Such inquiries into the definition of terrorism appear helpful at first blush, but they often end up supporting a double standard. As was noted in chapter 1, some people consciously keep their definition of terrorism flexible and subjective, while some do not want to prejudice a cause they consider worthy by suggesting that certain uses of violence may not be appropriate in support of it. There appears in some cases to be a willingness to accept terrorism if the end results look beneficial to the person, group, or government making the judgment. Finally, there is a reluctance to distinguish between legal and illegal uses of violence without first looking at the motives of the actors.

Dealing with Ambiguity

These kinds of hang-ups and preferences quite deliberately leave ambiguous the issue of who is a terrorist. That ambiguity must be recognized in coping with extradition cases because the cases inevitably get into matters of social justice and fairness. However, can we go so far with our definitions as to say whether crimes are crimes or not depends on what provokes them? If we do, we open a giant window for all sorts of tyrannies, large and small, for governments, groups, and individuals, including ordinary criminals, to play deceitful word games with us, to turn all our terms against us with a twist of propaganda.

If we are going to learn to cope effectively with the spread of politically motivated violence in our world, that cannot be the end of the story. We must find enough reasonably fixed reference points with regard to human behavior so that we can all see them, we can all refer to them, and we can all agree on how they should be applied. If the rules of social behavior only apply to some of us some of the time, and if we can walk around any of our definitions with a flip of meaning or interpretation, our society is destined to become increasingly fragile. Our conceptions of morality and justice, the spiritual and functional norms of behavior for our society, must be brought together in law. If they are not, we have no reliable map, and in a place where anything is forgivable, everything must be tolerable. Terrorism will grow like a mushroom in that environment, as our society progressively loses its bearings.

The Concordance of Laws

Italian authorities recently have seen the underlying issues of extradition as problems of concordance of laws. None of the democracies can knowingly send an individual to another country to be persecuted or abused. Thus, the greatest difficulty we have in reaching any extradition agreement is determining whether our laws respecting due process and our definitions of specific crimes and punishments will be more or less equally reflected in the treatment afforded any person we return to another country for trial. The more closely the laws of countries conform on the way each will deal with a given crime, the easier it will be for each to justify politically the act of extradition.

These are the kinds of ideas that fueled examination of the treaty issues in the Senate Foreign Relations Committee. The record of those discussions suggests that some members sought to formulate and agree to a revision of the U.S.-British extradition treaty which would have absolutely no legal effect in further constraining the freedom of political expression of the individual. Such a formulation, of course, would not hamper greatly the activities of the IRA.

Despite the problems that were exposed in the hearings on the U.S.-British treaty, extradition law provides an essential constraint on behavior, designed to provide a legal means to retrieve a fugitive from abroad. It sets ground rules respecting both the means that may be used to bring someone back to the country of a crime for trial, and the kind of legal framework that is acceptable from the viewpoints of both parties to a treaty with regard to the fairness of laws and the nature of due process. This is the only real means to date that governments have found for exporting effectively their concepts of criminal law and jurisdiction: entering into a treaty that sets acceptable rules and definitions, and binds both parties to them.

Informal Alternatives

Gross examples of efforts to bring individuals back to their own countries for trial or confinement have occurred in recent times. In 1984, for instance, the Nigerian government attempted to return a dissident former cabinet officer to Lagos by sedating him and shipping him back in a large crate, complete with an attending physician in the crate with him! In at least one case Israeli authorities have kidnapped an accused Nazi war criminal in order to bring him to Israel for trial. As I write there is a question as to whether Israeli physicist Mordechi Venunu was kidnapped from London in November 1986 and spirited to Israel. However it was done, Venunu surfaced in Israel in December 1986, crying foul.

In discussions among terrorism experts, it is common for some hardliners I know to suggest that the way to get terrorists into court for trial is simply to go get them and bring them in involuntarily. According to a *New York Times* report, Reagan administration officials have considered such possibilities. Moreover, State Department Legal Adviser Abraham D. Sofaer is cited as favoring " 'seizure' of fugitives in other countries if the chances for success were reasonable." Sofaer makes the point that no one should like the idea that the murderers of Americans "simply laugh about it and go on living their lives as if nothing happened."[14] In this instance, he seems to have been thinking of the specific case of Lebanon, where the government seems powerless to curb terrorist activity. Extraordinary measures to gain custody of a terrorist for trial are likely to be considered in these circumstances.

The legal standing of such procedures is not clear-cut, because the courts as a rule do not inquire into the way in which a defendant may have been brought before the bench. As one U.S. attorney put it to me, "The court does not question how you got the guy to come to court, unless a specific issue of mistreatment arises." Unless the delivery was accomplished by coercion exceeding the normal amount of force involved in arrest and detention, a court has little or nothing to go on. Nor is a U.S. court likely to look closely at the fact that a U.S. law enforcement officer, who has neither authority nor jurisdiction in a foreign country, detains an accused person and escorts that person back to the United States for trial.

In September 1987 U.S. authorities apprehended Fawaz Younis, one of the accused perpetrators of the June 11, 1985, hijacking of an Air Jordan flight with American hostages on board. The aircraft was destroyed on the ground in Amman, Jordan. Climaxing several months of careful effort to apprehend him, in September 1987 Younis was arrested by U.S. authorities on board a private yacht in the Mediterranean. He was immediately placed on board a U.S. vessel and returned to the United States for trial. At the time of writing Younis had assserted that he was mistreated in the process of his apprehension, and apparently x-rays of his wrists showed minute fractures. Thus, both the informal procedure used to apprehend Younis in international waters and the appropriateness of the amount of force involved may be tested in this single case.

Informal procedures to permit acquisition of a prisoner for trial have existed between governments for a long time. They have worked with varying efficiency in many cases either to speed up the process or simply to avoid the hassles possibly involved in formal extradition. For instance a number of accused drug traffickers have been escorted from Latin American countries by U.S. officials to stand trial in U.S. courts. Where, as in these cases, the subject matter was ordinary crime, the use of such procedures was not likely to generate much excitement, so long as the receiving state observed the rules of due process in detention and trial of a suspect, meaning that there was little or no prospect of political kickback.

Making Extradition Work in Terrorism Cases

Terrorism introduces the application of the political offense exception into extradition decisions on a scale never before required. As Judge Sofaer remarked in the *Times* article cited earlier, "The effort to apply law to modern terrorism is really in its infancy."[15] The first hurdle really is to get governments to agree on uses of extradition in cases where motives for crime are judged to be political. The approach used in the U.S.-British treaty revision—to remove violent crimes from coverage of the political offense exception—is one of the better routes to solving the international extradition problem. The more widely terrorism can be dealt with in the same way as other crimes, the more readily governments can cooperate in ways that eliminate the convenient way out that the terrorist now has. As Stephen Trott said, all the terrorist needs to beat the system is an airplane ticket.

An approach recently taken in revising the U.S.-Belgian extradition treaty appears to deal directly with the issue of the political offense exception. It does this by providing that people accused of acts of political violence will be extradited.[16] That can work, it seems to me, only if the two parties to such a treaty decide to ignore the political motive and deal with acts of violence as crimes. There is also a need to assure that the person extradited is not the victim of a false accusation. Given the danger of such accusations, and judging from the inability of international bodies to agree on a definition of terrorism, the conclusion of Belgium-type agreements with very many countries does not appear likely, at least for the foreseeable future.

The U.S.-British and U.S.-Belgian approaches appear essential to making extradition treaties work in dealing with terrorism. It is important that we succeed in such efforts to avoid falling into extensive use of extralegal procedures. Effective treaty procedures enable the law enforcement machinery to operate without resorting to devices and methods that resemble those of the terrorist organizations.

Another crucial aspect of making the international system work depends entirely on the state that is asked to extradite. Extradition treaties in general provide that a state asked to extradite an accused person may fulfill its obligation by trying that person and, if the person is found guilty, by meting out appropriate punishment. In January 1987 the United States asked the Federal Republic of Germany to extradite Mohammed Ali Hamadei to stand trial for the murder of Robert Dean Stethem. Hamadei is one of the four people identified by passengers as having hijacked TWA Flight 847 in June 1985, during which incident Stethem, a U.S. Navy diver, was beaten and shot by one or more of the hijackers. In June 1987, German authorities announced that they would not extradite Hamadei. Under the rules of the U.S.-German extradition treaty, Germany thus put itself under obligation to bring Hamadei speedily to trial, and if the court finds him guilty, to impose a sentence appropriate to the crime of murder. As of the time of writing, no trial date has been set for Hamadei, and the impression is growing that the Hezballah terrorists who kidnapped two German nationals in Lebanon in order to intimidate the Bonn government may have succeeded.

The Importance of Clear Rules

As was discussed in chapter 2, an important element to the future managing of extradition problems lies with the way decisions are made about safe haven or political asylum. If the United States or other nations use the language of the political offense exception in treaties to tell other governments that acts of violence against their citizens cannot be redressed because the perpetrators were acting politically, the definitional problems that impede action against international terrorism can only increase. And if the United States cannot agree with the other democracies on acceptable ground rules of extradition, the chances for working out the problem successfully with anyone else are slim indeed. Every government can exercise the right to say when someone has committed an act of political protest rather than a crime. But if everybody does it, any capacity to deal with political violence across national boundaries practically disappears. The number of usable hiding places among the democratic governments greatly expands and with that the likelihood that crimes will go unpunished. That number expands enormously as one looks at the diversity of political and legal systems governing our world.

This counsels a very sparing and judicious use of any political rationale for denying extradition. It also counsels the democracies to undertake an effort of the greatest seriousness to achieve a concordance of laws and practices that will assure equal treatment before the laws of any of the countries with which they have extradition treaties in force. Even when that is done, the great task remains of making appropriate arrangements with Communist and other centrally directed legal systems.

The fact we must cope with ultimately is that the attitudes of many governments toward the so-called political offense create a large protective circle around terrorism. The presence of the political offense exception in almost one hundred treaties between the United States and other countries suggests that there is an immense amount of diplomatic work to be done to change the situation. However, if governments fail to get together, the terrorists will enjoy unimpeded freedom of action. If, on the other hand, governments develop an international system to close the gaps between nations and create a common legal approach to crime in the global community, the benefits will be enormous.

4

To Deal or Not to Deal
with Terrorists

D URING February 1986, when the recently publicized Iran arms deals
were just getting under way, I attended a seminar in the Rayburn House
office building in which former Lebanon hostage Jeremy Levin and several
members of the audience sharply criticized the Reagan administration's policy
of no concessions to terrorists and its related practice of quiet diplomacy. Levin
asserted forcefully that in two cases, one his own and the other that of the
Reverend Benjamin Weir, nothing happened on their release until the wives
of the hostages "went public." He did not go so far as to say that going public
forced the government to negotiate, but I and other officials working to obtain release of the hostages had no doubt that forcing the issue was the goal
of the publicity campaign. Levin argued in effect that terrorists are at war
and that negotiating in a terrorist hostage situation is an appropriate response.
Levin observed at one point that cynics and skeptics of the no-concessions
policy believe anyway that when the chips are down the United States always
negotiates, and therefore it should abandon altogether the posture of refusing to do so. Voicing this same theme, Mrs. Peggy Say, sister of hostage Terry
Anderson, urged on her return from Damascus, Syria, in June 1986 that the
United States should abandon the no-concessions policy and "get in there
and negotiate."

These were only two examples of a mounting campaign by hostage families
and friends, which began in early 1984 and continued through 1985 and
much of 1986, to get the U.S. government to make a maximum effort to
obtain freedom for American hostages in Lebanon. The highly publicized
"nontrade" with the Soviets for Nicholas Daniloff in late 1986 added more
pressure, and at one point the hostage families and the terrorists were on the

same side, arguing that the United States should enter into a Daniloff-type deal.[1]

So long as the administration seemed to be making no visible effort, hostage families and friends felt compelled to push for negotiations, but those pressures had three rather perverse effects: First, by pounding on the administration to push it toward negotiating with the terrorists, the hostage families tended to legitimate the terrorists as parties to a negotiation. Second, the push to negotiate gave the terrorists hope that their demands might eventually be met. This at least encouraged them to hold out and prolong the captivity of American and other hostages. Third, the rising pressure for action appears to have goaded U.S. officials, who in my personal judgment were always working pretty steadily at trying to get the hostages out, into moving faster and less thoughtfully than they should have. Thus, family pressures may have put at risk operations that might have succeeded if pursued with the necessary patience; they may also have prompted ventures into dubious and high-risk activities.

The Pressure to Deal

The fact that such pressures were being felt was made clear to me by Lt. Col. Oliver North in a statement he made during a workshop I moderated at the Foreign Service Institute in October 1985. Explaining the policy of no concessions to terrorists, Lt. Colonel North said that it "appears to many as a cruel and heartless and insensitive policy. It is based on the greater good, but for the private American citizens, particularly those who have been long resident in Beirut, it is an approach that they find to be unacceptable." North said that the families of the hostages had brought heavy pressure to bear through both media and personal contacts to get the government to "meet the demands of the terrorists who hold their loved ones in Lebanon."[2] Secretly, as it emerged in his June 1987 testimony before the Senate and House Select Committees on the Iran/contra affair, North and others were already in early phases of the Iran arms deal.

At the same time that these pressures were mounting, the Reagan administration, particularly through the chairman of the Interdepartmental Group on Terrorism, Ambassador Robert Oakley, was conducting an increasingly skillful campaign with governments in Western Europe to promote international cooperation in combating terrorism. Supporting that campaign was the fact, demonstrated by a series of attacks in 1984–85 and by overall international terrorism statistics for those years, that Europeans more often than Americans had become the victims. European governments thus had more reason to cooperate. One of Ambassador Oakley's key points was the demonstration that the problem of international terrorism was not that of the United States alone. And one of the crucial pieces of diplomatic baggage he carried when traveling abroad to promote cooperation, which was often, was the policy of no concessions to terrorists, which the United States, at least to that time, seemed to have applied better than most.

The Policy of No Concessions

The no-concessions policy is probably the least understood policy of the Reagan administration and of several previous administrations. But each president from Richard Nixon onward has attempted to apply it. The first and most common misunderstanding about this policy is the notion that no concessions means a policy of no negotiations. That has never been the case, and it has never been possible, because in every terrorist incident the government's role is to find some way to resolve it. This means in practical terms that some effort must be made to establish communications, directly or indirectly, with the terrorists and then some way must be found to bring the incident to an end. Ambassador Oakley explained this policy clearly in July 1985, saying that "our refusal to give in to terrorist demands . . . does not mean that we are unwilling to pursue any reasonable avenue toward the release of the Americans."[3] During the October 1985 workshop, Lt. Col. Oliver North elaborated further, saying that "our policy is not one of no negotiations or no meetings or no dialogue with terrorists, but rather one of no concessions." We have passed the word, he said, "through untold media our willingness to meet with those who hold our citizens." It is important to note, however, that none of the testimony in the Iran/contra hearings suggests that U.S. officials ever met directly with any member of the terrorist group Hezballah, which continues to hold American hostages, or that any concessions were made to that group in the course of arms deals with the Iranians.

While such statements of willingness to meet with the hostage takers were useful things to say to hostage families, it is not always possible or necessarily sensible to establish direct dialogue with the terrorists. As we saw in the Tehran hostage situation, President Jimmy Carter chose to work, successfully as it proved, through the Algerians, because they had good connections with Iranian leadership, something the United States did not have and in the circumstances could not easily develop.

Dealing through Intermediaries

In the case of the hijacking of TWA Flight 847 in June 1985, President Ronald Reagan saw little choice but to work through Shia Amal leader Nabih Berri, who acted as intermediary, even though his public actions and statements made it perfectly clear that he was sympathetic toward the terrorists.[4] In this as in most cases an effort was made by the government to determine what the terrorists wanted and then to judge whether it was feasible to concede that.

Using such an intermediary, with close associations and even involvement with the terrorists in their activities, has been necessary on several occasions. For example, in early 1984 a young American U.S. Agency for International Development (AID) contractor and his wife were kidnapped by Tamil separatists in the Jaffna area of Sri Lanka. The kidnappers were members of the Tamil Eelam Liberation Force, a subgroup of a movement to establish an independent Tamil state in Sri Lanka. This movement has many sources of sympathy and support in the Madras region of India, whose population is mostly Tamil. Moreover, intelligence information available at the time suggested that India had permitted or actively assisted the establishment of camps in the state of Madras to safe haven and train cadres of Tamil separatists from Sri Lanka. From the negotiator's point of view, those Indian connections put Indian authorities in a potentially strong position of influence over the kidnappers.[5] Thus, efforts were made both through Sri Lankan and official U.S. channels to get the Indians involved in negotiating the release of the hostages, even though Indian authorities at the time denied that separatists were operating from Indian territory.[6]

The confinement of this young couple fortunately proved to be brief, and it is not at all clear whether the strategy of getting the Indians to put pressure on the Tamil Eelam separatists was decisive, but it unquestionably was one of the avenues that should have been pursued to obtain their release. Certainly in cases of this sort the leadership of a country such as India, which is known to provide safe haven, financing, training, or other forms of support to a terrorist group, offers a promising point of contact for reaching the terrorists.

The issue, posed rather harshly by the Iran scandal, is how much of that kind of traffic is prudent with terrorists, with terrorism-sponsoring states, or with states that have influential relationships with the terrorists? The answer to that question is not at all simple, but pragmatically it boils down to recognizing that when you have to negotiate with hostage takers or their sponsors you are being forced to do something you otherwise would not do. If you are the negotiator, the key judgment you must make is how little you can manage to give away and still get your people back.

The Task of Coercive Bargaining

Finding that kind of a formula is the meat of a negotiation with any terrorist group. And in this regard the very natural pressure of the critics of the no-concessions policy and especially of hostage families and friends proceeds from an incorrect assumption: that bargaining with a terrorist is like bargaining with anybody else. Only rarely, if ever, can that be the case, because terrorist incidents are not friendly bargaining situations.

What I mean is that negotiating and making concessions are natural elements of a bargaining situation, but if the negotiation is freely arrived at, the parties on both sides come voluntarily to the bargaining table. Each party comes to the table with something to give and something to get, and the purpose of talking is to find a balance that is satisfactory to both. It is easy in this kind of situation to apply win–win strategies, because quite willingly each party gives something that is desired by the other, each party gets something that is desired, and the interests of both parties are served. Everybody wins!

But only in the crudest terms do terrorist incidents work that way. Terrorists create abnormal, deliberately coercive bargaining situations in which they seek by intimidation, kidnapping, murder, threats, or all of these forcefully to extract a concession from the other party. The concession as a rule is not something the other party willingly would give up; it may be, and frequently is, something that party does not own or control. In the case of TWA Flight 847, Hezballah terrorists took Americans hostage to get their friends out of jail in Kuwait, but ultimately they settled for an Israeli release of certain prisoners. Hezballah's strategy, which proved partially successful in that Israel did release several hundred prisoners, was to take a group of people captive against their will and then use them as nonconsenting bargaining chips to extract concessions from an unwilling government. This hardly characterizes a natural bargaining situation; rather, the terrorists underscored the unnatural character of the case by beginning the TWA 847 negotiation with the brutal beating and murder of Robert Stethem.

Is the Policy a Catch-22?

The Reagan administration and others before it have adhered to a no-concessions policy for the stated reason that when you make the concessions the terrorists demand you set the stage for future terrorist events. This argument, as we have heard it often from the president and others, is that conceding what the terrorists want in order to obtain the release of kidnapping victims only tells the terrorists that kidnapping is a successful strategy and therefore encourages them to set up future incidents and take more hostages.

Since we usually negotiate through some channel with the terrorists and normally make some kind of concession to them, some people would view the stated U.S. policy as pure catch-22: We have no real choice but to make some kind of a deal with the terrorists, but if we do, it is very likely that we will encourage future terrorist attacks. This is what troubles many people, and up to a point the problem seems inescapable, but there is much more to the policy than that.

As we in the United States have flagellated ourselves over the outcomes of the Iran scandal, we have forgotten that no other government has options that are different from those available to us. Democratic governments especially cannot fail to make the effort to get their citizens back, and this means that most Western governments faced with hostage situations have bargained, and they have done so without apology.[7]

The issue, given that you may have no choice in an incident but to negotiate at some level, is really what you should be prepared to negotiate about. A closely related issue is what kind of posture you should convey to the terrorist. These two issues often tend to get confused with each other, but it is essential to keep them separate; you may indeed be prepared to make certain concessions, but you do not say that up front to the terrorists, because to do so is effectively to tell them where to begin the bargaining.

Avoiding Concessions of Substance

On the subject of what is to be negotiated, a no-concessions policy is designed to start the terrorist as low as possible on the scale of concessions and then to keep the bargaining as far as possible from any concessions of substance. For instance, it may be necessary to provide food and water so that hostages do not suffer, or possibly to provide fuel that would permit a hijacked aircraft to take off but could keep the situation calm and buy time for finding a way out that is acceptable. Put in these terms, it is clear that an ordinarily prudent concern for personal interests, the interests of the victims, or the interests of the countries involved compel a negotiator to approach a terrorist bargaining situation in this way.

In part, what a nation may have to concede can be influenced by its level of attack and by its negotiating posture. On the matter of posture, there have been persistent problems in the United States' dealings with Iran. One of the crucial errors of President Jimmy Carter in the Iran hostage crisis was to surface early and prominently as chief U.S. negotiator. Standing right out front, he gave himself no layers of protection against being manipulated by the Iranians. President Reagan appears to have seen that pitfall and tried to stay out of it, but by permitting the Iran operation to be conducted so close to the Oval Office, he created an exposure to manipulation by Khomeini's supporters that made him, as the experience proved, perhaps more vulnerable than Carter. In both cases, once the Iranians discovered that the president was prepared to make concessions they gained a dangerous capacity for controlling the course of events. That in itself is a potent reason to keep a posture of no concessions in place as long as possible and to protect the president's role and options by keeping the presidency far removed from any actual negotiating process.

The Issue of Legitimacy

There are other strong reasons for maintaining a strong policy of no concessions to terrorists. Denial of legitimacy to the terrorist group, as will be discussed in chapter 10, is a particularly important one. Part of almost any terrorist group strategy is to capture public sympathy and thereby gain support for their negotiation or their cause. This is a way of achieving legitimacy in the eyes of the public. If the group can do so it will have won a significant victory and biased any negotiation in some degree in its favor. As an example of this process, both Shia Amal leader Nabih Berri, in general a moderate who competes with the radical Hezballah for sway over Lebanese Shiites, and Syrian president Hafiz al-Assad enhanced their standing with their own supporters and with outsiders because of their role in negotiating with the United States to resolve the TWA Flight 847 hijacking.

Jeremy Levin, in his statement mentioned earlier, made an argument that bears materially on the legitimacy of the terrorists. In substance, he argued that the terrorist hostage situation should be treated like a prisoner of war situation and that a prisoner exchange should be undertaken whenever necessary to obtain return of one's own people. On that basis, the United States should arrange a trade of the group of Dawa party dissidents in jail in Kuwait for the U.S. hostages now being held by Hezballah and other groups in Lebanon.

The Dawa party group, incidentally, was convicted by a Kuwaiti court of carrying out six terrorist attacks, including bombing the U.S. embassy in Kuwait,
and three members of the group apparently have close family ties to Hezballah.

I objected in that discussion to the idea of prisoner exchanges, pointing
out that the United States is not at war with Hezballah, nor, perhaps more
to the point, is Kuwait. Thus, arguing for "prisoner" exchanges in such a
case would extend an aura of legitimacy to Hezballah which it clearly does
not deserve. The action would be in a class with trading "Cosa Nostra" leaders
now in jail in the United States for kidnap victims.

I noted in this discussion that the Soviet Union and the Warsaw Pact countries have tried repeatedly to get the activities of certain groups that engage
in terrorism covered by the Geneva convention in order to legitimate their
activities, including their terrorist crimes.

Both Jeremy Levin and another participant in the seminar commented that
the trend had already been set by Israel's trade of prisoners as part of the
deal to obtain release of U.S. hostages aboard TWA Flight 847. They were
absolutely right. In May 1987 the Israelis reinforced this pattern by trading
suspected terrorists for three Israelis held prisoner in Lebanon. Throughout
the negotiation in the TWA 847 case, both the U.S. negotiators and the Israelis
had tried to identify the minimum necessary concessions without destroying
the basic policy, but the number of prisoners returned represented a major
concession. That success in negotiation undoubtedly encouraged Hezballah
to go on holding American and other hostages and to kidnap even more in
succeeding months on the theory that eventually the United States would
make the deal they wanted—the release of the Kuwait bombers. Both the
deal to get the TWA 847 hostages back and the legitimacy the terrorists acquired from being part of the negotiation could only have made the next
stages of effort to get the American hostages out much harder.

Denying Terrorism as a Bargaining Strategy

Refusing to accept terrorism as a bargaining strategy is another important reason
for making no concessions. Specifically, it counsels against giving in to terrorist demands on any matter of substance. If you say that you are prepared
to negotiate with terrorists on their demands, you at least imply that political
crimes of murder, intimidation, kidnapping, hostage taking, or destruction
of property are acceptable tools to bring to the bargaining table. Yet every
civilized society, certainly all of the democracies, considers terrorist acts as
criminal acts. Thus, to abandon a stated policy of no concessions would be

to say, in effect, that you are normally prepared to bargain no matter how the other party gets you to the bargaining table.

Sending that signal to the terrorists is a far more serious matter than making a concession or two, because the signal really means that terrorist tactics have become part of the normal bargaining habit of society. That would be a fundamental encouragement to terrorists or to anyone else who finds voluntary bargaining processes frustrating.

In the final analysis the no-concessions policy is designed to keep governments, victims, and families from paying more than they should. It is meant to reduce their exposure to making concessions on matters about which they should not bargain under duress. It was foolish to assume that at any time a policy of no concessions meant exactly that, no concessions of any kind. There isn't any free lunch even for terrorist victims. Somebody always pays something. To resolve an incident in some satisfactory way, negotiators end up having to bargain, and that means to give, at least a little.

But we should not be dismayed by the discovery that the policy of no concessions is hardly pure. The notion that one human being or a government should confront another from a position of absolutely no give is not realistic either for our society or for our times, and it probably never was. Experienced officials in the United States and in other governments accept this, but they still favor keeping the no-concessions policy as a working premise for any negotiation with a terrorist, because they argue that there should be no automatic conveyance of legitimacy.

Achieving Effective Contact

Achieving an effective bargaining contact and dialogue with the terrorists may constitute a tougher hurdle than deciding on what, if any, concessions to make. You may in fact know exactly where the terrorists are. In hijackings or hostage barricade situations you usually do know, but establishing effective contact for bargaining purposes may still be elusive.

The Lebanon hostage cases have been particularly difficult in this respect. Ever since a few weeks after Jeremy Levin and William Buckley were kidnapped, U.S. authorities have known that the group involved is the so-called Hezballah or "Party of Allah," whose spiritual leader is a Lebanese Shiite named Mohammed Hussein Fadlallah. This group is known to receive financial support and sometimes instructions from Iranian leadership through Iran's ambassador in Damascus. This group is also known to headquarter in the Bekaa Valley near the pre-Roman ruin of the temple of Baalbek, across the street from Syrian Army headquarters. In sum, the group is sponsored by Iran, safe havened by Syria, and given sympathy and support by various groups in Lebanon.

Knowing that much about Hezballah, however, has not solved the problem for U.S. authorities of how to establish a working dialogue to obtain release of the American hostages. Hezballah naturally tries to keep secret the identities of any members actually involved in holding those hostages, and it tries to keep the actual locations of the hostages as uncertain as possible. The group is very suspicious of people who may approach its members on behalf of the United States, and it has a rational concern about being destroyed. Hezballah thus keeps its movements furtive and its plans secret.

The Problem of Ransom Payments

That description of Hezballah would sound much the same if we were discussing a group of ordinary criminals engaged in kidnapping for profit. And here we get to the nub of the no-concessions policy: Hezballah and other terrorist groups have understood all along that no concessions doesn't mean no deals. Private business, contrary to the policies of numerous governments, has a more or less established practice of paying ransom to the terrorists. Several governments, including France and the United States, have made or have permitted back-channel approaches through intermediaries or cutouts, meaning covert intermediaries, to indicate that a ransom might be paid. Such offers were circulated through underworld channels in Italy during the kidnapping of Brigadier General James Lee Dozier. Similar offers, according to public statements by Ross Perot, were made and backed by Perot's funds in the effort to obtain the release of American hostages in Lebanon. The release of Peter Kilburn, the librarian at American University in Beirut, was a particular objective of these efforts, before his captors murdered him as a gesture supporting Muammar Qaddafi following the April 14, 1986, U.S. raid on Libya.

The point here is that terrorists in Europe, the Middle East, and Latin America, where most incidents occur, have been paid ransoms on many occasions for the return of hostages, frequently businessmen. Selling back a kidnapped company executive in fact has become a thriving little business in places like Colombia. Adhering to an official policy of no concessions to terrorists must be seen in this context for what it truly is: a way to keep concessions to a minimum and to make the terrorist's job as hard as possible. Either is a good enough reason for keeping this policy and for encouraging business organizations to adopt it.

The Need for Secrecy

Establishing contact with terrorists and beginning a bargaining process with them is a delicate business that is best pursued in secret. A terrorist may surface from time to time, with a hood over his or her head, to get publicity and to try to influence the bargaining process, but the bargaining itself occurs elsewhere. Because bargaining occurs in secret, and because resolving an incident can be profitable, the possibility of acting as an intermediary often brings out, as a State Department friend put it, "every slippery character in the country." At one point, this source indicated, to get the Lebanon hostages back there had been more than a dozen such shadowy approaches, each proponent seeking to work out the case for profit, for political advantage, or for positions of influence. No doubt groups such as Hezballah have found such intermediaries useful for testing the waters as well as for passing along signals to U.S. officials as part of the coercive bargaining process.

Dealing with Criminals: The Case of Iran

A difficult problem for the government is that each such approach presents a dilemma: the person making the approach may be a politician on the outs with the leadership at home, a known criminal, an arms or drug dealer, or a con artist. As I commented in a recent article in the *National Review*, however, it is necessary to check each one out, because the person who makes the approach just may be in a position of sufficient influence and access to the terrorists to be effective in obtaining release of the hostages.[8] Thus, a senior State Department official commenting on these approaches said he didn't like any part of them, but he didn't dare object to following up because "this time just might be different."

When the National Security Council (NSC) staff and the Central Intelligence Agency (CIA) began their effort to work through Iran to secure the release of American hostages in Lebanon, they were well aware of everything discussed up to this point in this chapter, and they undoubtedly knew a great deal more. John Poindexter and William Casey, as the responsible cabinet-level officers, and Oliver North and Dewey Claridge, as action officers, knew fully in advance that most of the people they would have to deal with would be unreliable, self-serving, politically ambitious, and in some instances rabidly anti-American.

Finding Somebody with a White Hat

Knowing both Adm. John Poindexter and Lt. Col. Oliver North reasonably well from working with them as a member of the Interdepartmental Group on Terrorism, I haven't the slightest doubt that their efforts with the Iranians were part of an approved covert operation; but putting that issue aside for the moment, what were their choices? Could they have chosen a better group to do business with? No. The option was not theirs, because there weren't any "white hats" with real influence over the terrorists offering their services. Could they count on success in obtaining release of the hostages through intermediaries such as the Archbishop of Canterbury's representative, Terry Waite? With all due respect, they could not, but it was essential to assist Terry Waite's efforts to keep moral pressure on the terrorists, and it just might work. Could they have waited for a better time? Yes, but at the cost of indefinite confinement for five known remaining hostages. Would the hostages survive if they waited? Probably, but given the reported torture of William Buckley, the murder of Peter Kilburn, and the threats against the other hostages Hezballah conveyed on videotape, the prospect was hardly reassuring.

Once they started down the road of dealing with Iran, could they avoid helping the Iranians and possibly the Hezballah terrorists by making concessions? No. The question was only how significant the concessions would have to be. Could they have resolved firmly in advance what they would and would not concede in bargaining with Iran? Yes, but at the risk of rendering their negotiating position untenable from the beginning. Could they really change the course of events in Iran? Maybe, but probably not very much and certainly not very rapidly.

What Were Minimum Concessions?

In short, once the process started, the president, Admiral Poindexter and Lieutenant Colonel North, former National Security Adviser Robert C. McFarlane, and the CIA and Pentagon officials who were party to the arms transactions were stuck with finding out what the minimum concessions were going to be, and they were stuck with doing business with people who could not be trusted, who didn't deserve to be helped, and who were hardly going to be reformed by the experience.

In trying to fix blame for the Iran scandal, critics have made much of the roles of a hard-working and zealous lieutenant colonel of Marines and a CIA concerned about one of its own, William Buckley, and also about the secrets he might already have passed under torture to his captors. In my judgment, however, the compassion of the president and the sometimes strident public calls by hostage families to "do something" were the crucial elements leading to the approach to Iran. Oliver North, a regular and sharply questioning reader of the intelligence reporting each day, knew full well how deeply Iran had gotten involved in terrorist attacks against the United States. He had watched that pattern emerge over a period of more than four years. Moreover, other members of the Interdepartmental Group on Terrorism, particularly in the State Department, the Pentagon, the Justice Department, and the FBI, were tracking Iran's involvement, reading as a rule tne same reports. In light of what they were reading, two facts were clear. First, all members of this group had to appreciate that Iran was a key player in any scenario, short of a Lebanon raid, for getting the hostages released. A raid was deemed by most to be out of the question, because of the risks of harm to the hostages and the probability that Syrian air and ground forces would inflict substantial casualties on would-be rescuers. Second, as several were quick to assert after the Iran story broke in a Lebanese magazine, trying to do business with Iran was a risky, delicate, and painstaking task, and more than likely any attempt would fail.[9]

With all of that to consider, you might say that prudent people would have avoided the encounter, but every president for nearly two decades has had to wrestle with hostage situations, and each has discovered that one hostage or fifty present about the same challenge to the presidency. Leadership cannot be seen to be indifferent or inactive. Thus, the NSC and CIA players obviously did not feel that they had the luxury of free choice.

The electronic media, print media, and personal campaign of hostage families, mentioned by Lieutenant Colonel North during the October 1985 workshop, was driving leadership toward an approach to Iran. In 1985–86, led by Carol Weir, the wife of the Rev. Benjamin Weir, by Terry Anderson's sister, Mrs. Peggy Say, and by David Jacobsen's son, Eric, the hostage families mounted a blitz, including a petition with several thousand names, urging President Reagan to take more and more decisive action to free the hostages. In a letter to the president and in a televised statement two weeks into the Iran crisis, Mrs. Say recognized the pressure that that campaign had generated, saying that the hostage families had pushed for an effort to get their loved ones back which barred no avenue. Her point was that having pounded the table to get the president to do something, Americans could not then say, "We did not ask you to do that." She and many others had asked the president, she said, "to do whatever he could."

One can never say with certainty how the attempt to deal with Iran would have turned out in the absence of hostage family pressures. The family campaign, however, constantly indicated to the Iranians that the White House had to make some kind of deal. That perceived fact was an inducement to raise the ante and to stretch out the bargaining, or, as revealed once the story became public, even to renege on promises to release all of the hostages at once. Prolonging the bargaining of course increased the risk of exposure either by factions in Iran seeking to enhance their own positions or by critics of the Reagan Administration looking for ways to undercut his presidency. The first lead came from Iran.

What of Future Policy?

Senior officials in the Department of State are reported to have said at the time the Iran story broke that "we have no policy. The no-concessions policy has been destroyed." I took that view myself for the first few days of the Iran crisis but have since thought better of it. The cynic would say we cannot destroy a policy we never had, but that is the kind of moralizing throwaway line we cannot use in any attempt to erect a sane defense against international terrorism.

International terrorism remains with us, and, despite a recent lull in terrorist activity, it appears to be an increasingly popular tactic among weak, impatient, and misguided people who believe that such violence can be used in their causes without any consequences. Thus, the U.S. need for a workable policy stands, and the best policy the nation has found to date is a policy of no concessions. That policy never meant literally no concessions of any kind, but the United States must move real bargaining with terrorists as close to that position as it can get.

The nation's public posture must continue to be that the United States makes no concessions to terrorists. In any negotiation to resolve a terrorist incident U.S. officials should keep all concessions to a minimum and should avoid concessions of substance. Where U.S. leaders have control of the subject matter, they should be prepared to listen carefully to the grievances of people who feel oppressed to the point of taking the extreme measure of terrorism, because their complaints, as crudely put as they appear, may be telling us that some feature most people take for granted in American or other

Western societies is not working, at least for them. Against that eventuality, national leaders should be prepared to talk about grievances, but a precondition to any bargaining on the substance of terrorist grievances must be release of any hostages. Under terrorist pressure, governments should not alter their behavior or change their policy. They should in no circumstances bargain with terrorists about the release of convicted criminals or of individuals properly charged with such crimes. Nor should government leaders do an end run around their own stated policy by putting pressure on other governments to do these things, as U.S. officials clearly did through back-channel approaches to Kuwait. Governments should not pay ransom. Businesses should adopt a similar policy.

One stark lesson of the Iran experience is that private citizens or private groups should not compete with national leadership for control of the decision process. That was the effect of the publicity campaign of the hostage families. In these cases a country can have only one set of negotiators. To attempt otherwise blunts negotiative efforts and sends the wrong signals. This helps the terrorists, and the result is that negotiators end up paying more than they should, leadership loses prestige and public confidence, and the terrorists continue to hold our people hostage. A policy of no concessions will work only if our negotiators are free to play out each situation on merit.

All of those elements of a no-concessions policy make for some very tough sledding, and the key to achieving them is patience. The stakes always include the freedom or the peace of mind of individuals who, as hostages or as loved ones, are the unwilling and innocent victims of terrorism. Governments or business leaders should not let that fact push them, however, into taking the offensive when nothing appears to be happening, because nothing may be exactly what should be happening during the miserable, protracted time when negotiators are trying to get people back without paying more than they should. Hurrying the process because of public pressure is probably the most critical source of failure in the approach to Iran. The other side almost always wins if you hurry the bargaining, while winning helps to confirm the terrorists' choice of violence as a bargaining strategy.

5

The Quality of Mercy

H ow does a government deal with deliberate, systematic illegal acts by religious groups? In the history of the relationship between Church and state is there a precedent for persistent and willful violations by churches of the laws of the state? Has that happened without the Church's coming to any harm? In the tradition of sanctuary are there cases in which the state has willingly permitted the creation of safe houses in the community at large—that is, off Church premises? Is there a history of systematic defiance of federal law by units of state or local government? Does it matter that the laws being violated by these groups are not laws covering major crimes but nonetheless would get the ordinary citizen sent to jail for several months or even years? Does a church have some right to violate laws it doesn't like or to decide which laws of the state it will obey? If the Church extends sanctuary to someone it encourages to violate the law, is the Church also in violation of the law? If a private group that lacks the traditional religious cloak for the offer of sanctuary nonetheless offers such protection, should that group be treated legally any differently from the ordinary citizen? If a church decides to pursue its own political programs and foreign policy in a country, is it usurping the ordinary functions of government?

These are unusual questions to ask in the beginning of a chapter labeled "The Quality of Mercy" because they don't seem to have much to do with matters of the spirit such as compassion, charity, or mercy. They arise out of the stated goals, practices, and propaganda activities of the Sanctuary movement. In order to develop answers to these questions, let's start with some background.

The Idea of Sanctuary

Americans have made growing use of protest as a means of influencing or forcing major decisions, particularly since the end of World War II. Beginning in 1980, however, a new type of protest group began to develop around the old idea of the Church's offer of sanctuary. This group formed as many independent clusters of supporters around particular churches in different parts of the country, and soon it became known as the Sanctuary movement. By the end of 1985, the movement reported that it had acquired adherents in more than two thousand congregations around the country who were supporting about two hundred sanctuaries or equivalent facilities for selected refugees.[1]

Sanctuary is an old tradition of offering the safe haven of the Church to someone who pleads the threat of some injustice. As discussed in chapter 2, the granting of asylum by states and of sanctuary by churches usually has involved cases of significant danger to the safety or the liberty of the individual. It is seldom used in our time, and it never really has been a tradition in the United States. Nonetheless, many governments continue to offer asylum, even though the practice is endangered by the spread of international terrorism.

The present Sanctuary movement is associated with the churches and with church-affiliated groups. Its stated agenda is to provide assistance to refugees from Central America. However, much of its behavior, doctrine, and literature make the movement resemble a political action committee rather than any traditional church-based community service group. In essence, Sanctuary appears to be using the refugee issue as a lever to bring churches fully into the political process. To do that, the leaders of Sanctuary have adopted an activist doctrine of the Catholic clergy in Latin America called liberation theology.

The Theology of Liberation

In the United States, the relationship between the Church and the state has been guided by the establishment language of the First Amendment to the Constitution. I am not a lawyer, and the views presented here, therefore, will not be the views of a lawyer but of a layman. As I understand it the relationship between Church and state generally has been defined as one of complete separation, meaning that the state as an entity will not intervene in religion, and the Church as an entity will not intervene in governance. Government officials can be churchgoers, and churchgoers can influence laws and policy, but we are talking here about the defined roles of institutions.

Over two centuries of American constitutional history, the separateness of Church and state, if anything, has increased with the growing religious, ethnic, and cultural diversity of American society. At the same time, however, the intervention of church hierarchies in the political process has become commonplace. In effect the leaders of the country's churches have come to be regarded in the same class as other lobbying organizations—that is, as secular voices in the business of running the state.

About two decades ago, bishops of the Catholic Church in Latin America held a conference in Medellín, Colombia, in which they began to restate the nature of the relation between Church and state. Articulated in that conference and refined in Central America, Peru, Chile, and elsewhere, including the southern Philippines, was a new clerical concept called liberation theology. The theology of liberation, a "theology" only in the sense that it was developed by clerics, is a theory of political and social change. It considers development a "total social process" in which economic, political, cultural, social, and other factors must play a role. It argues that the way to help the poor is to transform society into a socialist state that is free of external domination. It asserts that the process is a class struggle to reform society and, some advocates say, to break away from traditional dependencies on capitalist countries. It also asserts, as the Catholic hierarchy of Chile did during the Allende regime, that the interests of Marxism and Christianity are parallel, and it undercuts the role of democratic values in the achievement of future peace and prosperity in the world's underdeveloped regions. The major unclear element of this concept is the role of traditional theology itself.

Dependency Theory

Liberation theology has an economic theory, for which it draws on the early writings and speeches of an Argentine economist, Raul Prebisch. As chairman of the United Nations Economic Council for Latin America during the 1960s, Prebisch formulated theories of international trade between Third World and developed countries that led to the so-called dependency theory.

In substance, Prebisch said that the terms of trade between advanced industrial countries and the relatively primitive, raw materials–producing countries worked to keep the latter in perpetual dependency. Many elements of Prebisch's theory were later shown to be factually weak, but it was too late; the idea had developed a life of its own.[2] Most significantly, it linked up intellectually with theories of revolutionary political change. As a result, it became a commonplace of the rhetoric of insurgency and part of the conventional wisdom of neoisolationist criticism of post-Vietnam U.S. foreign policy. Such linkages were likely to keep it around, whether or not dependency theory contained any arguments of consequence. It became an ideology for explaining the poverty and weakness of states, and it came equipped with its own whipping boys: the rich, industrial states.

The North Discovers Liberation

Although it was a Western Hemisphere invention, liberation theology did not attract much attention among North American clergymen until after the Latin American Bishops' Conference in Puebla, Mexico, in 1979. In that conference, Pope John Paul II collided with the activist clergy on the central premises of liberation theology, asserting that their mission was not to transform society but to carry out the traditional ministry of the church. Then, as outlined in a landmark study by George S. Weigel of the James Madison Foundation,[3] the Catholic leadership in the United States began to wake up to the political influence potential of a church-based theory of development, and they enunciated a policy toward Central America containing the following main propositions:

U.S. intervention in the region has been bad

Further U.S. intervention will lead to war

Struggles in Central America are largely indigenous

Those struggles should not be seen in the U.S.-Soviet geopolitical context

U.S. and Soviet interventions in the region are essentially the same

Poverty and human rights issues are a lot more important than national or regional security issues

Democratic forces cannot—that is, are unable to—mediate between authoritarianism and insurgency in the region[4]

Sanctuary Is Formed

At about the same time the American Catholic hierarchy was crafting its position on Central America, Protestant groups in the southwestern United States were also beginning to discover that region. The specific incident that brought Central America to their attention occurred in July 1980: a so-called coyote, a smuggler of refugees, abandoned twenty-six Salvadorans in the Arizona desert. Starvation, dehydration, and heat exhaustion caused the death of some of them before they were found. The plight of these refugees became a focal point for launching the Sanctuary movement.[5]

Ironically, the plight of twenty-six Salvadorans accomplished what the annual movement of tens of thousands of people across the Mexican border had not achieved in the preceding half-century: recognition of the severity of economic and social distress below the U.S. southern flank by the people in the immediate path of its most obvious manifestation, migration to the United States through Mexico. That blinkered perception of the nature of conditions on the land bridge from the United States to Colombia was to characterize the entire movement.

Sanctuary almost immediately adopted a confrontational style in its dealings with state, local, or federal authorities. This grew out of a judgment by some of Sanctuary's leaders that civil disobedience was the most effective means for attacking U.S. immigration laws and policies.[6] Some members were fond of referring to the sanctuaries they established as stops on an "underground railroad," but the movement really geared up to run a refugee-smuggling operation out of Mexico into the United States, and the aim was to maximize media attention. Meanwhile, the movement set out to fight government on overall policies toward Central America.

The operating style of Sanctuary was also established very early. As the official history of the movement reports, Jim Corbett, one of the heroes and a cofounder of the movement, learned on May 4, 1981, that a Salvadoran had been detained for entering the United States "without inspection," meaning that he had not come through border controls in the usual way. Corbett decided to call a high Immigration and Naturalization Service (INS) official to see if he could pay the Salvadoran a visit. In that call, Corbett pretended that he was another Jim Corbett, well-known in the region as a former mayor of Tucson and still at the time a county official, and the INS official agreed to the visit. While there, Corbett learned that there were several other Salvadorans being detained, and he went out to get necessary forms to designate a legal representative for them. While he was away, INS authorities, who had learned that he was not the Corbett he pretended to be, decided to move the detainees and then refused to inform Corbett of their whereabouts. The official bible of the Sanctuary movement says that Corbett was "shocked" to learn that the INS would resort to that kind of "trickery,"[7] conveniently forgetting, of course, his own deception. In time, Corbett began to run a "coyote" operation with the help of Catholic churches in Mexico, smuggling refugees selected out of groups waiting at those churches into the United States.[8]

Sanctuary's Public Agenda

The Sanctuary movement has developed since that point into a loose underground of churches and private individuals and groups who offer various forms of assistance to certain Central American refugees. But not to all. Refugees from El Salvador and Guatemala are the designated target groups. Mexicans, who continue to be the largest group of arrivals across the frontier each day, are not included. There appears to be some interest in refugees from Honduras and Costa Rica, but Nicaraguans are not on the target list, nor are Latin refugees from other parts of the hemisphere. Refugees from outside the hemisphere don't count at all, except that people in the movement express deep suspicion of the motives of the U.S. government in granting political asylum to refugees from places like Vietnam, Cambodia, Laos, Cuba, and other "Communist" countries because they believe that official policy creates a double standard by putting undue weight on admitting refugees from those countries.[9]

Sanctuary's highly discriminatory selection of individuals said to be deserving of help has troubled many people, including religious leaders. Richard John Neuhaus, director of the Rockford Institute's Center on Religion and Society, states the issue simply in an article for the quarterly journal, *This World*. "Most social movements," he says, reflect "some tension" between the way "they present themselves to the public" and their "less 'saleable' purposes." The problem in the case of the Sanctuary movement is that the group's projected image "contradicts the reality."[10]

The Real Sanctuary Agenda

The reality, continues Neuhaus, is that the Sanctuary movement is "very selectively concerned" about refugees. Rather, he suggests that a number of the "refugees" Sanctuary has presented to American media are activists from El Salvador and other Central American countries who are engaged in a "struggle against U.S. imperialism." The main battle they are pursuing therefore is political, and their campaign is "being orchestrated as ideological theater in cruel indifference" to the interests or the plight of refugees.[11]

Neuhaus has used very strong language to characterize a movement that has attracted so much support from church groups and congregations. What, then, is the problem? The problem, say religious researchers Kerry Ptacek and Laura Ingraham, is that Sanctuary is using an appeal to "religious sentiments" to gain support for activities that are "dedicated to opposing U.S. Central American policy," but the principal motive of Sanctuary, say Ptacek and Ingraham, is to promote "a strategy for radical change in the United States."[12]

The agenda of the Sanctuary movement, while somewhat differently stated, is the same one established by the Catholic hierarchy in the United States for Central America. Statements by leaders, extensive press and other media coverage, other writings, and the movement's own writings suggest the following movement program:

Withdrawal of the United States government from Central America because

Its presence is disruptive
Its policies are bad
It is incapable of promoting beneficial change

Reduction or elimination of the U.S. presence abroad, because U.S. military and business activities are destructive

Termination of U.S. opposition to Nicaragua

Withdrawal of U.S. support for the contra insurgency against Nicaragua's Sandinista government

Withdrawal of U.S. government support for governments in El Salvador and Guatemala to permit the so-called popular forces (the leftist FMLN) to take over

That the Sanctuary agenda turns increasingly inward on the United States itself was made clear by William Sloane Coffin in his chapter in *Sanctuary.*[13] He says that members of the Sanctuary movement cannot really distinguish between foreign policy and domestic policies, and the way to alter foreign policies, he concludes, is to change domestic policy.[14] Nor is that essential emphasis likely to be changed, as some Sanctuary advocates have indicated, if immigration policies are opened to permit ready arrival and acceptance of refugees from El Salvador. As Coffin suggests, he would keep the movement going until the agenda outlined above is achieved,[15] and that agenda on its face has little to do with the status of refugees.

It should be noted at this point that implicit in the agenda outlined above is support for terrorism and insurgency in Central America. I will come back to this issue a bit later.

Sanctuary's Propaganda Approach

Neuhaus referred to the Sanctuary campaign as "ideological theater." The first example of that idea can be seen in the mere fact that the United States is singled out as the worldwide bogeyman respecting the treatment of the world's displaced peoples. In 1986 and in most recent years the United States has taken in more displaced people than *all other countries of the world put together.*[16] Apart from its failure to acknowledge that fact, Sanctuary then goes on to turn a specific disagreement with U.S. authorities over the status of migrants from two countries into a blanket condemnation of U.S. policy in this field. Even if its members are right about some migrants from Central America, Sanctuary's treatment of the issue is reckless if not downright dishonest. The only possible explanation for this degree of blindness has to be that Sanctuary wants to use the refugee issue for propaganda purposes.

The approach of other Sanctuary promoters makes it clear that helping refugees is less important than specific propaganda goals. In early 1987, for example, Sanctuary began to promote vigorously a "D.C. Sanctuary City Campaign," with the object of getting the citizens of the District of Columbia to persuade the government to declare the nation's capital a sanctuary. Operating out of an office in northwest Washington, Sanctuary representatives called on the leadership of Area Neighborhood Councils and other civic groups and asked these groups to give them time in meetings, to permit them to raise money and to circulate a brochure, the main point of which was an attack on U.S. policy in Central America. In this instance, obviously the status of migrants from Central America was not at issue, because as early as 1980 there were already close to 2,000 Salvadorans and Guatemalans resident in the District of Columbia, and fewer than 350 of them had received citizenship. In March 1987, the District of Columbia school system reported that there were 3,000 Salvadoran students in District of Columbia public shools, and one estimate placed the number of Salvadorans in the greater Washington area at 150,000.[17] Declaring the District of Columbia a sanctuary to help refugees, therefore, practically speaking, is unnecessary, but getting that declaration to embarrass the U.S. government politically would be an accomplishment.

That the name of the game is propaganda was further illustrated in February 1987 when Amnesty International decided to adopt a Sanctuary worker, Stacey Lynn Merkt, who was charged by U.S. authorities with helping illegal aliens to enter the United States, as "a prisoner of conscience." Neither she nor other defendants deny committing the acts that brought the felony charges against them. Amnesty, which previously had refused to accept Sanctuary assertions of the risk to people returned to El Salvador,[18] in this instance reiterated Sanctuary's view that Stacey Merkt was being imprisoned "because of her humanitarian work" under laws that "directly facilitate the violation of human rights."[19] Why Amnesty selected her is not entirely clear when you consider that the six-month sentence she received is neither excessive nor unusual when someone is convicted of the felony charge involved.

Sanctuary Supporters versus Sanctuary Leadership

From this point onward, I want to split this discussion. First, I want to make it clear that I think there are many people associated with the Sanctuary movement who are genuinely interested in alleviating human suffering; and I believe that is their entire agenda, apart from the satisfaction that any healthy person derives from helping someone in distress. Second, I believe that the goodwill, the energy, and the financial resources of those people are being used by elements of the movement, including some of its leadership, to pursue their political agenda, and they are both misleading and failing to inform the larger community that supports them.

Misleading the congregations is not just a polite failure to inform. As two members of a tour group to Central America describe their experiences in the April 16, 1985, issue of the *Congressional Record*, members of church groups who try to get behind the information ordinarily available from Sanctuary movement propaganda sources are thoroughly guided. They are practically led by the hand through a biased exposure that involves elements of conditioning and manipulation. One member of this group called the process "brainwashing." But the process in this case obviously did not take, because these two visitors reached these conclusions:

The Center for Global Service and Education of Augsburg College in Minneapolis, Minnesota, "is working against the best interests of the people of Central America and of the United States"

"The travel seminar is designed, organized and conducted to overwhelm the participants with information which supports the anti-U.S. pro-Sandinista bias . . ."

"The poor, illiterate and semiliterate people of Mexico and Central America are being manipulated by the left to build hatred and fear of the U.S."

Liberation theology "is being used extensively not only to ensnare the suffering people in the revolutionary movement but also to corrupt well-intentioned people . . ."

"Reality in Central America is not as it was painted for us by our tour leaders"

Obviously not everyone is taken in by such carefully planned and guided presentations of information, but many are. These types of presentations make it clear that Sanctuary's ostensible goal of helping refugees is only incidental to promoting political change. That split in objectives places Sanctuary's affiliated congregations at large in the awkward position of providing unwitting support to an enterprise that is much more political than charitable.

Breaking the Rules of Sanctuary

I indicated at the beginning of this chapter that the Sanctuary movement is breaking the rules of sanctuary, and its members are doing so in several ways. First, members of the movement willfully break the law by bringing aliens into the United States and keeping them from registering, not so much to help the aliens but to force changes in the law. That action alone would probably qualify as ordinary civil disobedience, except that members of the movement both break the law themselves and encourage foreign nationals to break the law in a manner that is conspiratorial. The disobedience has ceased to be a mere act of protest.

Second, Sanctuary has created a system of safe houses,[21] both within and outside church properties, which are intended to be used by refugees, but by bringing in activists from groups it supports, such as the Faribundo Martí National Liberation Front, and helping them to promote their cause in the United States, the movement leaves itself open to terrorist use of its sanctuaries. The Faribundo Martí group has been responsible for numerous attacks, including the 1985 kidnapping of President José Napoleón Duarte's daughter and the shooting of off-duty U.S. Marines and civilians in San Salvador. With that history, one can rightly ask whether members of the Faribundo group are taking advantage of Sanctuary and using its facilities to promote violent activities in El Salvador.

Third, as Neuhaus, Ptacek, and Ingraham all note, the agenda of Sanctuary is almost entirely political. The key to that agenda is its emphasis on revolutionary change. Chapters 19 and 20 of *Sanctuary* articulate a rationale for fundamental change in American society. As Sloane Coffin explains it, if rebel groups in Central America were to be successful, their successes could light the way for change in the United States,[22] meaning that lessons learned from revolution in Central America could be imported into the United States.

Sanctuary's Arguments on Refugees

Sanctuary's battle with the U.S. Immigration and Naturalization Service, at first blush, appears to grow out of compassion and humanitarianism. The stated objective of Sanctuary is to get the INS to stop returning would-be immigrants from Central America to their countries of origin to face possible torture or death. *Sanctuary* begins with the charge that over one million refugees have left the region. The book then goes on to recite statistics on deaths and disappearances, attacks on nuns, priests, and other clergy, as well as on old people and children who have been killed by military bombardments and sweeps of the countryside.[23]

Sanctuary leaders argue that the sole reason for the chaos in Central America is the policy of the Reagan administration. According to Sanctuary numbers, more than half a million Salvadorans have come to the United States since Reagan came to office. Those people, Sanctuary says, qualify as political refugees entitled to asylum in the United States under international law, and they argue that the policies of the Reagan administration and enforcement of the Immigration and Naturalization Act of 1980 by the INS are sending thousands of refugees back to the region to face torture and death.

The facts do not support Sanctuary in this. Looking at El Salvador as the central case in Sanctuary's argument, the pattern of low-level violence that now keeps that country in turmoil has roots at least a century old. It is attributable not only to *machismo*—the masculine ego of the Salvadoran male, who often carries a weapon and uses it frequently to settle trivial disputes—but also to an established pattern of repression and exploitation of the Salvadoran people by governments. The 1977 report of the U.S. Department of State to the Congress on human rights describes a three-part picture of the violence in El Salvador, saying, "During 1977 terrorism [came] from both the left and the right, as well as from criminal groups." Regional scholars such as Cynthia Arnson trace the roots of modern repression back into the 1930s.[24] Only in the past few decades has there been any real movement away from that pattern, and the present government of José Napoleón Duarte has advanced the process of breaking El Salvador out of its oligarchic past more than any previous regime.

The argument that only current events and policies are responsible for the exodus from El Salvador doesn't hold up either. Population growth and lagging economic development have combined for years to make El Salvador a regional source of migrants, particularly into Honduras.[25] That country has been the host for thousands of Salvadoran squatters for several decades. According to State Department data, of the 500,000 estimated El Salvadoran refugees in the United States in mid–1985 more than 300,000 were already in the United States in 1979.[26] Projections of population growth and economic development for the region do not show much promise for improvement in the situations that have led to increasing northward migration in the past decade.

With regard to its actual help to refugees, Sanctuary's approach contains some glaring contradictions. First, the refugees the Sanctuary movement "coyotes" pick up in Mexico are already out of any danger that their home country might represent. Mexico, to be sure, is not much better off economically than the other countries, but the refugees are not threatened. Sanctuary then brings them across the border into the United States where, according to Sanctuary's charges, they are exposed to deportation back into the dangerous situation that allegedly exists in their home countries. Then, by putting them in hiding in the United States and using its anti-U.S. propaganda on them, Sanctuary frightens them first with the threat of deportation and then with the risk of return home. Where in this is there any real compassion, and what has happened to the quality of mercy?

The Intergovernmental Committee for Migration, based in Geneva, Switzerland, takes issue with Sanctuary's charges of torture and harm to returnees. The ICM sent questionnaires to more than six thousand people who returned to El Salvador during 1984–86, and of the more than five thousand who replied only thirty-five returnees said they had encountered problems.[27]

The INS bogeyman stories do not hold up. While many Salvadorans have returned to their country voluntarily, a great many of those who came to the United States from the late 1970s onward are still in the country. The overwhelming majority of them are illegal aliens or people who have not yet gained citizenship. They have not been sent back without recourse. In 1984, more than thirteen thousand Salvadoran claims for asylum were denied by INS district directors, but more than nine thousand of the claimants were permitted to remain in the United States pending an appeal of their petition. Thus, while the status of thousands of Salvadorans still awaits settlement, for those who have applied for adjudication, the rules permit them to remain in the United States until a determination is made.

The Refugee Burden of Proof

If Sanctuary is interested only in the welfare of refugees, a significant part of its reason for being may have been eliminated in March 1987 when the U.S. Supreme Court decided to ease the burden of proof on petitioners for asylum.[28] Under the Immigration and Naturalization Act of 1980, the INS had applied a rule that required petitioners to show that they faced "a clear probability of persecution" if they were returned to their country. The Supreme Court ruled in the case of *INS* v. *Cardoza-Fonseca* that petitioners for asylum need only show "a well-founded fear of persecution" in order to show eligibility for the grant of asylum.[29]

Coming Back to the Opening Questions

This chapter began with the question, how does a government deal with deliberate, systematic illegal acts by religious groups? The U.S. government, I believe, is responding with immense generosity. I say that because in the history of the relationship between Church and state, the Church has seldom, if ever, invoked sanctuary as a cover for violating the law itself. Sanctuary has been available for the possible victims of injustice who came to the Church seeking help, but that is hardly the same thing as the way the Sanctuary movement is trying to use the concept by going aggressively into foreign countries and finding people to bring back and hide. The tolerance so far displayed by government for Church activities of this kind goes far beyond historic precedents. Rather, abuses by the Church in the past have resulted in curtailment or termination of the Church right to extend sanctuary.

Nor in the past has the state permitted the concept of sanctuary to flow out into a system of safe houses in the community at large—that is, off church premises. The state would refuse to permit this for the obvious reason that creating such extralegal enclaves is an invitation to anarchy. Determinations by cities such as San Francisco, California, or Takoma Park, Maryland, to provide sanctuary to Guatemalan and Salvadoran refugees is a violation of law that has nothing to do with the historic privilege of the Church to offer sanctuary. That the state permits private groups in any degree to set up so-called sanctuaries off church premises is a further mark of government tolerance for dissent in the United States.

It probably is of some consequence that the laws being violated by Sanctuary are not laws covering major crimes. The crimes nonetheless are felonies. An ordinary citizen would be jailed for several months or even years if he or she were to run an alien smuggling operation like that described in the book *Sanctuary*. If a church extends sanctuary to someone whom it encourages to violate the law, it would seem that the church also is in violation of the law. Moreover, it would seem that any citizen of the country has a right to take strong exception to such persistent and willful violations of the law by any seemingly preferred group, especially if those acts go unpunished while other citizens are forced to obey the law or pay the penalty.

Sanctuary could not exist in the United States today without the tolerance of the state. Historically, as now, the state has seen to it that the churches that provided sanctuary were not harassed and that the people who sought sanctuary were protected from any violation of their status. The Church, for its part, did not make the laws and it did not encourage people to violate them. There is no instance I am aware of where the use of sanctuary would have been considered appropriate when, as in the case of aliens hidden by the Sanctuary movement, a legal remedy is open to them, but the movement has encouraged these aliens not to seek a legal remedy.

What Are the Ways Out?

What can concerned congregations do to promote their views? To influence U.S. policies toward Central America or any other region, the churches have few unique resources. They have a certain moral and intellectual sway over their congregations. They have a certain national-level presence through their councils. By joining together in ecumenical "supercouncils" such as the National Council of Churches, they have been able to penetrate more effectively the arenas of secular influence. To get at the body politic as a whole, however, the individual churches as such have no natural forum. The framers of the Constitution would argue that this is as it should be; it helps to preserve the separation of Church and state.

I think that churches in the movement must examine critically the way Sanctuary leaders and promoters have dealt with the lack of a natural forum. Specifically they have figured out how to use the capacity of the media to magnify or glorify events in order to parlay a selected list of chosen and groomed refugees into a national statement about U.S. policy in Central America. The problem with that is not that the churches are using media; evangelists going back half a century have used electronic media to propagate their faith. The problem is that Sanctuary has taken a small body of fact and magnified it through carefully staged media events into a large untruth. This clearly is use of propaganda techniques to pursue a political objective, and when the element of truth is so distorted the technique becomes a way of distributing disinformation.

I agree with others who have suggested that the concern Sanctuary expresses for the plight of the people flowing out of Central America must be dealt with in some fashion. To me the millions of churchgoers and others who believe in the broad spiritual objective of Sanctuary, to help people in distress, are to be encouraged and supported. Outside of a few very favored places the world is dominated by scarcity. Millions of people are born, live, and die without ever knowing any condition but a nagging want that is sometimes brutal. One bleak report of the situation says "there are 800 million hungry and unemployed people in the world today," a number that is three times the total population of the United States.[30]

In this respect, fate has not played any special tricks on Central America. It is a place like many others where most people don't have enough of anything but the will to survive. The churches should make this fact the central focus of their charitable and humanitarian programs abroad. In the past they have, and the churches and government have succeeded in many places such as Egypt, India, Sri Lanka, Brazil, the Philippines in boosting the human spirit and improving the human condition at least a little.

But the secret of success has always been to go openly to the people in their own country. If the churches are going to maintain an underground railroad with Central America, it should go the other way, to take resources and opportunity and hope to the people there, not to bring a selected few out for show, nor to mount a propaganda campaign that weakens the authority of governments in Central America. Those leaders already have enough trouble getting resources to improve their economies and finding ways to get and keep the willing cooperation of their people.

The quarrel here is not about the rightness of compassion, it is about the choice of means. Although, as Neuhaus comments, Sanctuary's "political analysis and the judgments that emerge from it are thoroughly wrong-headed,"[31] no one could argue if the Sanctuary agenda were pursued through the normal channels that are open to any citizen to try to influence national policy. The problem is that those elements of Sanctuary dedicated to the political agenda are trying to use the institutions of the Church through extralegal and underground means to foment radical political change.

Sanctuary Support for Terrorism

In this process, Sanctuary promotes terrorism. In its haste to create change in Central America, Sanctuary promotes violence as surely as any government it accuses of doing just that. It does so in three ways that I can readily see. One is by chipping away at the legitimacy and thereby undercutting the ability of regimes such as that of José Napoleón Duarte to deal with national problems. Doing that only prolongs the process of improving El Salvador's political and economic conditions, and it increases the proneness to violence of an already unstable society.

Sanctuary's direct support for terrorism flows from its assistance to and encouragement of the Faribundo Martí National Liberation Front and other antigovernment groups in Central America. In 1985, members of an FMLN-affiliated group attacked a streetside café in San Salvador and killed thirteen people. In that same year they kidnapped President Duarte's daughter and held her prisoner for two months. There is no record to my knowledge of Sanctuary leaders ever condemning the FMLN for those acts of terrorism. Rather, as noted earlier, Sanctuary brings members of the so-called popular forces to the United States and provides them with exposure to media and the chance to promote their causes. Those activities only buy the future rounds of violence.

Trying to help through providing "humanitarian" gifts looks like a way to avoid getting trapped into helping the terrorists, but it is not. There is no magic here. Funds that help the FMLN sustain its membership and operations give it confidence, increase its staying power, enable it to buy weapons, and help it get ready for the next round of killings.

The Track Record of Liberation Theology

That posture of support for terrorism should prompt church congregations and others who are truly concerned about the human conditions in many parts of the world to look closely at Sanctuary's political agenda. The movement has indicated in various ways its desire to import liberation theology into the United States. In this they are either genuinely naive or simply unwilling to look at the facts.

To me the first indication of that unwillingness to look at the facts lies in the failure of Sanctuary's political activists to study the box score of liberation theology. The record, in brief, is that after a generation of political ferment since Puebla, there is not much to show in the way of real accomplishment, but there are some real danger signs. For example, in Brazil, the prospect that a liberal government and a liberal clergy would make common cause against people with property led to a coalition of business and the military that lasted for more than a decade. In Chile, Allende's election was followed by the closest expression of harmony between the goals of the church and those of the state that had occurred since colonial times. The result much like Brazil, was a whiplash of conservative reaction that led to control by Pinochet. In Nicaragua, members of the clergy participated in armed struggle and entered the councils of state to create a regime as politically repressive as its predecessor. In the Philippines, the activist Catholic clergy, with the knowledge and passive acceptance of the church hierarchy encouraged the Moro Liberation Front and the New People's Army, whose insurgent attacks in turn reinforced the unimaginative and predatory instincts of the Marcos government, and helped bring the Filipinos to the brink of political disaster,[32] where it hovers precariously at present.

With this many examples, the idea should somehow get across that liberation theology is not a formula for either quick or guaranteed benefits to the mass of the people. It is rather a formula that begets unstable and often undesirable results because it provokes highly polarized responses on the side of its advocates and on the part of those who react against it.

In that context, we should question the reasons for importing liberation theology into the United States. The first questions are, whom is to be liberated, from what, and how? Liberation theology, as espoused by the liberal Catholic clergy in Latin America, reserves a place for armed struggle as the means to provoke political change. Is that what the activists in Sanctuary have in mind for the United States? If so, who specifically are the targets? What policy agenda is the goal? Who will decide when and where the struggle begins? Will the rest of us be asked what we think about the struggle or its goals? Will even the congregations who now unwittingly support that agenda be asked whether they wish to participate?

These issues are at the heart of the doubts I have about the intentions and the values of the political activists in the Sanctuary movement. It is not only that they are "thoroughly wrongheaded," as Neuhaus suggests—American society has been able up to now to handle a wide variety of views, even some that at root are antisocial—but the political activists in Sanctuary, it seems to me, have joined other extremists of both the Left and the Right in taking full advantage of the American system while failing utterly to understand it.

Sanctuary's political activists, along with extremists of the Aryan Nations, the KKK, the abortion clinic bombers, and others discussed in chapter 6, have either forgotten or have chosen to put aside the fact that the American system is not designed to work at the extremes. The thing that got the U.S. Constitution written and accepted, and the process that has kept it alive longer than any other documentary set of governing principles around today, is compromise. There is a special quality of safety in this process because it buys the opportunity to move the system toward goals that can be justified to other people in it.

In order to get and keep a role of influence in the American system, however, it is necessary to work with people. That is the essential consensus procedure that underlies the democratic process. If confronted on something that really matters to them, people will fight for it. Efforts to take the game away from them might succeed, but at the price of making enemies. At the first opportunity they will try to get back what they have lost. All decisions, all outcomes are unstable in these circumstances. The winners are temporary. The losers are angry. The chemistry is wrong. This is a volatile social situation, and it is one of the paths that leads to terrorism.

We must consider the desire of Sanctuary's political activists to import radical political change in this perspective. What should concern us most about that scheme is its capacity to politicize and polarize radically the American decision process.

The movement is a twofold demonstration of American tolerance for dissent, but it is an abuse of that tolerance. First, the members of the movement are taking every advantage of the leeway provided by the law for the individual to disagree. As breakers of the law, they are receiving sentences that, if anything, are light. Second, they are being given legal room in which to practice "sanctuary" on a scale that goes well beyond any historic precedent. The abuse lies in hiding behind that tolerance to take actions which undermine American laws and institutions.

These excesses are a clear reminder that the United States must reexamine its approaches to political and social change before its own institutions are undermined. If the American people are going to be involved in processes of change either at home or abroad, they must do so as a nation, essentially on the same side. This cannot be done by deepening the ideological schisms that are creeping in from the Left and the Right on American society. The Constitution of the United States does not contemplate, promote, or cater to particular ideologies beyond its support for the dignity of all people as guaranteed by the Bill of Rights. The liberationist ideology of Sanctuary is out of place in this context, no less so than the separatist and ethnic purist views of other extremists.

6

Abuses of the Power of the People

I N November 1986, reports the *Washington Post*, a meeting was held in Washington, D.C., at the call of a California law firm to set up an organization called the "Rehnquist Watch."[1] The objective of this meeting, reported the *Post*, was to create a group that would literally watch all of Supreme Court Chief Justice William Rehnquist's decisions and public actions and, in the language of a memo provided to attendees of the meeting, to act as a "moral counterforce to Rehnquist." The memo proposed to undermine the effectiveness of the chief justice and to "give pause to other Supreme Court justices about being associated with Rehnquist opinions." The *Post* took exception to this proposal, saying that it was "awfully close to the kind of harassment and intimidation one does not expect from lawyers." My objections to this proposal are stronger than that, because the memo cited by the *Post* as being provided by the San Francisco law firm, Public Advocates, set a tone that was potentially as chilling as a terrorist group planning meeting.

A Pattern of Dissent

Formation of the Rehnquist Watch, unfortunately, is representative of a growing pattern of popular attitudes and responses to public issues. It is a part of a pattern of dissent that says that institutional decisions do not settle issues, they only move the contest to a different forum. A growing number of people and groups in the United States are not prepared to go with the flow, unless the flow is what they personally want. They are in essence antidemocratic. For them, the game is to participate, to go on trying to participate after an issue, at least in institutional terms, has been settled, and to look on no decision as final, no matter how correctly it may represent the wishes of the majority or how fully it may reflect established public decision-making procedures.

Pursuing the logic of mass participation in public policy decisions, Public Advocates may have meant well in trying to create the Rehnquist Watch, but this enterprise is only another of the numerous danger signals we must hear and respond to in the United States in order to protect democratic values and institutions. From such an organized campaign to harass and frighten a public official the drift into uses of violence is easy. How far is an effort of this sort from support of actions that lead to, condone, or turn a blind eye to acts of terrorism?

This challenge is a mixture of old and new elements. The United States has had gun-toting, fiercely independent pockets of individualists from the beginning. Historically these groups espoused a basically Judeo-Christian ethic, and they shared the values of the Constitution. Mainly they wanted to be left alone. Some, however, such as the Ku Klux Klan, have mouthed constitutional values while pursuing a private racist agenda, and now a growing number of groups espouse value systems that they would impose by law or force on the rest of the nation. These groups are not above the use of violence to suppress opposition or to expand their followings. On the political right, these groups include the KKK, Posse Comitatus, the Aryan Nations and its subgroup called the Order, and smaller private groups such as those involved in bombings of abortion clinics. On the left, the groups include the Weather Underground, the United Freedom Front, the Revolutionary Fighting Group, the Armed Resistance Unit, and the Red Guerrilla Resistance. Many of the groups overlap. Profiles on all these groups, developed by the FBI and local law enforcement agencies as well as by private groups such as the Southern Poverty Law Center, demonstrate a remarkable fact: the rhetoric of these groups sounds different, but their methods are much the same. Electronic media and modern weapons technology have changed the tools available, but the basic instruments of human intimidation and repression have not evolved much since the time of the Spanish Inquisition.

Many of the agendas of these groups and others whose approaches lead them to use violent methods make it clear that American society has not yet thought through what it means to run a social system as a coalition of minorities. The only hope for a system as ethnically, culturally, and preferentially diverse as that of the United States is to achieve acceptable orders of satisfaction for all members through continuous resort to compromise. If compromise is not accepted as a consensus procedure, as I suggested in discussing the

Sanctuary movement in chapter 5, the alternative is confrontation that yields unstable decisions, unhappy participants, and new generations of grievance.

The Trend to Coercive Bargaining

The social change that is driving much of the national drift toward an increasingly polarized political process and a tolerance for violent approaches is the emergence of widespread habits of coercive bargaining. Coercive bargaining situations are different from the normal bargaining case, mainly because they violate the principle of mutuality. Under that principle, a mutual, voluntary exchange of concessions is made. In a terrorist hostage situation, on the other hand, there are usually two unwilling parties to a negotiation with the terrorists: the victims, and the persons pursuing the negotiation. What the terrorist does is to take something of value to the other parties—the liberty of the hostages and the citizen of the country represented by the negotiator—creating a coercive bargaining situation in which the best the other parties can do is get back to square one by making concessions that are likely to constitute net benefits to the terrorist. By taking the citizen of the other party hostage, the terrorist has created an artificial trade good and forced that other party to deal.

We recognize this coercive pattern in the terrorism case and are offended by it, but we readily fall into coercive bargaining modes in our daily lives. The more or less innocent examples are commonplace. Take the case of the father who says to his teenage son, "If you don't get out there and mow that lawn, you can kiss the car goodbye for your date tonight." Or take as an example (which I remember graphically from childhood) my own mother's saying to me, "If you don't stop that I am going to send you after a switch and give you a good whipping." There, coercively, she had me twice: I had to fret about what she would do to me while I went to collect the switch, and then I had to face the whipping. Coercive bargaining indeed! And it worked.

Coercive bargaining does work. To take another example, a businessman is fussing about the late arrival of parts from a supplier and is annoyed with an employee who has failed to follow through with the supplier. Our businessman picks up the phone and calls the supplier to say, "Look, all this delay is messing up my production program. If I don't have those parts by Monday, I will cancel the order and you can forget about any future business from us." He then turns to the employee and says, "Get those parts in here and have them on the production line by Monday afternoon, or you're fired." By Monday night, the problem is solved. Coercion tactics have worked again.

Undoubtedly you can think of examples of this pattern that range all the way from simple household situations to the conduct of national security affairs. We have terms for it: the *arm twist* is one, *saber rattling* is another. Confrontation is an extreme form, and the Cuban missile crisis that occurred in the second year of John F. Kennedy's presidency is a superb example of how strong words and forceful maneuver coerced an adversary (the Soviet Union) into backing down.

The Growth of Civil Disobedience

We recognize all these examples and we are largely inclined to accept the tactics involved, but new dimensions have crept in. Beginning in the 1960s, coercive bargaining became the central instrument of minority political action strategies. What became clear very quickly was that it did not particularly matter whether the cause was just or reasonable, factually supported, or widely approved by other people. Gains could be made by forcing opposing parties to bargain. The primary targets of this strategy were government policies and public policy decisions. The basic tools of this strategy were civil disobedience, gall, and a flair for publicity.

The leadership of North Vietnam was among the quickest to see the merit of this strategy and set about using this behavioral change in American society against the United States. Making common cause with American groups, notably the Weather Underground organization, and by appealing to the sentiments of the media and some elements of the public, Hanoi set out to win the war by using the coercion tactics of American protest groups against U.S. policy and leadership.[2]

Unquestionably Hanoi succeeded, and many Americans still do not appear to understand how thoroughly they were manipulated in the process. Moreover, some American protest groups saw Hanoi's success as their own; the strategy worked, even though it involved gross amounts of misinformation and active disinformation.[3] The tactic on the ground was simple: You don't have to be right, but you can win if you are willful and persistent enough. Coercion pays.

With the Vietnam War ended and with the streets more or less free of public protest, Americans were inclined to forget the whole episode, but two trends already visible at the end of the Vietnam War were bringing fundamental change in the way people express their discontent and in the way public decisions get made. First, the lessons of Vietnam protest had not been lost on groups throughout the West and the Third World. Those patterns of dissident action, so successful in bringing about the end of the war, had taken on quasi-institutional status for protest movements in general. Civil disobedience was becoming a norm for provoking decisions in any field of interest. Second, the environment of political protest was being invaded by politically motivated violence, ranging from isolated acts of terrorism to the formation of paramilitary protest groups in the United States and various active insurgencies abroad.

The Acceptance of Violence

Despite the assertions of experts, including FBI officials, that American public support for terrorist causes is lacking,[4] a stage has been reached of nearly institutional acceptance of low-level political violence. The path was through a growing acceptance of coercive bargaining tactics, coupled to many different sources of value changes, including a concern for human rights and social justice,[5] a loss of faith in government, and a tolerance for extremes of individual and group behavior.

Grave dangers are posed to the stability and the moral and philosophical character of American society by the arrival at this point, and these dangers are manifest in the agendas of various groups in the United States. It is essential at this point to look at those agendas, and for our discussion purposes I have placed the groups of greatest interest in clusters broadly representing the political right, the political left, and special interests.

Groups from the Political Right

The Ku Klux Klan (KKK). "Picture a time in the near future," says Linda Hunt in *Common Cause* magazine, "an America overcome by millions of 'minority terrorist hordes' who run unchecked over the land, looting, raping, murdering white citizens." Out of that chaos "a new 'white citizen's militia' rises up amid the ashes to create a 'Great White Nation' called 'Southland.' " The stuff of bad dreams? Maybe, but as Linda Hunt reports, "This is the future of America as envisioned by 45-year-old Glenn Miller," founder of the White Patriot party, a militant subgroup of the Ku Klux Klan.[6]

The KKK, for years an extreme right, racist group centered mainly in the southern states, has in a sense changed its agenda with the times. The KKK was formed in a post–Civil War era when the only racial or ethnic threat it could see was from newly emancipated blacks, but Hispanics now come close to outnumbering blacks, the ethnic diversity of American society has multiplied, and the "whites" are well on their way to becoming a minority. Scary, perhaps, but only if you insist on supremacy rather than equality.

The KKK is not the only group whose members assert that their freedom of action, their religious and cultural values, and their life-styles are in some way threatened by population changes in the United States. Other right extremist groups include the following.

The Aryan Nations. Based in Hayden Lake, Idaho, this group is white supremacist and anti-Semitic, and according to published sources "is committed to establishing a 'territorial sanctuary' in the northwestern United States."[7] Some read that as an intent to create a separate state.

The Order. A militant, paramilitary subgroup of the Aryan Nations, the Order is small, and most of its members are in prison as the result of arrests by the FBI in December 1984. Its goal is to carry out the Aryan agenda: defending white supremacy and eliminating blacks and Jews from society.[8] The Order declared war on the U.S. government in November 1984, asserting that it was dominated by Zionists.[9] Rules of engagement established by the group say that they will make war under the Geneva convention, but their rules go on to say essentially that anyone who opposes them will be treated as a combatant.[10] Bank robberies and counterfeiting appear to have been the Order's primary sources of funds. Like members of other groups who have spent time in jail, the imprisoned leaders of the Order probably stay in close touch with like-minded groups and individuals on the outside.

The Covenant, the Sword and the Arm of the Lord. A survivalist and fundamentalist religious group associated with and sharing the aims of the Aryan Nations, this group maintained an armed camp near the Missouri–Arkansas border until its compound was raided by the FBI and police in 1985. The leader of the Covenant, James Ellison, who was sent to prison on weapons and racketeering charges, appears to have maintained close contact with the Aryan Nations.

The Sheriff's Posse Comitatus. This is the name taken by a number of groups who share a common goal of abolishing the state and federal governments. The county sheriff is the highest authority they recognize; their name comes from the Latin, referring to the practice of the sheriff in the Old West of forming a posse of citizens to enforce the law. Violently opposed to taxation, the Posse Comitatus groups exist mainly in midwestern and northwestern regions.

The activities of right-wing extremist groups have been sharply curtailed by police actions in the past two years. Many of their leaders are in prison, and leaders of the KKK White Patriot party recently were placed under federal indictment. However, according to Stanley Klein, who until early 1986 was head of the FBI's terrorism unit, the problem of right-wing groups may be dormant but it "is not over by any means."[11] In fact, he suggests that the groups may be getting together, combining their efforts, and regrouping for future acts to be directed mainly against the government. Confirming Klein's concern, affiliates of the Aryan Nations carried out four bombings and attempted a fifth in 1986.

According to Steven Pomerantz, the current head of the FBI's terrorism unit, Americans have little tolerance for the use of violence to achieve political change.[12] That may be true in significant degree, but the extreme right groups represent a different kind of threat: they are prepared to use violence to resist change or to deflect the impact of changes in American life away from themselves. Their tactic is like that of an aggressive ostrich who puts his head in the sand only after surrounding himself with a mine field; anyone who trespasses will be blown away. As I see it, the consequences of using violence in that way are not really different from the effects of using violence to promote change. The likely victims, members of minority groups and government officials, won't be able to tell the difference either.

A disturbing aspect of the means the extreme right groups have chosen to support their activities is their co-option of a small number of U.S. military personnel and their theft or illegal purchase of weapons from military stores. On January 8, 1987, five members of the KKK were indicted by a federal grand jury in Raleigh, North Carolina, on charges of "conspiring to obtain weapons and explosives stolen from a U.S. military installation." This indictment also charged one of the defendants with plotting to get rid of Morris Dees, head of the Southern Poverty Law Center in Montgomery, Alabama, who has been urging federal action against the KKK.[13] The January 8 indictment brought to twenty-eight the number of KKK White Patriot party members charged in North Carolina alone during the past year and a half, and the charges largely involve attempts to obtain weapons from military installations.

The theft of weapons from U.S. military installations and their acquisition by extremist groups has become a pattern of great concern. Of equal if not greater concern, however, is the degree to which military personnel appear to have been involved. In a number of instances, military personnel have been charged with the removal of weapons from military arsenals for sale or supply to the extremists, with helping to train members of extremist groups in use of the stolen weapons or more generally in military tactics, and with participating with the extremist groups in their programs and activities.[14] Responding to an April 1986 request of the Southern Poverty Law Center, in November 1986 Defense Secretary Caspar Weinberger instructed U.S. military commanders that members of the armed forces "must reject participation in hate groups" such as the KKK and American Nazi organizations. Specifically, the Weinberger directive precluded "active participation, including public demonstrations, recruiting and training members, and organizing or leading" such groups. He said that these activities were "utterly incompatible with military service."[15]

Hate groups are not the only manifestation of a proneness to political violence on the political right which should concern us. For instance, when Indian Prime Minister Rajiv Gandhi was preparing to visit the United States in mid-1985, a plot was mounted against him by Sikh separatists. Happily, that plot was foiled by the FBI. Not surprisingly, when Attorney General Edwin Meese visited New Delhi in March 1986, Prime Minister Gandhi prodded him to do something about the training of Sikh extremists in private military training camps in the United States. What he had in mind, no doubt, was the fact that, according to FBI sources, the five Sikh militants arrested in the plot against the prime minister had received training at a private paramilitary training camp in Alabama on such subjects as the use of explosives.[16] For a fee of $350, they reportedly took a two-week training course at Frank Camper's Reconnaissance Commando School near Birmingham, Alabama.[17] Meese reportedly assured Prime Minister Gandhi that steps were being taken to control such camps[18]—not a simple task, because at the moment such training is not illegal. Moreover, efforts of the Reagan administration, in which I participated, to get legislation to prohibit training and support of terrorist activities and groups by Americans were soundly rebuffed by the Congress in 1984, mainly because of objections from the American Civil Liberties Union and from liberal members of the Congress.[19]

Groups from the Political Left

As might be expected, groups from the extreme left pose a different set of threats. Their motives and their geographic areas of activity are different from those of the rightist groups, although their methods are much the same. The leftist groups also generally tend to have or to cultivate foreign connections, something the rightist groups do not seek as a rule. Among the most important leftist groups are the United Freedom Front and the May 19 Communist Organization.

The United Freedom Front. This group engaged in a series of ten bank robberies and nineteen bombings or attempted bombings in the northeastern part of the United States during 1976–84. Group leaders Thomas Manning and Raymond Levasseur were arrested in 1984–85, along with most of the members, and are now both in prison. The group has a loose Marxist agenda but seems to be of the "armed struggle" school of terrorists. It has no clear goal but destruction of the present system. The UFF aims mainly at multinational corporations, claims sympathy for so-called freedom fighters in other parts of the world, and opposes U.S. policies in Central America and southern Africa.

The May 19 Communist Organization. This group includes Eastern seaboard remnants of the Weather Underground, the militant successor to Students for a Democratic Society, which was the most violent group in the United States during the 1970s. The Weather Underground established links with both Havana and Hanoi during the latter days of the Vietnam War, and May 19 appears to have extended those connections to include at least Nicaragua. This is also a group devoted to armed struggle, with no articulated design for future society. May 19 appears to have been crippled by the arrest of key people, Susan Rosenberg and Timothy Blunk, who received long prison sentences in 1985. There is also a West Coast arm of the Weather Underground called the *Prairie Fire Organizing Committee.*

Special Interest Groups

A third category of terrorist groups operating in the United States qualify as special interest groups. Most active among these are the following groups.

Jewish Extremists. The *Jewish Defense League* was founded in New York by Rabbi Meir Kahane and is rabidly supportive of Israel. It appears to be most active against Soviet, Arab, and former Nazi targets. Of seven incidents of domestic terrorism recorded by the FBI in 1985, four were attributed to Jewish extremists. A few days after the murder of Leon Klinghoffer in October 1985 on board the Italian cruise ship *Achille Lauro,* the regional director of the Arab-American Antidiscrimination League in California, a group that lobbies for equal treatment of Arabs and recognition of their causes, was killed and seven other people were injured in a bomb explosion. This attack was attributed by the FBI to Jewish extremists. The group carried out two attacks in 1986.

Puerto Rican Groups. 1. *The Armed Forces of National Liberation* (FALN is the Spanish acronym) is a militant Puerto Rican separatist group that has been credited with numerous bombings. The group was reputed to be the most active in the United States during 1982. Its bomb maker was explosives expert William Morales, who was arrested in Mexico in 1983. Morales remains in prison there, despite rumored efforts of Mexican drug dealers to arrange a trade of Morales for major drug ringleaders in jail in the United States.

2. *The Ejercito Popular Boricua (EPB), or the Macheteros.* This group has reportedly been involved in at least four murders and eighteen terrorist incidents in the past eight years. Describing itself as a proindependence terrorist group, the EPB is considered by the FBI the most violent group in Puerto Rico. It has claimed responsibility for a $7 million robbery of a Wells Fargo terminal in Hartford, Connecticut, using a fund-raising tactic that is commonplace for terrorist groups of both the Left and Right.

3. *Organization of Volunteers of the Puerto Rican Revolution (OVRP).* As the name implies, this group is militantly separatist. According to the FBI, it specializes in attacks on military recruiting officers. In November 1985 the group claimed responsibility for the shooting of the executive officer of the U.S. recruiting battalion in San Juan. The group also claimed that it had shot the officer in retaliation for the visit of FBI Director William Webster, and for the arrest of eleven Puerto Ricans by the FBI in August 1985.[20]

Like their rightist counterparts, leftist and special interest groups also have been crippled by arrests within the past few years, but the same thing must be said of them as of the rightist groups: they remain a serious threat, even though they are small. For example, in 1983 one of the Puerto Rican groups tried to demolish FBI offices in San Juan with a light antitank weapon. The attack failed only because the aim was poor, but the possession of this type of weapon means that a small group can do serious harm, and it can inflict damage at a distance. In 1986, the total number of terrorist attacks in the United States rose to seventeen, the highest since 1983. Twelve of these attacks are attributed by the FBI to Puerto Rican nationalists and Jewish extremists.

The Questionable Cases

Rightist and leftist groups with essentially domestic causes represent one broad category of supporters for terrorism within the United States. However, these groups, defined as terrorist by the FBI, are only part of the story. In part, the story depends on what you define as a terrorist incident. In 1984 the FBI counted thirteen incidents inside the United States as terrorist incidents. It did not include twenty-four bombings of abortion clinics and counseling facilities because the FBI said that it "found no evidence that those bombings had violated civil rights" nor, said the FBI, were there any indications that the attacks were carried out by "an organized group or a conspiracy."[21] I doubt seriously that the clinic operators, who were caught in the middle of a national political dispute over the right to life, felt that comfortable about the state of their personal liberties. I understand, however, the FBI's problem with trying to assess the motives of a lone bomber who may have acted only out of some personal grievance.

In terms of the purposes of this book, the problem gets even murkier when you look at overall statistics on bombings. In 1983, the FBI reported 687 bombing incidents in the United States and Puerto Rico. Only 22 of these were classed as terrorist attacks.[22] There were over 800 bombings reported by the FBI in 1984, and only 13 were categorized as terrorist attacks.[23] In looking at these numbers, I found it of some interest that there were very few human casualties associated with any of the bombings. The terrorists and the ordinary criminal bombers alike seemed to be satisfied to make their points through property damage. If that pattern continues, one could say that there is hope for us yet.

The Foreign Terrorist Groups

A fourth category of terrorist activity consists of foreign terrorists who operate in the United States with some sympathy and support from their own or other ethnic, religious, or cultural groups. This cateogry is growing, and its motives are becoming increasingly complex.

Most people are familiar with the sources of support for the Irish Republican Army, (IRA) which have existed in the United States for many years. The Irish National Liberation Army (INLA) and the Provisional Irish Republican Army (PIRA) also are active in the United States, mainly in fund-raising and weapons procurement. Eight PIRA members were arrested in Massachusetts on weapons procurement charges in 1986, and seven others were indicted on such charges. In chapter 3 I discussed the way IRA terrorists until recently were able to safe haven in the United States by hiding behind provisions of the extradition law and treaty with the British. Revision of the treaty in 1986 diminished that possibility.

Because of headlines reporting attacks on Turkish diplomats in the United States, many people are also familiar with the terrorist activities of the Armenian terrorist groups ASALA (the Armenian Secret Army for the Liberation of Armenia), and JCAG (the Justice Commandos against Genocide). Two lesser groups in the United States, the October 3 Organization, and the June 9 Organization, appear most closely associated with JCAG. Armenian terrorists carried out thirteen attacks in 1981–83. They assassinated the Turkish consul in Los Angeles and attacked his counterpart in Boston. In 1984 three Armenian terrorists were arrested in Ottawa, Canada, on a charge of attempting to assassinate the Turkish commercial attaché. The group JCAG alleges that the Turkish government, at the time what remained of the Ottoman Empire, committed genocide against the Armenian people in the early 1900s, and it seeks some acknowledgment and restitution from the present Turkish leadership. ASALA's cause is to reunite the territory of Armenia now divided between Turkey and the Soviet Union. These causes are viewed with sympathy by many Armenians in the United States, and prominent Armenians such as Governor Deukmejian of California have supported efforts in the Congress to pass a resolution designating an official day of remembrance for the Armenian genocide.

Three years ago, when I was newly arrived in the Office of Counterterrorism in the State Department, I approached an Armenian friend to discuss what might be done about Armenian terrorist activities in the United States, France, and elsewhere. In the course of our discussion, I asked him whether the many Armenians who live in the United States really supported the terrorist activities of ASALA or of the more militant JCAG. My friend gave a fairly long and honest answer, and it boiled down to this: "No, they don't support the terrorism, but they are not prepared to speak out against it."

From that perspective, I watched the evolution of the TWA Flight 847 hijacking with great interest, because the negotiator designated by the hijackers, Lebanese Shia Amal leader Nabih Berri, is a green card–carrying aspirant to American citizenship. His wife lives in Michigan, as does his daughter, an American citizen. As was discussed in chapter 4, it was clear where Berri's sympathies lay, and as far as the hijackers were concerned that was essential to his credibility. For me it underscored the fact that relationships with the rest of the world are emotionally and practically very complex for millions of Americans.

In many statements I have heard and read, U.S. federal, state, and local law enforcement officials are concerned about the impact the diversity of American society has on patterns of sympathy and support for terrorism. Particularly they worry about the possibility that terrorists from outside could enter the United States and find safe haven in their own ethnic communities. FBI officials have said that ethnic communities and foreign nationals from Iran, Lebanon, and Libya are of special concern.[24] For example, as the result of an FBI investigation, deportation charges were brought in early 1987 against several Palestinians for allegedly working on behalf of the radical leftist Popular Front for the Liberation of Palestine.[25] Such cases as the 1985 plot by Sikh separatists to take the life of Prime Minister Rajiv Gandhi and the assassination by Sikh separatists in Canada of a Punjabi minister show that the list of concerns could become a lot longer.

Terrorist activities driven from the outside are another source of concern. In 1985 the FBI exposed a plan involving a Libyan attached to Libya's United Nations mission and several "students" to carry out attacks against Libyans in the United States who oppose the regime of Muammar Qaddafi. Earlier Qaddafi efforts in at least one instance ended in an assassination. In 1986, according to FBI reports, concern developed about Iranian activities, mainly efforts of Khomeini agents to intimidate Iranian opponents.

Dealing with This Pattern

If we add terrorist groups inside the United States who go abroad looking for help and allies, we have a fairly complete picture of the pattern. As I noted earlier, leftist groups, more often than rightist groups, look outside for help, but that picture is imperfect. In August 1986, the *Washington Times* reported that a Chicago street gang called El-Rukn had been in touch with Libyan leader Qaddafi, apparently to see if he might have work for them to do in the United States. This article also reported that Louis Farrakhan, leader of the Chicago-based Nation of Islam, visited Qaddafi and that other Nation of Islam leaders attended a meeting with Qaddafi in 1983 for purposes of finding "ways and means that Libya could provide direct support to liberation fighters within the United States."[26] This meeting, which apparently was called for the ostensible reason to give Qaddafi a platform to explain his "Green Book" philosophy,[27] appears actually to have been created as an occasion for establishing relations between Qaddafi and anti-Western groups.[28]

The FBI lists more than twenty groups that are more or less active in the United States. This includes all of the groups I have discussed, plus others such as the anti-Castro group called Omega 7, three of whose members were imprisoned in 1986 on charges of conspiracy. Because the borders are open, agents of any of the terrorist and insurgent groups throughout Central America are able to move freely in and out of the United States. In March 1986, for example, five people were convicted in the United States for involvement in a 1984 plot to assassinate Honduran President Roberto Suazo. In July 1986, fourteen people were arrested in the United States on charges related to a plan to invade the country of Surinam. As was discussed in chapter 5, the Sanctuary movement has brought members of the Faribundo Martí National Liberation Front to the United States to promote its cause in El Salvador.

What all of this means is that American society is in grave danger if ways are not found and maintained to restrain the nation's ideologically varied, widely distributed, and well-armed range of special interest groups, some of whom are practicing terrorists. The FBI and other federal, state, and local law enforcement agencies have been doing a good job so far of keeping the extremists among these groups under control. They cannot continue to do that, however, if the American public increasingly goes outside the law to help dissident groups both in the United States and abroad. Other ethnic and special interest groups as well as the Armenians have a responsibility to assert discipline and to exert some degree of social control over the activities of volatile elements within their communities.

One of the ways to turn down the burner under this overheating vessel that is American society is to review and redefine the role of civil disobedience and other coercive bargaining tactics. The apologists for the current pattern of readiness to take to the streets remind us that it is a tradition. Yes, it is, for correcting violations of constitutional rights and for use on occasion to redress egregious violations of civil liberties. It was never seen by our forebears as an alternative decision procedure in situations where constitutional rights are guaranteed; rather, civil disobedience was viewed as a remedy in situations where constitutional guarantees had broken down. Nor is it likely that the framers of the Constitution ever envisaged the proliferation of armed groups in the country that has occurred in the past few decades. The coalescence of such groups as a direct and immediate threat to other citizens could hardly have been the intent of the right to bear arms.

With all the nation's problems, the constitutional guarantees have not broken down. They are being placed under stress, however, by the activities of groups prepared to operate outside the law or to ignore their own institutions in order to get their way, and to use coercion and force if they consider it necessary to do so. For this purpose, there are no practical differences among the White Patriot element of the KKK, the political activists in the Sanctuary movement, the antinuclear groups who run a spy network around nuclear facilities,[29] and the volatile elements of ethnic communities. The people who tried to set up the Rehnquist Watch are different only in degree. Each is making a personal decision as to when to uphold the law. All of these are abuses of the power of the people, and the pattern of abuse is contagious.

7

Getting Too Close
to the Story

IN June 1985 at Beirut International Airport, with much of the world looking on via the convenience of nearly real-time television coverage, a dramatic
interview occurred. Charles Glass, a reporter for ABC stood on the tarmac
and through the cockpit window of hijacked TWA Flight 847 interviewed
the pilot, Capt. John Testrake. Captain Testrake was one of the few people
still left on the plane, which had been hijacked to Beirut by members of the
Shiite extremist group Hezballah a few days earlier. Shortly after arrival in
Beirut, Captain Testrake had watched all of his passengers removed from the
plane to be hidden in several locations around Beirut by members of the Shiite
community. The immediate drama was created by a nervous, pistol-waving
hijacker who stood behind Captain Testrake as he talked. Had any distur-
bance occurred, the terrorist at any moment could have ended Captain
Testrake's life with a flick of his trigger finger.

ABC considered this interview the television news coup of the episode.
It was a coup, but it was also a good deal more. ABC had gotten into the
middle of an intense, coercive bargaining situation, in which the hijackers
were using thirty-nine Americans as bargaining chips. With this interview,
ABC captured the drama of a terrorist's threatening the life of a hostage. The
network, however, also gave the hijackers a valuable opportunity to intimidate
the American public, the U.S. government, and the families of the hostages
being held in Lebanon. In so doing, the interview gave the terrorists an essential
medium for improving their negotiating leverage with the United States.

Many writers and commentators have analyzed the reporting and increasingly have criticized the coverage of major terrorist incidents. Following their
experiences with nearly around-the-clock coverage for seventeen days of the

TWA Flight 847 hijacking and with the October 1985 hijacking of the Italian cruise ship *Achille Lauro*, media people themselves appeared to become a good deal more cautious about reporting future terrorist incidents. Even so, the September 1986 hijacking of Pan Am Flight 073, which broke a summer of respite from terrorist activity, showed most of the media back at their old stands with almost full-time coverage of the incident. Because Karachi, Pakistan, is so far from New York, there were delays in getting people and equipment into place, and the electronic media never achieved the hour-by-hour continuous coverage of the incident that had characterized treatment of the TWA 847 story. The temptation to go all out was strong, however, as is evidenced by the fact that the networks began using their prime-time anchor people to keep the public up to date on developments as they occurred.

Helping the Terrorists

Media people justify their close-in coverage of such news stories by saying that the people have a right to know, and that right, they say, fully justifies a report on anything that is happening. I don't intend to quarrel with their basic point; the public does have a right to coverage of the news, even though a right to know, per se, is nowhere specified in the Constitution. That's not the issue. The issue is, at what point does a news person, seeking to cover a story, cross over an invisible line and become part of the story?

Charles Glass, standing on the tarmac in the sun at Beirut International Airport that day in June 1985, did not just cover the news. He became part of it.[1]

By the same token, the reporters who visited the TWA Flight 847 hostages where they were being held captive were not just covering the news. To get there, they had to strike a bargain with the terrorists. In exchange for access to the hostages, the reporters delivered a message to the U.S. government and the American people for the hostage takers. The reporters didn't get to the hostages through skill, or daring, or even luck. They were taken to see, hear, and broadcast the statements of hostages who, because they were ignorant, frightened, or convinced, made statements that helped the hijackers establish themselves as the legitimate voices of Shia grievances.

These cases represent a growing list of instances in which the effort to cover the news has led willy-nilly into a process of making news. They also illustrate how, willingly or not, media people get cast as sympathizers or supporters of terrorist activity. In particular, the use made by the terrorists of electronic media revealed just how easily the terrorists could manipulate radio and television news.

Even more sympathetic and supportive of the terrorists, however, is the weight media give to specific stories. Television news reporters seldom allot the time or have the background information to comment reliably on the content of the stories they report. The viewer, therefore, often has no better index of the truth or importance of a piece of news than the amount of time the media give to covering the story. With this criterion of judgment, equal time means equal weight. And if Muammar Qaddafi, for example, receives time equal to that given to Secretary of State George Shultz, in the perception of the viewer what Qaddafi says is at least as important as what the secretary says.

There is also a common pattern of discrimination against U.S. spokesmen. Very often when an adversary of the United States is interviewed, that person—for example, Qaddafi—is allowed to deliver his own message. When the president of the United States or some senior U.S. official speaks, however, the media person often summarizes what he says in a voiceover comment. The senior official gets to mouth silently to the camera while a newsperson tells the public what he said, even as he says it. This kind of editing does not merely deny a public figure the opportunity to speak for himself, it permits the media person to tell the story the way he or she wants to tell it. Moreover, letting those in an adversary relationship speak for themselves gives their statements greater weight. The reason given for this kind of reporting is that an adversary has greater dramatic appeal than does someone on one's own side. That may be true at least part of the time, but the impact of this kind of reporting and editing is that the media end up helping the terrorists.

Another facet of the pattern is the tendency of many media people to view the U.S. government as an adversary. Thus, what U.S. officials say in a crisis situation is frequently treated as suspect. Anything that looks to be less than full disclosure runs a fair risk of being labeled a cover-up, no matter whether at that moment there may be very good reasons, including the safety of hostages or the sheer delicacy of a negotiation, to withhold information. Thus during a terrorist incident, frequently by a combination of speech, body language, time given to specific elements of coverage, and commentary, the media manage to convey the impression that the statements of the government involved in dealing with a terrorist incident ought to be regarded with skepticism and perhaps suspicion, while the terrorists involved may deserve at least understanding.

No doubt because he understood these dynamics very well, Palestine Liberation Front leader Abu Abbas arranged an interview in a secret place with NBC in early 1986. Effectively, he at least bartered his appearance for the opportunity to speak for himself following the piracy of the *Achille Lauro*. NBC knew at the time that Abbas was wanted by U.S. authorities for the murder of Leon Klinghoffer during the hijacking, but the network refused to disclose the whereabouts of Abbas.

Letting the adversary speak for himself sometimes double-crosses the media themselves. In their coverage of the effects of the April 14, 1986, U.S. raid on Libya, the electronic media must have regretted the unquestioning hearing they gave Qaddafi's spokesmen. For the benefit of the media, Qaddafi's aides were given the opportunity to parade people whose injuries were faked and children who were substitutes for Qaddafi's own, thereby gaining sympathy for Qaddafi as a victim and injured party.

What Is the Problem?

In my view the media sins in covering terrorism are not unique to this subject. The errors and distortions that concern me are visible in news coverage of any dramatic, fast-breaking story. The ease with which a story can become distorted was clearly illustrated to me during the academic year 1964–65, when I was a graduate student at the University of California, Berkeley. Berkeley became the birthplace of the Free Speech movement, which was led by U.C. student Mario Savio. In 1964 there were more than thirty thousand students enrolled at Berkeley, but the overwhelming majority of those students never took part in Free Speech activities. Generous estimates of the number of students who were involved at one time or another in active or passive protest reached a maximum of about three thousand. However, news coverage of protest events, particularly those involving dissident professors, gave the impression that the entire population of Berkeley was in turmoil, which was simply not the case.

I go back to the mid-1960s for an illustration of media distortion because that period proved to be a seminal one in the development of modern terrorist groups as well as protest movements. Terrorist organizations such as the Red Army Faction in Germany, the Red Army in Japan, and the Weather Underground in the United States have their roots in Vietnam protest. The approaches of these groups to terrorist activity appear to have been influenced significantly by the media successes of that era. Their terrorist tactics are descended from proven strategies for attracting media coverage of protest events.

The Scope of the Problem

The scope of the problem to be dealt with, if any improvement is to be made in the way the media handle terrorism, has been set by the statements of media people themselves. At one extreme is the reported remark of the well-known journalist Seymour Hersh at the National War College: "In all my stories I violate national security. I'm not worried about it. I don't care."[2] At the other are the comments of columnist Georgie Anne Geyer: "We could start," she said, "by recognizing that we are not a neutral force in a country of limitless security and sanity."[3] Hersh was asserting what many media people argue: No one can prove that anything I have said has had any adverse effects. Geyer was saying something more to the point: Let's wake up to the fact that ideas have consequences.

The primary source of trouble in media coverage of terrorism is stated very well by Katharine Graham, board chairman of the *Washington Post*. She favors the fullest possible coverage of terrorist incidents because, in her view the attacks cannot be ignored, there is no real proof that attacks would stop if the media reduced coverage, and the public has a right to know. Her starting position sounds like that of Hersh, but she moderates that considerably by saying that the problem centers on how the media can do a good job of covering the news without becoming a "participant in the crisis."[4]

Getting Too Close

That, it seems to me gets to the heart of the difficulty, because many of the common problems we see in the coverage of any terrorist incident, including distortions of scale and focus in stories, arise when the media get too close. It is a natural and indeed a competitive impulse of a reporter to get as close as possible to a story in order to assure the best possible coverage. But getting close enough to do that may mean that the reporter gets so close that he or she becomes involved.

Real-time reporting of actions officials may be taking to resolve an incident is one of the most risky ways of becoming involved in a terrorist incident. In the early 1970s, a group calling itself the Hanafi Muslims took over a mosque in Washington, D.C., and seized a number of hostages. As they struggled to resolve the incident, the authorities managing the crisis at the scene were startled to discover that one radio reporter was reporting live and in detail their preparations to rescue the hostages. Terrorists involved in an incident frequently use the media to keep themselves informed. In this instance, had they heard the report of a rescue attempt, the effort itself might have been damaged, or hostages, police officers, or bystanders might have been harmed.

A second example can be found in what occurred during the early phases of the TWA Flight 847 hijacking in June 1985. When the aircraft with all its hostages on board was on the ground in Algiers, electronic media people began to speculate about movements of U.S. Delta forces—forces trained for special operations—in the Mediterranean. The charge was made at the time that these reports of Delta Force movements persuaded the hijackers that their safe haven on the ground in Algiers was no longer safe. The timing of their move is consistent with that theory since they left Algiers after these reports started circulating, but the hijackers themselves have not commented on the reasons for their move. In any event, they forced the TWA 847 crew to fly them to Beirut and shortly after arrival farmed the hostages out in different parts of the Shia community. Dispersal of the hostages made it difficult if not impossible to mount a rescue.

A third example is taken from much more recent events and indicates that perhaps media people have made little progress toward recognizing how easy it is to get too close to a story. As unfortunately was revealed in the Pan Am Flight 073 incident, part of Pan Am's standard operating procedure for dealing with a hijacking called for the flight crew to escape, if possible, thereby forcing the hijackers to keep the plane on the ground. The escape of the pilot and copilot in this case bought Pakistani authorities several hours of ground time in which to mount a response. Media reporters subsequently described in detail the manner of the flight crew's escape. Even if some terrorists already knew about Pan Am's escape procedure, as the hijackers in this case clearly did not, reporting on that procedure made it easier for future hijackers to anticipate and thwart such a tactic.

During a January 1987 interview on the ABC "Evening News" with one of the TWA Flight 847 hostages, anchorman Peter Jennings got very close to a pending court case. He interviewed a former hostage on that flight about his knowledge of Mohammed Ali Hamadei, who had just been arrested in West Germany. Hamadei, one of four accused hijackers of TWA Flight 847, was also the subject of a U.S. extradition request that could bring him to the United States to stand trial for the murder of Navy diver Robert Dean Stethem. Anticipating that possibility, Jennings asked a series of questions about the former hostage's knowledge of and confidence in his ability to identify Hamadei, thereby getting in front of the future efforts of a court to establish that Hamadei was among the culprits. I think that this interview might have been dropped if the legal department of ABC had briefed Jennings and the producers on the potential legal implications of his line of questioning. In that vein, one media anchorman has had second thoughts, I am told, about his interview of Shia Amal leader Nabih Berri during the TWA Flight 847 hijacking in which he asked Berri if he had any messages for the president. With that question, he thrust himself into the middle of an intense, very sensitive negotiation.

The Right to Know

Part of the problem with managing any dramatic, fast-breaking terrorist incident is that many people assert a right to know. Hostage family members, self-proclaimed experts, opposition politicians, and others are often eager to get into the act, and the entering wedge of their effort to get involved is the argument that they have a right to know what is going on. Some people, including media people, see that as a right to participate. For example, in summing up right after the event, and in a degree trying to head off criticism of media performance during the TWA Flight 847 hijacking, former NBC anchorman John Chancellor argued that media coverage of the incident had helped to resolve it. It interested me that he ended up applauding media participation in the incident, not media coverage of the story.

That kind of confusion is natural. It is difficult for the most honest individual to be detached in fast-moving, emotionally charged situations. It simply is impossible to be detached and involved at the same time.

The media rely heavily on the argument that the public has a right to know to justify close-in news coverage. However, the right to know, as I noted earlier, is not mentioned anywhere in the Constitution, and there is, in fact, no way that such a right, if it existed, could be enforced. Nor is it specified anywhere just how such a right ought to be served or when in the evolution of a story the public ought to be informed. In any event, the right to know can hardly be interpreted as a right to know everything instantly.

The right to know is perhaps better described as the right to inquire. The individual and media have the right to raise any question they may want to, but the people being asked those questions are under no obligation to answer them. In fact, the legal obligation to answer questions applies only to someone under oath in a court of law or in other similar proceedings. Even in those situations, tribunals asking questions are likely to enforce some rule of germaneness to the issue at hand. So the right to know is almost immediately constrained by what individuals are willing to tell you. It is further constrained, of course, by legal protection of the right to privacy.

Where public officials are concerned, the media often argue that full disclosure is the only appropriate service of the public's right to know. This is at least partly a self-serving challenge of any concept of official secrets. Other governments, notably the British, have laws governing official secrets. The United States seems psychologically and politically unable to arrive at one. This puts a burden on public officials to take personal blame for any effort to protect sensitive official information. Even so, it seems to me that the public has a right to know that security and other vital systems and strategies the public pays to create for its own protection will not be weakened by disclosure. In the context of this study, the public should be able to assure itself that, even if it obtained such information, the media would refrain from reporting force movements or other actions that could harm those movements, damage their effectiveness, or cause harm to hostages.

It can be argued that in pressing their claim to guardianship of the public's right to know, the media have no special legal standing. Article 1 of the Constitution guarantees freedom of the press, but it does not identify any individual or group whose members have any special claim to protection. Freedom of speech was guaranteed well before electronic media were invented, and the media have no expressed right under the Constitution that is greater than the right of the ordinary citizen. Thus, in constitutional legal terms, everybody possesses the same rights.

The Impact of Media Coverage

On the broad issue of publicizing terrorist incidents, media people frequently argue that their close-in reporting of a terrorist crisis was beneficial to resolving the incident. There is not a terrorist incident that I'm aware of, however, in which the resolution was directly or in a significant degree traceable to news coverage. On the other hand, it appears reasonable, as some media people argue, that a terrorist group, interested in publicity for its group and cause, is not likely to harm its hostages if it can use the media to get its story across to the targeted audience. The terrorists are likely to sit tight as long as there is some prospect that their demands might be met. This unfortunately raises the prospect that media coverage can give the terrorists false hope and cause them to prolong an incident, thereby increasing risks to hostages and property when frustration eventually sets in. The very nervous state of terrorists as an incident progresses was made clear in the conclusion of the Pan Am

Flight 073 incident, when failure of an on-board generator appears to have caused the terrorists to panic and to start shooting passengers.

The Perceived versus Proven Risk

It is fair to say, however, that many of the concerns expressed in this chapter and elsewhere about media coverage of terrorism have grown more out of perceived risks than out of examples of real harm done by news coverage. Until we talk with the TWA Flight 847 hijackers, for instance, we are not likely to know for sure whether the final move they made from Algiers to Beirut was caused by concern about Delta Force movements. This is an important question for German authorities to raise with Mohammed Ali Hamadei when they bring him to trial. Without the benefit of interviews with captured terrorists or defectors, we cannot establish to what extent media coverage of incidents may have prolonged them. We can be reasonably confident, even so, that media coverage helps the terrorists get some of what they want from an incident, and terrorists behave as if they know all too well the immense boost that media coverage can give to their legitimacy and effectiveness. Saying that many terrorists are media wise, Katharine Graham points out that terrorists have arranged press pools, granted exclusive interviews, given press conferences, provided videotapes and recordings, and timed news releases to fit media needs. Media responses to these moves can provide great sympathy and support to the terrorists. As she concludes, it is up to the media to assure that they do not give the terrorists "unwarranted exposure," that in providing appropriate coverage the media "do not glorify them."[5] The need to stay out of such traps should generate extreme caution on the part of the media as they cover future incidents.

The Media Dilemma

In trying to cover the terrorism story correctly, the media face a difficult and persistent dilemma: some analysts have said that terrorism "is a combination of propaganda and theater,"[6] and to the extent that that is true the media are an essential ingredient of the incident, as designed by the terrorists. Once an incident begins, therefore, the media often may be caught, led like everyone else, by the unfolding of an incident.

Terrorists stage media events. The ABC interview on the tarmac at Beirut International Airport is a clear example. The gathering of media people for a visit with the hostages from TWA Flight 847 is another. NBC's interview with Abu Abbas obviously was staged by Abbas to get an American audience. And the shooting of passengers on the ground outside the Pan Am Flight 073 plane is a chilling example of terrorists' using media to intimidate negotiators. There is probably no way the media can cover such a story without being used by the terrorists.

Governments also use the media to manage terrorist incidents. Negotiators seek to convey specific impressions of events to the terrorists. Officials look to the media for readings on the situation that may bear on the terrorists' chances of success. The media become the vehicle for putting across real negotiating postures, for testing the waters, and sometimes for efforts to intimidate or influence the terrorists or their allies.

Governments use the media in wartime to practice one of the classical war-fighting strategies: deception. An attempt at peacetime use of this strategy backfired in late 1986 when U.S. officials tried to unsettle Qaddafi through the psychological warfare tactic of leaking false stories of a possible U.S. attack. But in exposing this scheme the media confused strategic deception with "disinformation" and tended to obscure the fact that deception remains a legitimate tool of warfare. The only thing the media really can do to protect themselves is to check stories as carefully as possible. Users of deception, meanwhile, should remember that the best use of the strategy is to stick as close to the truth as possible.

The Pressure of Competition

The competitive aspects of news coverage create the conditions for many of the mistakes. During one incident I helped to manage, a group of us watched a CNN reporter deliver a particularly sensitive piece of information about the case. One of my colleagues quipped, "There they are, thirty minutes ahead of the best intelligence service in the world!" The impulse to be first stimulated. reporting on Delta Force movements in the Mediterranean during the TWA Flight 847 crisis. That impulse can lead an editor to use a story before checking it or thinking through its implications.

Competitive factors have increasingly made coverage of the news part of the circus. As one magazine writer put it, a terrorist attack is far better entertainment than anything scenario writers can make up. In this context, a dramatic terrorism story has real potential to affect network ratings, and getting there "fastest with the mostest" can affect network competitiveness. The push to get in there and cover the story, therefore, is almost irresistible, and getting there first often means getting out front, trying to run ahead of the story, getting as close as possible, and, often, getting involved.

What Can Be Done?

What are the answers to the problem of a growing pattern of excessive, too involved journalism, whether print or electronic? One answer is to improve and maintain the reporting standards of the profession, particularly to reestablish and maintain the distinction between editorial opinion and news. With that it might be possible to get the style of reporting Jack Webb used to insist on in "Dragnet": "Just give us the facts." It is difficult if not impossible these days to get a news report that is not laced with commentary, and too often a journalist no longer seems to feel obligated to inform the public that the front-page story he or she has written is a mixture of fact, fancy, hearsay, opinion, and preferred statements of the case. Thus, the old maxim "Let the buyer beware" has become "Caveat lector"—let the reader beware!

This is not just a broadside criticism. In dealing with the terrorism case, the general standards of the profession, if applied rigorously, would tell a reporter when he or she is getting too close. Those standards should sound a warning when the boundary between gathering facts and getting involved or manipulating a source is about to be crossed. Those standards should provide some guidance on how to avoid exaggeration or distortion, and they should give a journalist some handle on how to be fair to the public. Too often the standards slip in the frenzy of covering a fast-breaking, emotional story.

A fundamental solution requires disciplined coverage of stories to keep the reporting journalist from getting too close and becoming involved. How close is too close? The answer is a matter of judgment, but there are some useful alarm bells journalists and editors might set: clearly if the reporter begins to manipulate either the participants or the elements of the story, the reporter is already too close. Can you interview a key participant in a hostage crisis and ask that person leading questions about management of the incident without beginning to manipulate the story? As a journalist, is it possible in the heat of a terrorist incident for you to interview one of the principals without introducing your own judgments on what is important, on the nature of the event, or on the actions and decisions of the players? The odds are against it, and it seems to me that this particular case leaves the journalist with two choices: to hold an interview with a principal in such a crisis but to avoid talking about the issues, or to avoid doing such interviews until the crisis is over. The latter looks like the prudent choice, given that people's lives are often at risk in such crises.

Many print and electronic media people I know are looking for appropriate ways to solve the kinds of problems I have mentioned. Moreover, journalists do not inevitably rush into print or onto the air with every story. The best ones I know are careful about checking sources and are wary of giving an inaccurate impression with a story. I am aware of several instances in which journalists have withheld stories to avoid danger to hostages or kidnap victims. When I was working in the Office of Counterterrorism in the State Department, I was called very late one night by a newspaper reporter who wanted to check a story with me. He had a report, he said, that a prominent foreigner had been kidnapped in Florida and was being held for ransom. Within minutes I was able to confirm that the story was true but that there was great concern among law enforcement officials and the family that any publicity could get the victim hurt or killed. I suggested that the reporter sit on the story until a safer time, and he did.

Some Courses of Action

Media people seem to feel that to some degree they are trapped, that there is not much they can do about the tendency to get pulled in by a terrorist operation. But there are specific things both journalists and media managers can do to protect themselves and their reporting, to limit danger to hostages, and to protect the public.

In my view, the most urgent step is for television news producers, editors, and anchorpeople to do serious contingency planning about how they will approach coverage of a terrorist incident. Among other things, contingency planning should help them avoid getting caught with cameras rolling but no game plan. Trying to meet this problem, NBC developed a set of guidelines as a result of its experience with the TWA Flight 847 hijacking and other incidents. In the article cited earlier, Katharine Graham did a good job of avoiding any statement of guidelines while laying out the most common pitfalls to be avoided. Such conceptual guidelines deal with the main sources of difficulty that many critics as well as media people themselves see a need to confront. Some of the main principles are:

Don't make bad matters worse

Don't give details that might harm hostages

Don't talk about specific hostages or their connections

Don't talk about military or police movements

Don't go live and lose control of the story

Don't speculate, especially about possible counterterrorist actions

Don't exaggerate the importance of a story or risk lowering reporting standards by just filling time

Don't become part of the problem

Such operating principles or guidelines are hardly perfect, and they are difficult to apply equally to all cases, but they can help the media avoid trouble and perhaps even improve the quality of news coverage.

Support for principles of this type appears to be growing both inside and outside the media. Among the major networks there were signs of real soul searching following coverage of the TWA Flight 847 incident. At least one anchorman expressed concern about overkill and about unintentionally being of help to terrorists.

Going Live at the Scene

A decision to go live at the scene of a crisis is literally a decision to suspend editorial judgment and to let the situation present itself. One senior network news executive producer has concluded that live coverage of a terrorist incident is an abdication of editorial responsibility; it is dangerous, he says, because it turns control of the story over to the terrorists. This realization has caused him to question just what would be lost if the media were to reduce or eliminate live coverage in order to retain editorial control.

The answer is probably very little. People in the television audience do not spend all of their time glued to their television screens, and even during the most gripping of crises the live coverage of an event is likely to catch a random segment of the audience, depending almost entirely on the time zone, whereas the replay at programmed times is likely to be seen by more people. Therefore, broadcasts could be delayed several minutes or maybe even a few hours to provide some opportunity for the exercise of editorial judgment on how to handle a story. There is no doubt that real-time or near real-time news coverage has value, but the bulk of that value seems attainable without surrendering control of the story.

Guidelines, of course, can be only indicators. Media people are quick to point out that every terrorist incident is different and that therefore it is not possible or even desirable to try to apply hard and fast rules. I agree with that, but guidelines and contingency planning for the coverage of crisis situations will force the media to think in advance about their actions and help them plan for possible sources of trouble. I believe the media should use exercises and simulations the way other institutions increasingly do to improve their responses to crises. Preplanning and the use of guidelines to handle coverage of incidents can greatly reduce the likelihood of careless error. The quality of coverage will improve as a result.

Finally, it has become increasingly clear to many analysts of terrorist incidents and crisis management that ways must be found to keep the officials who manage incidents and the media that report them closer together. There are three sets of issues. One concerns the handling of fast-breaking developments. A second relates to news coverage that can give the terrorists a platform. A third relates to contact with and handling of information about hostages or victim families. These are not easy matters to deal with. Developments such as phases of a negotiation in progress can be sensitive, and their premature revelation can be potentially life threatening. Yet one of the ways media can stay out of such danger zones is to know enough about what is happening to avoid them. Information sharing cannot be complete, but the question government and media need to answer in some cooperative way has to do with what amounts and broad categories of information they might share in specific cases. Both terrorism and media experts have suggested that an information center be set up by government incident managers as a routine way of dealing with media information needs. To make that work, both media and government would have to do something about the normal suspicions that pervade their relationship.

The first hurdle to such cooperation is the common tendency for media and government to approach one another as adversaries. As the lead federal agency in managing international terrorist incidents, the State Department has reorganized its Office of Counterterrorism to provide a stronger information program particularly for use during terrorist incidents. Other federal agencies and many state and local law enforcement agencies have responded in various ways to the need to inform the public. These approaches should help by enabling incident managers to understand and to anticipate the media's most urgent information needs and to find acceptable ways to meet them. If media people don't feel they have to fight for each small piece of information on a story of vital interest to their competitors and their editors, the whole relationship should become a lot smoother.

When Should Sensitive Facts Be Published?

One of the media arguments for reporting information such as the Pan Am flight crew escape procedure is that such information would become public in time anyway. And since that is so, why not publish it? A colleague who writes frequently on terrorism issues asserts that the terrorists already know such things in any case. Thus there is no reason to try to keep the information from them. His assumption is that what he knows the terrorists know. If we use the logic of the media or the logic of my colleague on the protection of defense secrets, however, or even of family secrets, we would not have any.

A more prudent approach is to try to limit circulation of information that can be harmful to you or people you value. When dealing with or countering terrorist attacks, the longer information that might help the terrorists can be restricted, the better the chances are of avoiding or effectively managing an attack.

The Outlook

Reading the carefully hedged positions of those in the print and electronic media on the substance and utility of guidelines, I think I can predict that media coverage of future terrorist incidents will not differ radically from that of the past. On one hand, the media are captive to events; but on the other, I sense that many media managers are so caught up in a reflexive defense of the First Amendment that they are not looking soberly at the real dangers flagged by Georgie Anne Geyer respecting the effects of what the media tell people. This leaves us with too much concern by the media about form, but hardly enough about substance.

The coverage of terrorist incidents, in the estimate of one journalist I interviewed, has revealed terrible vulnerabilities of the American media that other people, terrorists or not, can exploit. The media are crisis driven, he says, and despite the appearance that media excesses during the TWA 847 episode taught them something, the only thing that made coverage of the *Achille Lauro* piracy different from that of the TWA hijacking was the fact that the reporters couldn't get to the ship. Despite the fact that good contingency plans can be developed in advance to cope with 80–90 percent of crisis situations, the media will not use them, he predicts. They will not plan out how to cover a story until they see how the story will play, and that, as a rule, will be too late.

That summation is unfortunate, because experienced crisis managers have learned that planning ahead on how to deal with the commonplace problems of an emergency frees up more time and concentration for handling the unexpected. The media, I think, can apply that principle as well as anyone else.

By studying the characteristics of the media, terrorists can always know where to get part of the help they need to stage a successful incident. The terrorists will be helped by the fact that the start of an incident is a siren call that the media cannot fail to heed. But answering that call unreservedly is potentially as disastrous for the media as it nearly was for Ulysses. If the media continue to get too close, as they have, an incident sooner or later will go really sour, a journalist will get hurt or killed, a plane will blow up, or hostages will die. Seamen learned to stay far from the rocks when the sirens sang. The media must learn that too, to protect their own interests, to avoid aiding and abetting terrorists, and to serve the public.

8

The Dirty Little Wars

How do you tell the difference between terrorism and rebellion or insurgency? In chapter 1, I discussed the problem of definitions, pointing out the basic differences that exist between these forms of violence. My definitions mainly distinguish between the two by placing terrorism in a category of violent crimes—principally against persons—which should be dealt with under the penal code, and by placing insurgency in a class of small-scale military or paramilitary activity that should be dealt with under the international rules of armed conflict.[1] This distinction is not perfect, because terrorism is used as an instrument by insurgents, but the two broad classes of violent behavior I have defined are still the correct ones. Nonetheless, you often hear someone say, without further qualification, that "terrorism is a form of warfare."

Calling terrorism "warfare" sits comfortably on the mind, because it suggests a kind of structure and discipline to the problem that ought to aid one's analysis of it. Terrorist incidents usually are small, brief episodes that are not clearly linked to specific plans or goals. Thus the incidents lack visible order that, even allowing for the confusion of battle, analysts have been able to distill from the "art" of war. That lack of order in terrorism is made even more patent by the random patterns of terrorist attacks, in time, place, and choice of victims.

We persist, nonetheless, in placing terrrorism among the classes of modern warfare. In doing that we complicate the personal, political, and institutional tasks of dealing with it because we don't have any rules stating what is permissible in a terrorist act, whereas, even though they may be disregarded, we do have rules of war that we use to judge the conduct of armies and of warring nations. As we will see later in this chapter, we also create a natural place for terrorism in the structure of most insurgencies.

All of those complications come together in the way we look at the "dirty little wars." As Neil Livingstone, author and lecturer on terrorism, commented to a panel at the National War College on October 8, 1983, the "prospective battlefield of the next 20 years is more likely to be an urban wilderness" than the traditional fields of war so studied by strategists like Clausewitz.[2] Thus, by the conventional rules of war fighting, terrorism may not be war, but we can expect it to do war's work.

The Classes of Attacks

Because the experts fall so readily into the habit of talking about warfare, the ordinary citizen doesn't get much help from the professional or scholarly communities in trying to make judgments about the moral or legal yardsticks that should be applied to terrorism. My definitions suggest that terrorism as a form of political violence must be treated as an illegitimate instrument in warfare. By failing to make that clear, we leave the field to propagandists of all leanings, and the Western democracies tend to lose more than the radicals and extremists in the resulting plays on words.

Take, for example, a conventional act of war: the mining of Corinto Harbor in Nicaragua by contra rebels, reportedly with the help of the CIA. Many critics of U.S. policy in Central America have called the operation an act of terrorism, but that charge is a deliberate confusion of the issue. Such a mining operation is generally a legitimate act of warfare, and when an insurgency such as that of the contras conducts such an attack to disrupt the shipping of the government with which it is at open, declared war, the mining of that harbor does not qualify as terrorism; it is war! The wisdom of any U.S. involvement in this operation is a separate issue, but the fact that any U.S. government part in it may have been ill-advised does not make the attack terrorism.

Still, the mining of Corinto Harbor puts the issue of what is terrorism in the ambiguous light that is so commonly shed on the behavior of the actors in dirty little wars. Practically everybody reserves the word *terrorism* for what their enemies do. In that regard, the word *terrorism* is not different from the more classical term *atrocity*. In the history of war, it was always the enemy whose troops committed atrocities, and being able to make the charge stick was a matter of some consequence to the legitimacy of one's own side. *Terrorism* has assumed that role almost entirely for the small-scale conflicts of our day.

As I stated in chapter 1, most of us are able to distinguish broadly between acts of warfare and acts of terrorism. The problem, as I indicated in that discussion, is use of terrorism by insurgents. Consider some cases:

In the mountains of northern Luzon, a cadre of the New People's Army ambushes a patrol of the Philippine Army; a young army lieutenant leading this patrol and most of his force are killed

The whole southern half of Angola is under the control of Jonas Savimbi's National Union for the Total Independence of Angola, UNITA organization, which has been conducting a protracted war against the government of Angola for more than two decades

Not far outside of Kabul, in Afghanistan, Afghan rebels attack a Soviet supply column headed toward the capital city to provide food and equipment to the Marxist government of that country

Back and forth across the border between Honduras and Nicaragua, members of the Nicaraguan Democratic Resistance—the contras—fight a desultory war against the government of Nicaragua, attacking supply lines and disrupting military operations

Next door, in El Salvador, members of the Faribundo Marti National Liberation Front carry out a surprise raid on a government barracks, killing Salvadoran soldiers and an American advisor

These events and situations, viewed through the eyes of a military tactician, are all related to straightforward acts of warfare. But look at the following actions by groups that also purport to be insurgencies:

While they were stopped at a service station in Namibia on May 15, 1984, two American diplomats were killed in a bomb explosion believed to have been set off by the Southwest African People's Organization, a group fighting for Namibian independence

In the Philippines during November 1984, members of the Moro National Liberation Front claimed responsibility for taking an American expatriate hostage

In June 1985 elements of the Faribundo Marti rebel group carried out an armed attack on a streetside cafe in San Salvador, killing thirteen people, including six Americans; and in September 1985 an affiliated group kidnapped President Jose Napoleon Duarte's daughter

On August 6, 1985, members of the Mozambique National Resistance attacked a funeral cortege, killing thirty-three people

The groups responsible for these attacks all claim the status of insurgents, but in these instances they are clearly resorting to terrorism.

All the acts described in these two lists fall within the context of the "dirty little wars." They are "little" because the acts seldom if ever engage the full forces of a government. They are "dirty" because they are fought with hardly any rules.

The Age of Insurgency

Since the end of the Korean War, the world has been in a more or less formal state of peace. But whereas of old, the intervals between wars were literal times of peace, the time since the end of the Korean engagement has been filled with small-scale conflict. Only a short while after the end of the Korean conflict, France suffered defeat at the hands of Indochinese rebels at Dien Bien Phu and that marked the beginning of creeping American involvement in Vietnam. France went on from Dien Bien Phu to the "savage war of peace" in Algeria,[3] in which the Algerian people took the country's largest department away from France, and France itself was almost torn apart in the struggle.

In the Western Hemisphere in the late 1950s the stage was being set for a new approach to regime change in countries of particular interest to the United States. The old era of authoritarian regimes was passing and along with it a habit of regime change by palace coup. Pressures for change, for opening and liberalizing regimes in many countries were mounting. Few of those countries had much in the way of democratic tradition. Thus, the means to achieve regime change without conflict were often not ready to hand. We were entering an age in which insurgency has become the stock means for changing the policies of a repressive or inattentive regime, to depose an unwilling autocrat, or to achieve ideological change. In countries of interest to it, the United States got involved.

Cuba

In 1958–59 pressures from liberal groups and the media in the United States mounted to do something about President Fulgencio Batista's regime. Batista had been in power too long; his legitimacy had virtually disappeared; his days were numbered by the most generous assessment of his staying power; and moderate political opposition to him was growing. At that point, a revolutionary figure appeared in the Oriente province. Discovered and romanticized by the *New York Times*, Fidel Castro was made into the liberal alternative to Batista.[4] His real credentials and background were not examined closely; therefore, when the United States withdrew support from Batista, who then fled the country, Americans were greatly surprised when the first thing Castro did was to imprison and murder the great bulk of any effective opposition. His plan was to capture and keep power,[5] which he has done by continually suppressing all opposition or forcing it into exile, in effect by using terrorism against the Cuban people.

Cuba was the first, shall we say, successful postwar venture of the United States into regime change by insurgency—a success in the sense that leadership actually was changed, but all the future problems the United States was to experience with that process were exposed in the evolution of the Cuban case. The U.S. government found itself at odds with significant elements of the public and with the media. It did not have any clear fix on the anatomy of such situations, how they developed, or on what actions were most critical at what stages of the changeover. This was in part due to the fact that there were not many good examples to look at for purposes of mapping the process. Of equal if not greater consequence for its later involvement in regime changes, the United States applied rather simplistic ideas of how democratic principles get planted or used in another country.

More importantly, however, Americans were reacting to events rather than scheming to shape them. U.S. officials were treating the Cuban case as an immediate crisis, and they were not looking at it as an example that could become an important precedent. It appears to have been too early for anyone to have a clear game plan. Specifically, as the shortcomings of the Castro regime became evident, U.S. officials displayed no long-term strategy to influence Castro's behavior. The collapse of the Bay of Pigs invasion attempt rather seemed to put a chill on efforts to moderate Castro's behavior, and it bought him an extended period of freedom from outside pressure in which to consolidate his power. Those were to be our manifest failings in important future cases.

Iran

From the beginning of his administration, Jimmy Carter faced growing political pressure to dump the Shah. To his opponents in the United States, that the Shah had slowly advanced Iran out of the Middle Ages and had created a climate for a growing middle class was of little consequence. Unknown to U.S. officials, and representing a major U.S. intelligence failure, the Shah was already gravely ill with cancer, and the end was only a matter of time.

History does not record its alternatives, so we can never know, but it seems to me that the United States had two real options at this point, either of which could have been superior to what actually occurred. First, the Shah, ill or not, was already in trouble. Decisive action was needed on his part either to reduce the speed and social stresses of the Westernization programs he was pressing on Iran, or on the part of the United States to strengthen his hand to help him weather a very unstable phase of the process. This balancing act would have been difficult in any event, but something like it was essential if the regime were to have any chance at all of surviving. Secondly, if succession did not occur from within the ruling family, there was no real procedure in Iran for selecting a successor to the Shah by consensus. In that sense, Iran was not ready for either a change of leadership or a change of regime. The process needed more time, and by communicating decisive support the United States could have helped the Shah buy time. Instead, wavering signals from the United States must have helped to undermine the Shah's confidence. His own responses to increasing turmoil in the mid-1970s were indecisive, and he lost the confidence of his military forces. The Shah's departure brought the Ayatollah Khomeini to power and placed Iran in the grip of a fanatical extreme fundamentalist dictatorship. Supporters of the Shah in the military, the civil government, and other sectors were murdered in a systematic purge.[6] By the time of the U.S. embassy takeover in November 1979, Khomeini was well on his way toward eliminating all effective opposition.

Nicaragua

During the late 1970s, the family dynasty led by Anastasio Somoza clearly ran out of time. His family and immediate supporters seemed to have forgotten even the informal consensus procedures that had extended some legitimacy to the regime of his father. As a possible alternative to Somoza, the Sandinistas had been around for generations without making much progress. They were only one source of growing opposition to Somoza, but without examining their credentials the United States withdrew support from Somoza and gave the Sandinistas the field. The Sandinistas had not been particularly secretive about their intentions, but once again the United States seemed to have been surprised by the speed with which they consolidated their hold, suppressed and intimidated all sources of opposition within Nicaragua, and drove the nucleus of an insurgent opposition into exile. Although the Carter administration initially held out its hand to the Sandinistas and provided foreign aid, the Sandinistas established close ties with Cuba and the Soviet Union. They created a repressive regime with a human rights record that already surpasses the worst excesses of the Somoza family.

The Lessons to Be Learned

The record in these three cases has distinctive properties: In every one the regime deposed had a long history of U.S. government support, through a succession of Democratic and Republican administrations. In every case the old regime was opposed by protest groups and the media in the United States which brought pressure for the withdrawal of U.S. support, and this pressure affected, in my view adversely, the timing and substance of U.S. actions. In each case the earliest casualties, by death, imprisonment, or exile, were supporters of the old regime and other significant sources of political opposition to the new leadership. The consequence of that pattern of repressive action was the effective suppression of any democratic infrastructure. Thus in every case, from any viewpoint of promoting democratic values or human rights, the results have been catastrophic political change.

The Role of Protest

In each of these cases, as well as in others, the perceptions of the leadership respecting the likelihood of future U.S. support were strongly influenced by public debate in the United States. The public life expectancies of Batista, the Shah, and Somoza inevitably were shortened by such pressures. The choice of successors in significant measure was guided partly by protest activities and partly by the media. Moreover, one outgrowth of the resort to protest activities in these and other cases, especially following Vietnam, was the evolution of an adversarial relationship between the U.S. government and protest groups. For protest groups, to face the government in that frame of mind is now almost a reflex.

The reflexive negative reaction has become so immediate that when the United States joined with eastern Caribbean nations to make the October 1983 landing in Grenada, media and protest groups were both poised to castigate the Reagan administration. They had a natural target in the administration's forceful rhetoric against Communism, and they saw the Grenada invasion as slavish adherence to that doctrine. The capture of several tons of documents during the landing, however, provided detailed information from Grenadan government archives about the plans of Maurice Bishop to impose a repressive, Marxist-Leninist regime.[7] The captured records provided too much evidence for an adversarial treatment of the decision to go into Grenada to be credible or sustained.[8]

Looking at Future Choices

Given the track record represented by the cases just discussed, the question naturally arises as to whether Americans learned anything or could adapt from these experiences. The answers always will be a bit murky because cases inevitably are different.

Given that, several aspects of the Cuban, Iranian, and Nicaraguan experience are relevant. First, in all three cases the United States waited too long to act, and then it acted too quickly. Stable processes for consensus building and political succession are not quickly reached or revised. They call for long-term patterns of influence, not abrupt changes of course. Second, abrupt and, in these cases, politically extreme shifts in leadership left the United States without significant influence over the situation at its most crucial phase, installation and setting the course for new leadership. Before that break in continuity of influence could be remedied in the Cuban and Nicaraguan cases, close ties were established with the Soviet Union. Third, unless you are going to invade another country, the patterns of effective influence are at the margins. Exerting influence over leadership from the sidelines, even with considerable resource leverage, requires patience and time.

The Situation in Southern Africa

Taking such lessons seriously, the United States ought to be proceeding very cautiously on the problems presented by apartheid in South Africa, but the prognosis is hardly encouraging. To be sure, the Botha regime in South Africa is running out of time and has practically exhausted the patience of the rest of the world with its stubborn obtuseness and repressive reactions to the need for change. It is on the verge of having waited too long and thus may be facing abrupt change, but there are many whites in South Africa who understand this and are seeking change via the political process. Unfortunately, the changes they have achieved have proved neither fast enough nor dramatic enough to satisfy either protest movements and governments in Europe and the United States or the growing numbers of increasingly militant blacks throughout southern Africa.

White South Africans have expressed concern that any future black regime will be inattentive to their rights or repressive, and that is more than likely to be the case. The probable chosen instrument of succession in South Africa is the African National Congress, the majority of whose members have sought change through the political process. However, the militant, extremist, terrorist wing of the ANC under Oliver Tambo has a Marxist agenda, and if the ANC does get control in South Africa, that extremist element can be expected to try to take charge, to eliminate moderate elements around it, and to impose a monolithic regime. My concern about Tambo's Marxism has nothing to do with "godless Communism." His Marxist approach practically guarantees that he will install an authoritarian regime if he gets any chance at all. His effort to do that no doubt will be opposed by others, particularly the Zulus, but to improve his chances Tambo will seek and will likely receive open Soviet support.

If the United States and the Europeans monitor the evolution of black rule in South Africa after an ANC takeover with no more diligence or interest than they have shown in the past, the militant ANC leaders can count on several months or even a few years of tolerance from the United States and Western Europe. American and European protest groups who have worked for the overthrow of apartheid will remain silent, and if the Nicaragua experience is any indication, protest groups will actively oppose any efforts by their governments to act against even obviously repressive moves by the ANC. That window of freedom from criticism and outside opposition will provide all the time extremists in the ANC will need to wipe out opposition and consolidate their power against any real challenge from either moderate blacks or whites. After years of effort to break apartheid, South Africa will have advanced only to the extent that blacks are then repressing other blacks. That is hardly a step forward, but the pattern already has been set in Angola, Mozambique, Malawi, and elsewhere in the region.

This of course is only one possible scenario for the future of South Africa. It is not inevitable. The seeds are there, in the ground, and such an outcome is in disturbing degree consistent with experience.

Change in the Philippines

Political change in the Philippines offers some hope that the protest cycle of regime change can be moderated or broken beneficially. Ferdinand Marcos stayed in power long after even his friends had concluded he should step down. He had shown a remarkable ability to achieve and sustain workable consensus; in fact, informal consensus building was a prime source of his strength in the earlier years. Even after his declaration of martial law in 1972 he had the support of the majority of Filipinos, because many believed that the political process had gotten out of control; it had become corrupt, self-serving, and violent, and there were hardly any clean hands in Philippine politics. However, during the four and a half years (1971–76) that I observed his performance from the perspective of a senior officer of the U.S. embassy in Manila, Marcos increasingly turned to old friends and cronies to help him keep power. They helped him in exchange for the opportunity for unrestrained theft or acquisition of control over the Philippine economy. In charge of economic and commercial affairs for the embassy, I watched that process at first hand, and the losers often were foreign businesses, many of them American. But the most common victims were other Filipinos.

By the early 1980s the Marcos regime was ripe for change, but there was no effective opposition in sight. Benigno Aquino, whom Marcos had jailed on declaring martial law, was considered dangerous to Marcos's ambitions because he was of the same political school as Marcos. Aquino knew how to play Philippine politics and play them ruthlessly enough to grow rich and powerful in his own central Luzon district of Tarlac. In the view of young political activists I knew, the problem with Benigno Aquino was the problem with most active politicians on the landscape at the time: they would have run the country in the same corrupt style as Marcos. In that sense, Philippine democracy had run down.

A decade and a half of martial law had some cleansing effect. Jail made something of a popular hero of Aquino, and assassination made him a martyr. Corazon Aquino, who slowly emerged as opposition leader after her husand's death, was a natural sort of choice. Judging from their mood when I visited Manila briefly in early 1984, Filipinos pretty generally were ready for a change, but not a radical one.

Had the prospects been pushed, the radical alternatives were there, in the New People's Army in the north and the Moro National Liberation Front in the south, but those alternative forces were not allowed to gain control. Instead, the Philippines is in the hands of moderates who appear committed to restoring Philippine democracy. Had Marcos been dumped in the way that Batista, the Shah, and Somoza were, the outcome could have been radically different. The New People's Army was looking for any opportunity to grab power, but because there was an orderly handing over of leadership authority without a significant break, NPA extremists who tried to assert control could not succeed. Had they done so, the people who now hold the future of the Philippines in their hands would be in jail, in exile, or dead, because they would have been seen as natural enemies by any extremist group that might have come to power.

Unfortunately, the jury is still out on the future of democracy in the Philippines, and being helpful is not a simple matter for the United States or anyone else. The leading political figures and families, both supporters of former president Marcos and of President Corazon Aquino, seem to have learned little from the two decades of increasingly corrupt leadership that ended with Marcos's departure. Rather they appear to have gotten quickly back into playing old style Philippine politics, a game of every man for himself. In that regard, their worst enemy is not the New People's Army but their own cupidity and lack of vision. Having been given a reprieve by the departure of Ferdinand Marcos, they seem bent on giving it away through squabbling among themselves. Getting Filipinos of influence to work on the same side is the main task, and outsiders cannot do much about that.

The Impact on American Power

An important feature of the American approach to political regime change is the pattern of protest activity that grew out of the Vietnam War. That pattern developed in the 1960s and early 1970s into a sort of "gung ho" style of protest that is aimed at getting things done quickly and visibly.

From the mid-1960s onward, the United States became increasingly involved in Vietnam, getting more and more deeply engulfed, while never quite able to reach a consensus at home about the usefulness or the pertinence of this engagement to American interests. In the end the United States withdrew, not because it was defeated but because it ran out of consensus to sustain the engagement. That, of course, from Hanoi's point of view, was victory.

In the meantime, in more respects than merely the habit of protest, the Vietnam experience had permanently changed American character. First, the Vietnam experience altered the way Americans think about the outside world and their role in it. On the one hand, there were popular pressures for a lowering of the American profile abroad, while on the other, political activism had introduced a sort of people-to-people involvement of Americans in the affairs of other countries. Second, Vietnam altered the way Americans deal with each other internally. As I noted earlier, an increasingly confrontational approach of people to government had grown out of the Vietnam experience. Third, Vietnam changed the way Americans make decisions. People increasingly tended to take controversial issues to the streets in protests and demonstrations. Fourth, Vietnam changed the American perception of the role of conflict in the management of human affairs. Americans' relations with each other became increasingly contentious and polarized. And none of that is as yet settled, but it is all very real.

In this context, since the withdrawal from Vietnam the United States has been involved in a nattering kind of dialogue with itself, seeming to be certain that it wants to, and indeed must, influence processes of change abroad, but appearing to be unwilling to get involved deeply or long enough to make that influence effective. It commits itself in a desultory way to the support of insurgent activity in Central America—aid to the contras against the Sandinistas—but seems unable politically to deliver anything like a firm pattern of support.

The Change in Defense Outlook

Most radically changed in all of this was perhaps the Defense Department itself. Coming out of World War II, the U.S. military was organized for war on a scale that no other country had ever achieved. By the end of the Korean War the United States was well launched into the global strategy that has guided its relations with the Soviet Union ever since—a continuous pattern of escalation and refinement in the art of nuclear standoff, the game of deterrence. For a bit more than a decade, the only game was deterrence, but slowly the world had changed. Shortly after Fidel Castro took over in Cuba, one of his principal lieutenants, Che Guevara, went abroad to export the art of insurgency. Che met his own destiny in Bolivia, but the Montaneros of Argentina tried his approach in protracted urban guerrilla warfare with the government. That in combination with a repressive set of responses by the government left political scars on the Argentine character that may never go away. Argentina's experience was not exceptional. Across the River Plate, in neighboring Uruguay, the Tupamaros failed utterly to achieve their political objectives, while succeeding in almost destroying Uruguayan democracy.

These experiences made it very clear that small-scale warfare could destroy governments, could destroy stable political regimes, could change the course of history for countries. Although neither Che Guevara nor other revolutionary philosophers such as Mao Zedong had succeeded in packaging the exportable revolution, the rules of statecraft clearly had changed. The message was getting around that insurgency was the way to do it, but the specifics of any campaign pretty much had to be developed on-site.

The Impact on Military Thought

On emerging from the Vietnam War, the Pentagon was in a psychic state of some disrepair. Attending the National War College as a student in 1970–71,

I found that my military peers, many of whom were combat veterans of Vietnam, felt badly bruised by the experience, badly bruised in two senses: One, that they had fought the good fight, and the United States was not winning. Two, that the United States had gone into that war with an inadequate consensus, and everything they had fought for was being lost in the collapse of national support. They understood very well what was happening to national feelings about the war, but they were convinced that the reason the nation could not develop a consensus favorable to continued engagement was a failure of leadership.

During 1981–83, as chairman of the Department of International Studies at the National War College, I saw that the state of confusion and anger that existed a decade earlier had evolved into a cautious new stance for the senior middle-grade military officer. The constant theme of the military officer in the 1980s was that the United States should not get involved in a military way anywhere in the world unless the American people were solidly behind it. The decision for war in this analysis had become not the calculated judgment of leadership respecting the balance of national interests, but rather something like a popular expression of enthusiasm detected through a Harris poll.

This frame of mind moved Americans toward becoming detached observers, always distant from the conflict. The dirty little wars are natural vehicles for doing that. If the United States is going to fight only popular wars, it will predictably stay out of all the little ones because they are not big enough and visibly consequential enough to engage the American people; the nation will never get a consensus.

Secretary of Defense Caspar Weinberger turned this widely accepted military attitude toward engagement into a national stand. The confusion of national attitude toward small encounters such as guerrilla warfare in Central America or in Angola, Afghanistan, or Indochina only reinforced the Pentagon in its cautious stance. Thus, by the end of the first Reagan administration, in view of the pattern of small-scale conflict that persisted in many parts of the world, the United States was awkwardly postured. Deterrence was working at both strategic nuclear and conventional force levels; the nation carried a big stick, but it was so grossly oversize that no one saw fit to try to justify its use in the seemingly trivial engagements presented by modern insurgency.

We the people, the media and the government had reasoned ourselves into a first-rate quandary. The best judgment of military officers continued to be that these little engagements do matter to U.S. interests, and the roster of conflicts now occurring adds up impressively in those terms. What, however, can you do, when your police power and authority stops at the frontier, and your military power is too grossly configured for the occasion? If the people didn't like it, U.S. leadership would not make war. But the little wars were seen mostly as not important enough to waste good political chips in building consensus. The Congress, following flip-flop public guidance, turned the support light on and off for insurgency in Angola, and it did the same, only more often, in Nicaragua, for wholly domestic reasons. Americans had become dabblers, voting for a pattern of political change by refusing to take any clear stand, by declaring themselves politically unable to cope with the process of sustained involvement. Strategic deterrence, it seemed, was a functional reality. Conventional military power apparently had become a functional irrelevancy.

Coping with Insurgency

Americans told themselves that they were unable to act as the world's policeman. That was true, but not so from any technical point of view. Due to the way decision processes had developed since the Vietnam War, the whole American decisions structure had been rendered insensitive to small-scale conflict. The Congress chose to regard all international conflict management decisions as war decisions, and opponents of U.S. military involvement abroad used rhetoric that almost automatically inflated any potential military move into the bogeyman of a new Vietnam. Such rhetoric of fear had psyched the United States out of Vietnam, and Americans were using that experience to psych themselves out of the future in Central America and in southern Africa.

The addition of U.S. Marines to UN peacekeeping forces in Lebanon seemed a constructive use of U.S. military power, but in the end it reinforced a cautious stance. Progressive erosion of their security and de facto change of the role of the Marines in Lebanon in the face of growing resistance led to a disastrous terrorist attack. In that attack, 241 Marines were killed and many others were wounded, and as a result the unit was withdrawn from Lebanon.

Under the doctrine that bears his name, President Ronald Reagan tried persistently to buck this tide. He launched with some success a highly publicized "covert" effort to help the Afghan rebels, but that remained his only real success in this field. He was able to do that because there was no real popular opposition to assisting the rebels against an obvious Soviet invasion. In Central America, however, he ran aground on the basic confusion discussed earlier in this chapter which pervades the American approach to regime change. The Central America problem had the added fillip that church groups, elements of the Democratic party, rightist extremists, and others set themselves up to run alternative foreign policies in competition with the government.

Moreover, the executive could not make decisions to attempt small applications of force because the Congress insisted that any use of force anywhere in the world was warfare that demanded they be consulted and approve essentially on a case-by-case basis. In this process the Congress was moving more and more into executive decision making, seeking direct involvement. That might not have been a bad idea except that the Congress had begun to prove during the Vietnam War that it could not make either rapid or durable decisions in this field, and it has repeatedly demonstrated its inability to do so. Instead the Congress got into a mode of backing away from insurgent activity for what were increasingly partisan political reasons, but also out of distrust of the executive, which derived from members' belief that they had been misled on the Tonkin Gulf.

The Lebanon experience with the Marines did not inspire confidence that military power could be used effectively on a small scale; rather, it added to congressional mistrust of the executive. Such mistrust, as well as differences of view on policy, showed up clearly in the domestic political quarrels that ensued over Nicaragua, or, with the congressional prohibition on aid to Jonas Savimbi in Angola.

One consequence of the mistrust and competition for role between the Congress and the executive was that a bipartisan approach to issues concerning foreign policy aspects of political violence became virtually impossible to achieve. Instead, congressional decisions on such issues as aid to Savimbi's National Union for the Total Independence of Angola, UNITA forces, in Angola or later to the Nicaraguan resistance became highly politicized, even ideologically loaded as between liberal and conservative stances.

A Boon to Terrorists

Because small-scale conflict decisions have been rendered bulky by developments in congressional, executive, and public attitudes, the field of fire for small-scale insurgent and terrorist activity has been greatly enlarged. The chance to avoid conflict, to support measures to reduce or ameliorate it in a timely way, has been practically eliminated, and in areas of particular interest to the United States insurgents are almost inevitably allowed the opportunity to get out of hand before the United States can muster a clear consensus to act, either to support the efforts of another government or to take action on its own. Insurgencies operating against governments of interest to the United States, therefore, have considerable latitude to carry out their strategies before the United States will be expected to become excited enough to react.

On the other hand, any insurgency that the United States tries to help is probably in trouble, mainly because the nation is likely to have immense political difficulty defining and delivering the kind of support a group may need. Moreover, any decisions made in the United States about support for such a group are likely to be made more in light of internal political considerations than of defined group needs. That means that neither times, nor amounts, nor duration of assistance are likely to be tailored to the needs of the insurgents.

International consensus procedures within the United Nations or the NATO alliance are even more difficult to engage than are those in the United States, so that insurgent attacks on an established government anywhere are likely to receive little concerted attention. The international system is not geared to deal with widespread acts of insurgency, nor is it capable of voting on the same side in making judgments about which insurgent activities are contrary to the common interest.

What all of this means is that if an insurgent group is smart it can sustain a very large window for its activities for an indefinite period of time. Unless the government being challenged is able and willing to fight back effectively, or it receives outside help for doing so, the insurgency can take its time, and keep itself fed and protected, wait for the opportunity to make a decisive strike, and hand the outside world a fait accompli. All the insurgents have to do is keep their operations below the excitability thresholds of the major powers and bide their time.

This insurgent operating mode, however, is a natural environment for terrorism. While the attempt to mount a military engagement on some field of battle can prove fatal to the insurgents in that they can be beaten decisively, or their attacks will prompt governments to mount a counterattack, setting off a bomb in a government building or kidnapping a foreigner is not so likely to goad a government into a decisive response. My point is that terrorism becomes the preferred technique in this setting because it is the most tailored means of protest the insurgents can use. It is both the cheapest and the safest instrument for keeping an insurgent enterprise alive.

Closing the Window

This insurgent opportunity and the pattern of terrorism it sustains can be dealt with only by closing the window. If the U.S. and other governments continue to deal with the global conflict environment as they now do, both the pattern of insurgency and its terrorist operating mode will spread. It is correct to say that the United States, or for that matter any other single country, cannot act as world policemen, but the nation must find an effective way to manage conflict in the international environment before it is too late.

The U.S. experience since World War II suggests a half-dozen essential steps toward a national strategy for dealing with the dirty little wars. First, the United States must apply a long-term strategy that does not change greatly from administration to administration. Second, and crucial to the first step, bipartisan approach to foreign policy must be restored, thereby reducing the ideology- and preference-driven swings in U.S. posture. Third, dependent in some measure on the first and second steps, the United States must make more lasting decisions about its support of causes, groups, and governments abroad, particularly as these decisions involve resource commitments. Fourth, as a leading world power the United States must apply itself patiently, recognizing that American influence in many cases is limited and can best be exerted over time. Fifth, the public needs to join in a bipartisan approach, rather than try to pursue independent foreign policies in places like Central America.

Finally, a reaffirmation of national goals is needed which will bring the public, the executive, and the Congress into harmony. The vital interest of the United States, which I define as the ability to live and prosper in cooperative arrangements with others, is being steadily eroded by the pattern of terrorism and insurgency in the world, and by the internally contentious and indecisive handling of it. We cannot go on working at cross purposes. The partisan, reactive, impatient, and short-sighted things we now do will defeat us and bring an end to democracy.

9

Global Issues:
The Catalytic Factors

B ETWEEN 1981 and 1983 there was an intense flare-up of opposition, mainly in Europe, to the basing of U.S. Pershing II and cruise missiles in Germany, Belgium, the Netherlands, the United Kingdom, and Italy. Through rallies, marches, sit-ins, and public protest events staged for the media in major European capitals, opponents of these deployments conducted a sustained effort to persuade the governments of the five countries about to receive these missiles to overturn their commitment to the deployment. Much of the campaign was aimed at and received full media coverage in the United States.

It was no surprise that through this pattern of protest many Europeans expressed their opposition to the idea of stationing nuclear weapons on their territory. Nor was it a surprise that the sources of opposition to these deployments represented many different sectors of European opinion. The surprise lay in the ability of organizers to make opposition to the deployment of U.S. intermediate-range nuclear weapons in Western Europe a rallying point around which groups with widely different causes could get together.

As opposition to the deployments of these weapons gained momentum in the summer of 1982, peace groups joined with the environmentalists, with the anti–nuclear power groups, with church groups, labor organizations, women's organizations, and others. This was not entirely a concerted program of opposition, but at times it was a fairly coordinated one.

Opposition to the deployment of intermediate-range missiles received substantial financial support from the Soviet Union, as indicated in intelligence reports at the time. It was natural that the Soviet Union would take advantage of this opportunity to neutralize U.S. intermediate-range ballistic weapons by political means rather than having to face them in military strategic terms.

Supporting European opposition to the deployments, even to the tune of many millions of dollars, was a cheap option for the Soviet leadership.

The Soviet part in this pattern of protest was never admitted, of course, nor was it acknowledged or even necessarily known by the protest groups. Neither was the involvement of various European terrorist groups in these protests publicly acknowledged, but much of the violence associated with antinuclear protest activity during this period was not merely incidental, caused by inadvertent excess. It was actively promoted by terrorist groups, such as West Germany's Red Army Faction and the Italian Red Brigades, whose members were seeking, with only limited success, to use protest demonstrations as cover for more vicious acts.

The Link to Terrorists

Recent analysis suggests that the terrorists may have achieved more than was thought at the time. To illustrate, in July 1983 Green party leader Petra Kelly made a speech in the Bundestag in which she warned the government of Helmut Kohl against "genocide" and charged that his government was "'criminalizing' the 'nonviolent' peace movement." These and other terms she used were "all themes in RAF [Red Army Faction] texts." The terrorists may not have been able to take over the peace movement or to use its demonstrations for terrorist activities, but they had succeeded in creating much of its rhetoric.[1]

In German elections held during January 1987, Christian Democrats campaigned against a possible "Red–Green" linkup between socialists (Red) and the peace movement (Green).[2] No comment appeared, however, about the apparent Green–Red Army Faction connection, which also is indicated by the fact that a senior Green party member of the Bundestag, Otto Schily, is the former attorney of the Baader-Meinhof gang, which evolved into the Red Army Faction.

The striking feature of the loose coalition of opposition groups that grew up to protest the deployment of nuclear weapons was the fact that the groups ordinarily had little in common. Protest activity in Italy during the peak of the antideployment effort is illustrative. Italy's "verde" (or Green) peace group worked with Autonomia Opraria, a labor union movement, and had the help of Red Brigades members and sympathizers as well as the so-called United Communist Cells. The latter is a terrorist group, which claimed responsibility for the murder of two policemen in Rome in early 1987 and published a proclamation at the time announcing its intent to cooperate and seek solidarity with Action Directe in France, the Red Army Faction in Germany, and other terrorist groups in Europe.[3]

The obvious range of ideologies, goals, and objectives caused me to wonder, what brought all of these groups together in working, cooperative arrangements? Were the Greens just "stumbling into terrorism" in their extraparliamentary opposition because they were looking for help anywhere they could get it? Were they "walking with the terrorists," including borrowing their rhetoric as a matter of mere convenience?[4] Or did the Greens and other peace advocates have a more calculated agenda? Was this all the product of a blinding expediency?

The Unity of Activist Agendas

I was really interested in learning where, in terms of their normal agendas, these groups see a payoff for joining hands with extremists in the antinuclear movement. The answer to that question is still not very clear, but I set out to answer a second, closely related question: Which values of the groups as individual organizations showed the highest compatibility with the values of other groups? The more I studied the problem, the more I became convinced that the unifying force among them was not any blanket commitment to violent methodologies. Rather, it was each group's commitment toward one or more of the global issues. I will come back to the global issues themselves after doing a little more groundwork.

Somebody once tried to sum up the involvement of diverse groups in the peace movement by saying, somewhat facetiously, that "everybody is interested in everything." You don't have to look closely at many people for long to appreciate that such an observation, if notionally true, is practical nonsense. Most people frankly don't have enough time to be interested in everything, and in the high-intensity information environment in which we now live most people's attention spans, except for their particular interests, are often transitory.

Many people will be interested in almost anything when it is the subject of a fast-breaking or dramatic news story. In quieter times, however, people are likely to pursue sustained interests in only a few subjects. Relatively few people take the time for the constant scanning of information that is necessary to stay current on a wide variety of topics. Moreover, an increasing number of issues have become politicized, which tends to polarize and separate groups rather than bring them together.

The rallying force of the global issues was demonstrated anew to me in 1985–86 by the efforts of U.S.A. for Africa, a group of young people, media people, actors, singers, rock groups, and others, to gather support for the starving children of Ethiopia. Having spent several weeks in that country in 1976, including a visit to a UN refugee camp in the lower Wabe Shebele River basin, I understood their desire to help these children, because in those camps people live under some of the worst conditions in the world. Recent photographs show that the poor conditions I saw, if anything, have gotten worse. The charitable fund-raising effort of this group centered on the creation and sale of the recording "We Are the World," and the very successful campaign demonstrated once again that people could get together around a common cause of this sort regardless of where they stood ideologically on other issues. As one writer put it, "People who normally wouldn't drop a dime in a poor box" contributed willingly.[5]

The True Believers

Psychologists tell us that there are many layers in the human personality and that there is no natural law requiring us to be consistent. Some months ago I spent a couple of hours exchanging thoughts with a young Washington journalist who seemed to live quite comfortably on two distinct planes. As I talked with this young writer and listened to his comments, I came to the conclusion that although he represented a very liberal news organ and his published views were of similar perspective, his personal views were really conservative. I told him I had concluded that he clearly led at least a double intellectual life. He responded that he was indeed conservative about everything except his media role. On anything to do with media, including the content of his stories, he was liberal, but on anything having to do with home, family, and personal values he placed himself to the right of Genghis Khan.

This encounter revived for me the thought that apparent ideological distances between the far Left and the far Right are often not as extreme as they seem. This line of thought rekindled an interest in people's reasons for the causes they espouse.

In the 1940s and 1950s a self-educated scholar, longshoreman, and writer, Eric Hoffer, wrote perhaps the definitive work on this subject, *The True Believer*. Many people found Hoffer's work offensive because his main message for some was a little hard to take. He said that people who feel strongly about some particular cause are fairly easily recruitable to many different causes, given the right motivational triggering. His point was that ideas of ideological purity and exclusiveness were largely illusory. The deeper and more pertinent implication of his analysis, even though he did not state it in these words, was that people's commitment to causes is driven more by emotional and egoistic forces than by ideology.

Hoffer's conclusion was that a true believer in anything is susceptible to recruitment into anything else. People who are able to take one thing seriously are able to take other things seriously, and the key is the capacity for getting deeply involved. It is this kind of energy that is transferable from one cause to another and that provides the operational stimulus for common cause.

The Global Issues

If Eric Hoffer has put his finger on the psychological machinery that brings cause-oriented people, especially from wealthy elites, the middle-class and academic groups, to combine in the ways they do, what are the subjects that normally arouse them? As I mentioned earlier, I believe the combining force is found in the global issues.

What are the global issues? Simply put, they are concerns that transcend all national boundaries and focus on the whole human condition. They are hunger, poverty, population crowding, scarcity, economic disparity, the environment, human rights, the fate of humanity, and the quality of life.

The global issues constitute a large, emotionally charged agenda. There is something, one or more somethings, on that agenda for practically everybody, regardless of race, creed, color, national origin, or political affiliation. Unless you've stopped living and thinking at least a little bit about the processes and the implications of life, you will be concerned about one or more of the global issues.

The issues are often emotional and the slants romantic. Dire predictions are common. There is often more chicanery and demagoguery on these issues than there is real illumination. Feelings are at times the only "facts" you have to work with. Perceptions are realities in their own right.

What makes the issues global, as several thinkers and commentators have pointed out, is a set of more or less common properties. What people do affects everybody, everywhere. No one country or group of people can solve the problems unaided. All countries must take part in solving them. There are no quick fixes; the solutions require enormous, continuing effort. Extraordinary cooperation among countries and coordination of efforts are essential. Problems cut across old organizational and functional lines. New and heavy demands are placed on national agencies and on international institutions. These issues affect our interests in areas where previously we saw no problems. They call for extreme acts of patience and endurance and they demand new national and global strategies.[6] They require a redirection of both material and spiritual resources, and they are proving to be immensely important to both our sense of well-being and harmony with our surroundings and to a growing measure of our physical security.[7]

Most of the global issues are familiar, and the data are generally known. I could devote at least another book the size of this one to the global issues themselves, but I think that only an outline is needed for the purposes of this discussion.

Population

Human crowding, the so-called population explosion, is one of the oldest issues on the global agenda. Malthus sounded dire warnings about population outrunning the food supply as early as 1790. At that time, the world's population was still short of 1 billion people, but that number was reached in about 1830. In little more than 150 years since reaching the first billion, the world's population has climbed rapidly, reaching 5 billion in 1986. Various studies project a continued rise in human numbers to more than 6 billion in the late 1990s, and to almost 8 billion by the year 2030.[8] This means that as we enter the twenty-first century three people must share the earthly resources that were available for one at the end of World War II, and six or more people will be standing where Malthus saw only one when he considered the world already to be in grave trouble.

The population issues center, however, not so much on the numbers as on the meaning of the numbers. Malthus and others since his time, including the pessimists in the so-called Club of Rome, have been expressing concern mainly about overrunning the carrying capacity of the earth. In effect, they have suggested that technical limits on agriculture will be reached before the population foreseeable in present trends can be adequately fed or economically supported.

Some economists argue that more people mean more output. Thus, if each person provides only for his or her own necessities, the population explosion is largely self-sustaining. Even if the materials, the inputs needed to support the individual are only land, water, and sunshine, however, there are obvious practical limits.

A major problem for any effort to make predictions in this field is the fact that we don't know precisely what the practical limits of the earth's carrying capacity really are. The supply of solar energy is, of course, fixed by the earth's size and relation to the sun, but how efficiently we use it is a function of applied technology. Over the long run the land area of the earth's surface changes slowly in response to geological and weather forces, while in the short run the supply of agricultural land is being rapidly cut into by the scramble of people for living space and by erosion. But significant increases in food production are possible with techniques that are already established, and to just what extent increasing output can compensate for shrinking land area and rapidly expanding human numbers remains to be seen.

With that kind of an information base, there appears some room for us to manage our future, but one fact is clear: everything essential to human life on this planet is getting more scarce, either absolutely or relatively. Moreover, for people who are already at the margin of survival, for the miserable bustee dweller in Calcutta who lives practically on the street, for the boat person in China, or the favella dweller of São Paulo, Brazil, conditions are already so bad that they may well conclude that any increase in numbers is only a net addition to their own misery.

We may not either attain or effectively use the carrying capacity of the earth in the foreseeable future. However, the fact of a large, underfed, under-privileged mass of people is already an immediate global population challenge. Awareness that the mass is large, growing, and increasingly miserable in many places is a moral albatross hanging on the necks of all thoughtful people. Fixing those population problems may not be our highest priority, but living comfortably with them is something only a hardened few of us can achieve.

Meanwhile, the population issues have been restated, by both supporters and opponents of birth control, by supporters of the right to life, and by people who either approve or disapprove of abortion. These versions of the population question are personal, individual, emotional, and religious, and on these levels, the Malthusian question of numbers is largely irrelevant. Feelings run high in debate at these levels, and the choice of weapons has ranged from the constitutional amendment to the pipe bomb.

Food, Poverty, and Hunger

The issue respecting food is a corollary of the population problem. Whether we are about to stare in the face one of the four horsemen of the Apocalypse is a stark question for the future. Views on prospects for food production are conflicting. Most experts seem to have concluded that food supplies will be adequate for the next decade or so but that many countries will have severe production and distribution problems. Both the optimists and the pessimists on world food production, however, appear to see crisis in the future.

In reality, for many milllions of people, the crisis exists now, and both sides in the controversy over world food supply conditions seem somehow unable to grapple with that fact. One writer suggests that the number of hungry and unemployed people now exceeds 800 million.[9] Many are being permanently damaged by undernutrition every day. Even when there is a market surplus, as the economists define it, this crisis goes on, because misery lies with those who cannot pay, those who are too weak to enter the market. The crisis hovers inevitably around them, and the worst cases are found in parts of Ethiopia, the sub-Saharan drought belt called the Sahel, and in the crowded cities of the Indian subcontinent. In trying to deal with those cases, we have not really applied the lessons learned in the United States, with such programs as food stamps, that governments need to supplement market forces to overcome various common frictions of the marketplace. The social objective is equitable distribution of food, not just economic clearing of the market.

The outlook on food prospects is very uncertain. On one side, there is some cause for optimism because average crop yields for the world's agriculture are well below what is possible even for mediocre lands. The technology to increase food production already exists. On the other side, however, the problem is how to get resources and techniques to people on the land. Whether the poorer countries can afford the energy inputs and other capital costs of increasing food output remains unclear.

We are a long way from any solution to this problem now, and we are probably headed in the wrong direction. As I see it, the trend of overseas development policies in the United States and in other advanced countries has been away from any effective grappling with the global food problem for more than a decade. The concept of assistance for economic development that dominated U.S. programs in the 1960s has been largely abandoned in favor of mere feeding programs. On this point, the public programs of U.S. Aid, the food and nutrition programs of various churches, and other private efforts such as U.S.A. for Africa have a common failing: what is now done in the way of providing food to the poorest of the poor is charitable, but it leaves them as they are—with a little more food in their stomachs but with no better tools to use in winning survival from the earth and with no better prospects for the future.

The Environment

Concern for the effects of human activity on the environment is an issue we have made for ourselves mainly in the last century, significantly only in the past fifty years. Before that time, with the exception of cutting down large tracts of forest in both temperate and tropical zones for fuel and housing, people were probably having a limited effect on the conditions that support life as we know it. In the past century, however, human activities have made or contributed to many risks to that life support band of conditions, and both ordinary people and the scientific community seem to know all too little about some of those risks.

The main categories are air, water, and soil pollution. Types of pollution include acid rain, toxic wastes, nuclear wastes, noise, rising levels of carbon dioxide in the earth's atmosphere. There are others, of course, associated with our continually shrinking living space.

The debate over what to do about acid rain—rain combined with the airborne sulfurous by-products of burning coal to produce electricity—has more or less set the tone of these problems. Acid rain is the identified culprit in the pollution of lakes and streams in the northeastern United States and parts of Canada. Various experts think they pretty well know what causes it and, in technical terms, how to stop it. The debate on what to do has become quite polarized, however, between environmental groups on one side and public utilities and government on the other. At present, public policy decision processes seem politically immobilized by such questions as "who pays" for the cleanup and for the transformation of power production, by ideological and economic objections to tighter regulation by government, and by concerns about related energy cost and employment issues.

What Americans and others have learned so far about the effects of corrective action on environmental problems is cause for optimism. Recovery rates for lakes and rivers have proved to be much better than imagined. Lake Erie, the Potomac, the Hudson, and the Wisconsin rivers and others have gotten back many fish. Lake Michigan, largely given over to eels a few years ago, now supports at least five types of salmon and other game fish.

Those successes, however, have been hard-won, and one of the prices American society has paid has been the spread of protest strategies as a means to provoke public policy decisions on environmental issues. Those strategies have worked to get decisions that often are emotional responses to technical issues; and the decisions are unstable because they have been coerced from unwilling participants, frequently business firms and utilities. Consequently, people on both sides of the leading cases have been slow to see and to apply the basic factors that must be considered in dealing with the environmental and other global issues: the problems are common. Costs must be shared, because benefits are common. Lasting decisions cannot be achieved without consensus. Problems big enough to affect the global environment cannot be fixed either cheaply or in a hurry.

There are also problems in relations between rich and poor countries over the environmental issues. Leaders of developing countries and environmentalists alike have become sensitive to the possibility that industrialized countries will export their polluting industries, either through the activities of multinational firms or through cultivating sources of the products of such industries in underdeveloped regions. With the advanced countries getting, so far, most of the wealth and other benefits from industrialization, the developing countries feel that the rich should pay for much of the cleanup. There seems little doubt that the longer corrective actions are delayed the more the burdens of material and social costs will fall on the poorer countries.

Energy

Although two energy shocks have occurred in less than a decade, this problem is not only still with us, it is arguable that except for price effects on demand and the damper of worldwide economic conditions on consumption, little has changed. The United States still does not have a comprehensive energy strategy, and the prospect is that continuing low energy prices (in real terms a gallon of gasoline is cheaper now than it was at the beginning of World War II) will nudge the advanced countries back into the conspicuous energy use habits of the past. Congressional legislation in 1987 approving a 65-mile-per-hour speed limit on superhighways is one indication.

The main emphasis of U.S. energy policy is still on direct substitutes for oil, but applied research and development work on synthetic fuels has been derailed. Research and development in areas such as solar energy have languished. Fusion research, whether on laser or other systems, is underfunded. Nuclear power production is being destroyed by debate while we wring our hands over such problems as waste disposal, which technically is a fairly straightforward problem to solve if we will just get on with it.

The picture is not entirely bleak, but neither is it very positive. Useful work is being done on energy from biomass in Brazil, India, and elsewhere. Hydropower is receiving close attention, at least in Brazil, and possibilities are being reevaluated in the United States. Despite the tough climate created by environmental and other cost pressures, nuclear power has been increasing its role in energy supplies worldwide, although that trend may have been reversed by the Chernobyl accident in the spring of 1986.

In the meantime, the use of energy is and will be heavily skewed toward the advanced countries. In this regard the rich are very rich. The work of energy specialists such as Dr. Howard Odum of the University of Florida, Thomas Robertson, a private Washington consultant, and their colleagues shows that the United States now uses eight to ten times as much energy per capita in an average day as do the countries of Central America.[10] Moreover, the rich countries daily increase the embodied energy of their economies, storing it in the forms of machinery, equipment, food reserves, and economic infrastructure, including transportation, communications, and developed real estate. This energy in the bank and control of the technologies needed to put it there are the biggest factors between being very rich and being very poor. Because the poor use the great bulk of the energy available to them just to survive, their energy bank accounts stay small, often embodied in little more than mud huts, subsistence food supplies, and meager possessions.

The Global Common

More and more the weaker members of society see the world's resources distributed in ways that go against their interests. In fact, a friend of mine once commented cynically that the only thing the poor get a lot of is scarcity. While this picture is unremittingly true for the goods and services that affect survival, it is also true for sharing the global common—those global features such as radio frequencies, air spaces, sea passages, sea floor resources, inner space, and the riches of Antarctica which are the common heritage of all but also end up mainly in the hands of the rich. In fact, a steady process of reallocation is occurring, for example, of radio frequencies and commercial air routes, toward the Third World. But the rich countries have the edge simply because they got there first, developed the technologies, and in general occupied the global common. The frustrating feature of this situation for the Third World is having to negotiate to receive a proportionate share of property that they believe they already are entitled to in common with the rich.

The Impact of Global Issues

Seeing the same 15–20 percent of the world's people enjoying the lion's share of all resources, whether food, energy, metals, money, or sectors of the global common, many people of the poorer countries, especially among intellectual

elites and the clergy, view the disparities between rich and poor with a growing bitterness. Many people in the United States and in other wealthy countries are sympathetic to that view.

The politics of the global issues lie right here, in human reactions to the
great disparities created by historic allocations of opportunities, wealth, and
resources. The skepticism of U.S. policies encountered among elements of
the American public, and the decision-making troubles commonly experienced
on such issues in the United Nations organization manifest these politics. So
does the receptivity of liberal elements in many countries, including the United
States, to anti-U.S. propaganda.

One of the major recruitment pools for young people who get recruited
and trained as terrorists or insurgents springs from this situation as well. Poverty
is a binding matrix. Breaking out of it is hard, and in the poorer countries
the chances are few. A terrorist group that offers income, training, travel, excitement, or just escape can look very appealing. A group offering those things
with some chance to uplift one's family, to improve the situation of an ethnic
group, or to redress some deeply felt grievance has potentially powerful appeal. Groups with money and organization, such as the Popular Front for
the Liberation of Palestine, the Italian Red Brigades, or, closer to home, the
Aryan Nations or the Black Muslims are well positioned to recruit young
people who see no other hope and train them to violence.

Human Rights

The global issues converge on the broad ground of human rights, and to understand this thought a bit better it is helpful to review briefly where most of
us come from on this subject. The debate of the past two administrations,
with the seeming 180-degree shift between the Carter and the Reagan policies,
has had really very little impact on underlying American attitudes, because
the wellsprings of opinion on this subject run very deep. On this point, it
is well worth a look back at a few of the things Americans have been saying
to themselves for a long time.[11]

> Establishing the liberties of America . . . will have some effect in diminishing
> the misery of those, who in other parts of the world groan under despotism,
> by rendering it more circumspect, and inducing it to govern with a light hand.
> —*Benjamin Franklin*

Providence . . . has chosen you as the guardians of freedom, to preserve it for the benefit of the human race.

—Andrew Jackson

We must take up and perform, and as free, strong, brave people, accept the trust which civilization puts upon us.

—William McKinley

America will come into the full light of day when all shall know that she puts human rights above all other rights, and that her flag is the flag . . . of humanity.

—Woodrow Wilson

Following these traditions, Franklin Roosevelt articulated the Four Freedoms, and former secretary of state Cyrus Vance in effect elaborated the concepts of the Four Freedoms into three sets of "complementary and reinforcing rights":

1. The "right to be free from governmental violation of the integrity of the person"
2. The "right to fulfillment of such vital needs as food, shelter, health care, and education"
3. The "right to enjoy civil and political liberties"[12]

As we see readily in these attitudes, which bridge two centuries of the nation's history, a concern for human rights, and acceptance of a vested national responsibility to protect and to promote them, are constant faces of the American character. That concern, however, has evolved with American society to such a degree that a basic recognition of the rights to political and civil liberties that founded the American democracy has slowly become recognition of fundamental rights to certain minimum qualities for the whole human condition.

The emergence of this very broad "bill of rights," which tries to encompass the needs of the whole person, has been articulated with a growing clarity since World War II. And in the past two decades the broad bill of rights, not merely the traditional one, has become the benchmark against which success or failure in the performance of other governments is measured. Such a model now forms the basis for judging the legitimacy of U.S. policy, especially respecting political and social change abroad, and for gauging the moral rightness, and perhaps the political wisdom, of U.S. support for the leader-ship and the policies of other governments.

Concern for human rights has been a continuing part of the American character, but the projection of U.S. power in defense of human rights is something the nation has never done comfortably, artfully, or successfully, except perhaps in the context of general war. The rising trend of human rights violations around the world thus has created increasingly acute problems of national perspective and of foreign policy: at the same time that our concern for human rights has increased both in level and in nature, our willingness to send people and resources abroad to deal with these problems has declined absolutely and relatively. The cacophony of voices within the United States, each of which, with the amplifier of media, presumes to speak for all, tends to confuse the issues, not merely respecting where and in aid of what to send resources abroad but also respecting where and how to apply diplomatic energies with greatest effect.

Meanwhile, the global issues focus ever more sharply on human rights. All the indexes of power and wealth place the developed countries of the West, followed by Japan, the Soviet Union and the Warsaw Pact group, and a few others among a critically advantaged fifth of the world's people. Look-ing downward from the top, we see the United States, the Organization for Economic Cooperation and Development (OECD) group, the Soviet Union, and Eastern Europe. Looking upward from the bottom, we see sub-Saharan Africa, Asia and the subcontinent, and Latin America.

Misery and the Causes of Violence

This map of the human condition, which demonstrates our success to date in treating the global issues, has some other frightening dynamics. Where in the past two decades have the bulk of the insurgent uprisings been? Where on this map are the happenings or the origins of the incidents and the stated motivations for the rise in international terrorism? Where on this map are the most numerous, persistent, and egregious violations of human rights?

It cannot be mere coincidence that where responses to the global issues most severely operate against the interests of ordinary people the resort to violence is increasing. By suggesting that, I don't mean to subscribe to the so-called root cause theory, which says that "terrorism is a byproduct of misery, oppression, hunger, and other terrible situations" that cause people to lose hope for any solutions other than the violent ones.[13] In fact, millions of people have grievances at any one time, but fortunately for world peace the overwhelming majority who suffer the impact of scarcity and repression are patient, resigned, or even forgiving. Violence is growing around the worst human situations, but it generally is not being generated by the victims.

The global issues are catalytic factors but not root causes for violence. Two different users of violence come out of the pits created by the great disparities. One is the recruit from this pit. Mostly he or she is a young person who can be used by almost anyone who is prepared to harness the emotional energy generated by poverty and repression. The other is the educated, usually well-off individual. Again, mostly, he or she is a young person who is either hagridden by conscience or buoyed up by grandiose visions of reform. Either type of recruit sees low-level violence as the path to correcting the disparities themselves or to establishing a new order for that purpose. Both types of recruit happen to be fair game for exploitation by people who promise beneficial change, and whether the exploiter is coming from the political left or the political right may be relatively unimportant in the appeal of such a promise.

In the discontent that grows out of the ways the global issues are being handled lies the recruitment pool for insurgencies that seek to overthrow their country's government, for terrorist groups that seek to promote an insurgency or to serve their members' own ambitions, for governments that see terrorist tactics as a cheap alternative to negotiation, and for states allied with the Soviet Union that see the pool of discontent in many countries as a natural source of allies and instruments of low-level warfare against the West.

The global issues are a potent catalyst for patterns of sympathy and support in the United States for terrorists and insurgents who go against governments with poor human rights or political and social development records. The perception, however sensible, that Salvadoran president José Napoleón Duarte may be unable to curb human rights violators from the right has led numerous American church groups into an alliance with antigovernment insurgents who practice terrorism. Perceptions among younger Catholic clergy in Latin America that the established institutions cannot greatly improve the human condition has led them to espouse liberation theology, including the idea of the violent overthrow of established governments. The lack of support the United States has found in the United Nations organization on actions to counter terrorism stems in great measure from the belief of Third World governments that the global issues are root causes of terrorist activity.

Practically all of the long-term solutions to the problem of international terrorism must deal with those perceptions of the impact of the global issues on human conduct. Many other sources and motivations of violence exist, but this one is the most compelling because it is the most human; it is the easiest for most people to understand and therefore to justify; and it gives a legitimacy to violence that, it is increasingly obvious, we cannot afford to ignore.

Politics of the Global Issues

Global issues are catalytic factors in a complex chemistry of protest in the United States. Since the era of Vietnam War protest activity, the protest strategies developed in that era have emerged as almost reflexive tools for effecting political and social change. Protest and civil disobedience have become far more common as means to influence decisions than they ever were in U.S. history. The inability or unwillingness of the government to take appropriate action, as defined by the protestors, on environmental or other issues affecting the basic human condition seems to goad them into ever stiffer positions of opposition to the national leadership.

The most serious manifestation of that stiffening attitude is the drift toward violent solutions. In Germany, the Greens have become a political party of respectable weight in the Bundestag, but they decided some time ago on a two-part strategy: in a manner parallel to that of the agenda of the New People's Army in the Philippines, they seek to promote change by getting their members elected to parliament, but if the pace or the content of change is not adequate in their view they plan to take the issues to the street. Moreover, the extremists among them want the issues pushed to confrontation with established authority.

For the American extremist, the strategy is not much different. Leaders of the Weathermen (now the Weather Underground) in the 1970s saw the process as a natural escalation to violence.[14]

So far only the extremists have gone that far on the path to violence, but some manifestations of the trend in that direction are proving to be difficult to manage. A number of protest groups, religious organizations, and members of the Congress increasingly appear to have concluded that government cannot be trusted to deal with sensitive matters such as human rights, and they have set up their own independent connections with opposition groups or other sources of pressure on governments abroad. As we see almost daily in Central America, opponents of official U.S. policy have set themselves up as purveyors of an alternative policy, a third force at work, at times openly and derisively in opposition to official policies. These groups also are directly confrontational with the leadership and policies of other governments. There are similar indications in Germany of an activist tug of war with government over the control of foreign policy.[15]

The categorical losers of efforts to run an alternative U.S. policy in Central America are the ordinary people of those countries. Governments of the countries with responsibility for refugees' pouring into the United States are distracted from developmental tasks that would have real future impact on the ability of the economies of those countries to provide jobs and opportunities. U.S. resources are blunted in their effects by stop-start, tug and haul policy changes, and the country's efforts abroad are neutralized, not by its enemies, but by its own citizens.

In this perspective, the politics of the global issues emerge as a principal barrier to taking decisive actions to correct the endemic problems they represent. Skepticism and doubt about the will of governments to use resources effectively leads to the resources' being denied. Unwillingness to permit someone to grow rich through running a large project, for which he or she would grow rich in any of the developed nations, prevents such projects from ever being started. Impatience with the pace of change causes resources to be withdrawn from the process, and the development process staggers for want of fuel. Disagreement with a national leader over the speed or the degree of responses to human rights violations causes the U.S. Congress or private groups or both to undermine the moral position of the leader, making progress on the issues much harder to achieve.

The effects of the U.S. policy approach obviously differ from country to country, and the potential weight of U.S. assistance varies as well in light of local sytems, cultures, attitudes, and states of development. But the broad effects of these approaches as I just outlined them are visible in several countries.

It must be obvious that no country can run its foreign affairs in that manner and succeed. If the United States continues on the path now suggested by relations between private groups and the governments in Central America, it will end up with no policy, no program, and no effective pattern of influence over countries that are important to their own people as well as to regional peace and progress. Confusion about how to deal with the global issues has brought the United States to this impasse, and some future decisions on how to deal with them clearly is essential to get the nation out of the present mess.

The solutions to the global issues require the same sort of national response I outlined for dealing with the dirty little wars. National development, of the United States or any other country, takes time, and any organization or government that gets into it must have long-term policies and programs. We can't get that or sustain it without a bipartisan policy that brings Congress, the executive, the public, and leading public institutions into agreement on national goals. We need to back those goals with long-term resource commitments aimed at promoting economic and social developments that are compatible with local societies; not mirror images of the United States, but not threatening to it. Somehow we must balance the equities of the global system, and that means we must find equitable ways to divide up and use the world's resources.

If we cannot do that cooperatively, if the contest between East and West continues as now to be a competition for power, with the waste and resource misuse that that competition sustains, then all our assistance choices will be harder. Sustained effort on the part of the United States will be more critical.

The security and the credibility of Western values and institutions will suffer most in this situation. Why? Because Westerners are the ones who claim to value the person. That will not be meaningful if those in the West cannot advance the human condition. Thus the West will go on being the natural target of political violence, because the spoken as well as the implicit promise of its system will generate grievances when the West fails to keep the promise. That is the power the global issues have over us, and it is imperative to take thoughtful, sustained actions to deal with them.

10

The Matter of Legitimacy

O NE of the charges made against President Reagan by opponents during the weeks after the Iran scandal surfaced in late 1986 was that trafficking with Khomeini's people in Iran had enhanced their respectability and standing to the disadvantage of the United States. By arranging secret meetings with Iranian representatives, the United States gave Khomeini's government the opportunity to exploit that recognition, even if it was informal and not intended to be public. In a degree that is correct; but if the United States talked at all to the Iranians, it was also inescapable. There was no way that representatives of a U.S. government could talk to Iranian officials whether or not they represented dissident factions, without enhancing the standing of Khomeini's regime in the world community. The questions are really: When is that an appropriate step? When is it not an appropriate step? And of about equal importance, for whom is it an appropriate step?

Legitimacy and standing are critical issues to any party to a negotiation. That a negotiation may be about to occur informally between governments, between a government and private groups, or between private groups and individuals does not matter. What does matter is that each party to a negotiation is perceived in the eyes of the other party and in the eyes of its sources of support as being legitimately engaged in the negotiation. That being so, whatever one does to improve or diminish the legitimacy of the other party, or to improve or diminish one's own legitimacy, changes the terms of the bargaining.

The usual terrorist effort to use the media to achieve a standing and a legitimacy before the targeted government or audience is therefore a sensible strategy for the terrorist. The first question of any negotiation (why should I bargain with you?) can be partially answered. If media treatment of the incident goes well from the terrorist's point of view, possibly the legitimacy of the terrorist can be wholly established before any negotiation begins.

Americans, and indeed many other people, tend to be careless about this nicety of bargaining, and therefore give away bargaining chips they need not surrender. What I'm really saying here is that conveying legitimacy to the other party to a coming negotiation is itself a negotiating chip of considerable value. This is inevitably so, because conveying legitimacy means that you are obliging yourself to bargain seriously with the other party, and you are upping the ante on what would be appropriate for you to concede in the outcome of any bargaining session.

As an example of how important this matter of legitimacy can be, the North Vietnamese, at the beginning of Paris peace talks to end the Vietnam War, sought a way to indicate that their status was equal to that of the United States. Hence the Vietnamese staged the debate and cultivated the media publicity that went with it about the shape of the bargaining table.

One of the penalties of the diverse manner in which the United States conducts its relations with other groups and governments abroad is that legitimacy is frequently given away before the negotiator can do anything about it. The negotiator seldom has control of how and when that might occur, because other elements such as the media, members of the Congress, religious organizations, former ranking government officials, and environmental or other special interest groups manage publicly to impart a legitimacy that the U.S. negotiator must reflect in approaches to the other party. Thus a standard tactic of foreign governments or groups, particularly in the Third World, is to get American domestic groups to speak out for them, giving them a standing that is often influential on negotiations, on policy actions, and on legislation. Some of this obviously is out and out lobbying, but a lot of it is simple maneuvering to gain stature, which is usually of great value in the outcome of any negotiation.

The Case of Fidel Castro

Examples of this strategy and its results are numerous. Going back nearly thirty years, Herbert Matthew's reports in the *New York Times* in 1958 and 1959 were the first steps in conveying legitimacy to Fidel Castro. Castro at that time was leading a ragtag band in Cuba's Oriente province, and his band had no particular chance of success. However, by playing up Castro's activities and his goals, and especially by suggesting organization, strength, and capability that romanticized Castro and his followers, the *New York Times* portrayed Castro as the legitimate heir to the then ruling President Fulgencio Batista.[1] More or less in sequence with the appearance of those stories, several things began to happen. First, pressures were increased inside the United States to dump Batista, who had already undermined his own legitimacy by corrupting and then setting aside Cuba's democratic system. Second, the efforts of Batista's opponents within the existing political system in Cuba to unseat the president got lost in the shuffle when American attention shifted toward Fidel Castro. Third, the U.S. ambassador in Havana, charged with conducting relations with the Batista government, found his hands more or less completely tied.[2] Fourth, Americans in general did not look closely at Castro's credentials, because on the face of it the *New York Times* had already given him high standing. Fifth, and most critical of all, Fidel Castro's belief in democracy and his good intentions tended to be taken for granted, and his immediate acts of repression in Cuba, the murder, imprisonment, and exile of hundreds of moderate Cubans, were neither examined closely nor heavily criticized.

The *New York Times* quite naturally has resisted the notion that its publicity of Castro was a significant factor in his initial success, but the world often works that way, and the *New York Times* didn't invent the way the system works. The system works the way it does because most Americans don't know a great deal about events even in a nearby place like Cuba. Thus, a well-written story can have perhaps undeserved impact, and it follows that a badly thought-out story can have some badly thought-out effects. In that light, the initial laying on of legitimacy, therefore, was a potent step toward Fidel Castro's success in taking over and keeping power in Cuba, which he has now done for twenty-seven years without change of regime.

The Case of Roberto d'Aubuisson

As a second example, in early 1984, shortly before Duarte's newly elected government took office, U.S. intelligence authorities uncovered a plan to assassinate Salvadoran president-elect José Napoleón Duarte and U.S. ambassador Thomas Pickering. The aim in Duarte's case was to prevent him from taking office. The plotters were associated with the extreme right political faction of Roberto d'Aubuisson, whose "death squads" had been charged with numerous acts of political murder, torture, and kidnapping. These acts included the kidnapping and torture of Napoleón Duarte himself to keep him from taking office when he had won an earlier election.

In light of the threat, the United States, specifically the lead foreign affairs agencies in Washington, decided to send a high-level official to San Salvador to confront d'Aubuisson with the evidence. The object was to persuade him to moderate his behavior but specifically to stop the plan.

While the high-level official was still en route to San Salvador, a member of the White House staff decided that in light of his known association with d'Aubuisson Sen. Jesse Helms should be briefed about the situation. Shortly before his arrival in Salvador, the official was notified via a radio telephone call from Washington that a member of Senator Helms's staff had called d'Aubuisson and informed him of the intended visit and its purposes.

As I learned later from the account of a participant in the meeting, the report d'Aubuisson received was quite complete, and it was clear that d'Aubuisson was ready for the meeting. In this instance, d'Aubuisson not only had been warned, but also his standing and legitimacy vis-a-vis the high-level official had been materially enhanced by the intervention of the office of a U.S. senator. That d'Aubuisson's followers had been involved in plotting a criminal act against the U.S. ambassador and the president of El Salvador, along with a long record of terrorism against the Salvadoran people, was greatly diminished in significance by that intervention on d'Aubuisson's behalf. A large chunk of the moral high ground the official had under him when he left Washington had been yanked away, not by d'Aubuisson, but by the office of a U.S. senator.

The Case of the New People's Army

That giving the other party legitimacy changes the terms of the bargaining is important to remember in assessing the significance of the late December 1986 visit of Congressman Stephen Solarz (D–N.Y.) to the Philippines. This visit occurred in the midst of efforts by Corazon Aquino's government to negotiate a cease-fire with the leadership of the New People's Army. Congressman Solarz, chairman of the House Subcommittee on Asian and Pacific Affairs, wanted to meet with the leaders of the New People's Army rebels in the northern Philippines to judge for himself where they were coming from and where they were trying to go in the negotiation. According to a report from Antonio Zumel, leader of the Communist rebel group, Congressman Solarz met with the group for several hours of what were described as "very frank" talks. This was the first time on record that any American official had ever met with the rebels.[3]

Based on a talk with a member of his staff, Congressman Solarz went into this encounter well aware of its potential for exploitation by the NPA. Moreover, he was aware that Philippine defense officials were worried about the meeting of a U.S. congressman with leaders of the NPA because they feared the rebels could use the publicity to enhance recruitment. Thus,

Congressman Solarz and his staff sought to avoid any adverse impact on the negotiating stance of Aquino's government by keeping the meeting secret.

That effort was probably doomed in advance, because Zumel and doubtless other leaders of the NPA saw the publicity potential of the event immediately. While the prior understanding was that they would keep the meeting secret, Zumel acted as his own spokesman to publicize the meeting. As a result, only a matter of hours before they were to meet with Aquino in formal negotiating session, the rebels received the immense tactical opportunity of meeting with a member of the U.S. Congress. What they may have discussed is of less importance than the fact that the visit had real potential for enhancing the legitimacy of the rebels, giving them a standing vis-à-vis the United States, but more importantly vis-à-vis the Aquino government which they had never possessed before. Any positive publicity the NPA received as a result would help to gloss over the harassment, intimidation, and murder of numerous Filipinos by the rebels en route to the bargaining table. Therefore, the visit could bias the terms of the bargaining between the rebels and Aquino's government more in favor of the rebels. As Zumel probably saw it, the visit could only help by making the point that the leadership of a significant element of the New People's Army was recognized at least semiofficially by the United States.

In that sense, if Congressman Solarz met Zumel, he could not avoid giving away one of President Aquino's bargaining chips, or at least diminishing the value of it. I am informed that President Aquino agreed in advance to the visit but that the U.S. embassy in Manila refused to have any part of it because of concern about appearing to enhance Zumel's standing. I conclude that Aquino probably went along with this encounter, deciding to live with the likelihood that her government would have to pay a price for it in future dealings with the NPA.

Legitimacy and the Terrorist

Legitimacy is so important to the success of any terrorist venture that the terrorists must make its achievement a strategic goal. It does not follow, as some have asserted, that terrorists know more about this than other people, including governments. It is clear enough, however, that they need legitimacy; they know this, and they look for any convenient way to achieve it. On that point, the real breakthrough for the TWA Flight 847 hijackers came with the visit of media people to the Shiite community hiding place where the hostages were being held. Giving members of the hostage group the opportunity to speak for them was a clever legitimating step by the terrorists, and at that stage in the incident the possibility that the media would refuse to go along was nil.

Out of a desire to be fair and helpful, some former hostages as well as members of hostage families and friends often help the terrorists gain legitimacy. Although I have seen no report that former hostage David Jacobsen ever did so, many American hostages taken by the Lebanese group Hezballah who so far have been freed from captivity have stated in some way that they forgave the kidnappers or they have failed to condemn them, or they have found ways to rationalize, sometimes on the advice of family or friends. Hostage families have argued that the hostage takers have grievances and therefore must be dealt with, thereby asserting, perhaps without intent to do so, that bargaining with those who solve their problems by kidnapping and torturing other people is somehow normal.

The Management of Grievances

I have trouble with this whole idea, because it implies that people who have grievances can live by rules that are different from those for people without such causes. We have to be careful with that kind of idea, because in our world its implications are explosive. First of all, at any one moment millions of people have grievances, and if the normal response to grievance becomes some form of violence then the world will quickly become uninhabitable. Fortunately, only a small number of people respond by resorting to violence, and even fewer direct their violence at others.

This isn't to say that you and I or others affected by terrorist acts don't have to deal with people who take the violent path to resolving their grievances. It is hard to duck dealing with them in some fashion. But legitimacy concerns the moral and ethical tone of such dealings. It is one thing to recognize that you have no choice but to negotiate with a terrorist who is holding someone you love at gunpoint, but it would be ridiculous to suggest that in moral/ethical terms the bargaining situation is normal.

If people are not prepared as a general rule to make and to defend such distinctions, the problem of dealing with terrorists becomes even more difficult and dangerous. In a terrorist incident, the aim is to coerce and intimidate both the victim and the government by a violent act. People who are unable to make clear judgments about the appropriateness of that resort to violence will not be able to muster any ready moral/ethical defenses to protect their own position in the encounter. The terrorist often will use rhetoric on a victim to create this result, to strip away the individual's moral defenses and thereby add a sense of shame and remorse to an already acute state of terror. This same tactic, directed against a government whose citizen is being held hostage, can have the effect of undermining the legitimacy of that government, making it look inept, repressive, inhumane, insensitive, or unprepared.

My point about the way Americans so often deal with questions of legitimacy was made in a striking way on January 27, 1987, the evening of President Reagan's State of the Union Message to the Congress and to the people. ABC anchorman Peter Jennings announced on the evening news that ABC planned to get representatives of the Ayatollah Khomeini's government in Iran to critique the president's report to his people. Recognizing that one must deal with Iran's leadership, even though it has created the most active terrorism sponsoring state of our time, is one thing. Inviting it to participate in internal American processes and extending that order of legitimacy to it is something else entirely.

Achieving legitimacy, or having legitimacy conveyed by others, tends to mitigate the coercive nature of the bargaining situation created by a terrorist kidnapping, hijacking, or other incident. The more standing the terrorists can achieve, the more legitimacy they can appear to acquire. The more normal the bargaining situation can be made to appear, the greater is the pressure that is exerted on the target group to make concessions. It is almost axiomatic to say therefore that step one for the terrorist is to acquire legitimacy by whatever means. Even when the media would argue that they are only exposing what "bad guys" the terrorists really are, the terrorists on the whole seem to think they gain from the exposure. They obviously do gain when the media use apologists as commentators to argue that the terrorists' grievances justify their actions.

The negotiator who is about to face a terrorist incident negotiation should approach the issue of legitimacy from the beginning as an important question. It should not be assumed away as it frequently is. It should not be conveyed as if it were the due of the terrorist. The effort of a negotiator from beginning to end should be to avoid conveying more legitimacy to the terrorist than is absolutely essential to resolving the incident. Particular effort should be made to avoid mixing the means of the terrorist with the grievance or the demands of the terrorist. Whatever the apparent legitimacy of the demands or the complaint, the means being used must be treated as illegitimate.

The Value of Legitimacy

In summing up this chapter, I want to make a few main points to be sure we are on the same wavelength. First, legitimacy is a thing of value, and we should always get something for it, if we have any role in extending it. Second, one of the most unhelpful things we can do to our negotiator is to preempt or devalue the legitimacy chip by saying or doing things that change perceptions of legitimacy as between the parties. Third, we must not assume that the best way to play this chip emerges immediately and automatically in an intense crisis situation. It may not. Thus the best strategy may be to stand back, to wait and see where the terrorists are trying to go and how they seem to be planning to get there, before making a concession or deciding how the bargaining will be pursued. Fourth, as we look at a negotiating situation, we must always look for the legitimacy indicators and for efforts of either party to change the legitimacy weights. We must not give our own player's legitimacy away by meddling, making independent approaches to the other side, or by using intermediaries on the theory that they are neutral in their effect on legitimacy. Anyone who approaches the other party in your name may be able to play or to damage your legitimacy chip. Finally, as individuals, even vitally interested ones, unless we have overpowering reasons for getting involved in a negotiation, we should stay out of it. Leave the representative to do the job.

The Right of Self-defense

In the latter part of chapter 1, I struggled for some time with the position taken by Martha Crenshaw,[4] because I agree with one of her basic premises: democratic values and human rights are worth defending through a very broad range of means, and if we are pressed, in extremis, we must be prepared to use them. Thus, finding legitimate premises for the uses of power in your own defense is a vital matter. My problem with the concept of "legitimate" versus "illegitimate" uses of terrorism was the ease with which a world that shuns precise definitions in this field could either turn the distinction against the democracies or use the substance of her argument to justify uses of violence democratic societies would not find in any sense acceptable. I could see the United States ending up with a value system quite suitable to Robin Hood in Sherwood Forest or to the sheriff in a small Western town, and that was all very appealing for a moment, but I shuddered at the thought of this logic's being transported to the streets of a modern city, where a million people would be within range of the shootout at the O.K. Corral and the incidental casualties would outnumber the outlaws by a hundred to one. In October 1987 that kind of vision of random and widespread violence caused many people to react in horror to a new Florida gun law that would permit practically anyone to carry a concealed weapon or even openly to wear a sidearm.

With that thought, the time had come for me to face the single fact I had been circling throughout the preparations for this book: legitimacy is the central issue in managing the whole problem of political violence, no matter whose side you are on. People avoid defining terrorism for fear that the definition will work against them. And it will, most likely by limiting what they can do without inviting criticism or sharp public scrutiny. Here you come upon an ironic point of agreement: neither the terrorists nor their opponents want the term defined in such a way as to include what they do. For the terrorist that would mean the denial of legitimacy. For the rest of us that would mean denial of violence as a means to defend ourselves.

Many writers and commentators on terrorism have been looking for a way to retain the right to defend ourselves and still stop the terrorists, and they have not always been imaginative about it. I have friends and colleagues who have talked seriously about assassinating the terrorists, a treatment that in their view was not alone reserved for the international criminals like Abu Nidal. I have heard government officers and private citizens, including lawyers, argue the utility of "informally detaining" terrorists to bring them back to the United States to stand trial, and I don't have any problem with that procedure myself in cases where U.S. authorities have a valid warrant for the arrest of the individual involved. Authorities who do this, however, must be careful to assure that the rights of the accused terrorist are not thrown over the side. On one occasion it was seriously suggested that the way to get hostages back from Hezballah in Lebanon was to kidnap the families of the hostage takers and trade them back for the hostages. To the person who made that suggestion, the notion that in doing so Western authorities would be behaving like the terrorists did not seem relevant.

I have been particularly startled when these ideas come from people who have grown up in a community—American society at large—where people mostly don't seem to think that an occasional public hanging is in the public interest. What the inability of Americans to make up their minds about capital punishment means in this context is that Americans don't want to legislate the role of violence in society but they do want to retain access to it. That is the dilemma, and the dilemma is in two parts.

No Easy Way Out

We start by having limited, if any, control over the philosophical universe we operate in. Our best ideas are copied, mirrored, borrowed, and sometimes twisted by other people for their own reasons. They are reshaped and reused by dictators and democrats, charlatans and clerics, thugs and teachers, media and mimics, and they are recycled to us in the myriad forms created en route. It is dangerous to play games with the meaning of a word like *terrorist* in this environment. Even a sober, thoughtful effort to define terrorism so as to avoid interfering with the normal exercise of police power by sensible people will likely be misinterpreted by someone with a different agenda. If you don't deal with the subject carefully, you should be prepared for adversaries and critics to question your legitimacy.

The United States does not control enough of the world's people or territory to enforce its definitions in any case, and that leads us to the second dilemma: if you reserve the right to use violent methods, no matter what you call them, you leave the door open for others to do the same. I have a basic quarrel with the National Rifle Association, because I don't believe that Americans need even 10 percent of the weapons that exist in private homes in the United States to defend ourselves from hooliganism or runaway authority. I agree with them on one issue: controlling the resort to violence lies more with moderating human behavior than it does with eliminating weapons.

That means Americans must stop kidding themselves about the role of violence in society. It must be delegitimated for all but the most extreme circumstances. It must be brought down from its romanticized treatment as the almost casual remedy for almost trivial grievances. U.S. laws and courts already do the first half of this in the way they seek to control the use of weapons by police officers and in the rules of engagement they define to limit the uses of deadly force. Many Americans are miles from tackling the other half of this problem, however, and they will remain so until they recognize that the resort to violence by ordinary people is already approaching the limits of social control.

Legitimacy is the key. If people are not prepared to set standards for their society under which the resort to weapons and other violent remedies is controlled through strong, clear sanctions against them, then everyone must be prepared to live with the full flowering of violence as a means of making and enforcing decisions. Such a choice means that all of us will confront life on an increasingly crowded planet where no one has a place to hide.

11

Taking Terrorism
Too Seriously

S INCE the takeover of its embassy in Tehran on November 4, 1979, the United States has made terrorism a major foreign policy issue. The central concern of Jimmy Carter's administration was to obtain the release of the American hostages held by the Ayatollah Khomeini's government. When Ronald Reagan was inaugurated on the day those hostages were released, he declared that the effort to combat terrorism was a high-priority matter for his administration. The domestic rhetoric and the dialogue with foreign governments emphasized terrorism as a matter of pressing mutual concern. Early in his first year, President Reagan imposed the most extensive economic sanctions ever applied against any country in peacetime against the government of Libya's Muammar Qaddafi. In successive meetings of the leading western economic powers, the Economic Summit Seven,[1] the United States pressed with increasing persistence for a coordinated attack on international terrorism.

As the United States discovered fairly quickly, the rewards of this effort were few and far between. Jimmy Carter had already learned that even in the case of the gross violations of international law and custom represented by Iran's takeover of an entire embassy, there was no chance of a uniform condemnation from the world community. The ayatollah no doubt was encouraged by that lack of unanimity, and the captivity of the American hostages in Iran probably was extended because of it. Ronald Reagan fared no better with sanctions against Libya. The Europeans, whose cooperation was essential to any assured impact of sanctions on Libya, simply did not want to play. Even American oil companies and American workers in Libya's oil fields ignored a ban on travel to that country. In a fairly short period, with at least passive cooperation of most European countries, Qaddafi had worked off most side effects of the U.S. sanctions program. Further Reagan administration steps, begun in early 1986, to isolate Libya received limited European cooperation after the April 14, 1986 raids on Tripoli and Benghazi.

The Struggle for Attention

The Reagan administration, and indeed many Americans, did not seem to understand why the Europeans were being so uncooperative. Some media, particularly American, were quick to attribute the lack of response to Reagan administration rhetoric, asserting that spokesmen like Alexander Haig both overstated the seriousness of the problem and delivered only empty threats. A shocking 1983, in which more Americans were killed in terrorist attacks than in all previous years of record, and which included bomb attacks in London, Paris, Beirut, Kuwait, and Rangoon, caused U.S. policy planners to think there might finally be some chance of concerted action. But even the attempt of North Korea to kill South Korea's head of state and key members of his cabinet did not excite universal condemnation. The heads of governments, it seemed, could not be turned by mere sound and fury in remote places, nor even by a certain amount of blood on their own streets.

U.S. policymakers, displaying a usual American pragmatism, continued to push European governments, searching for a persuasive logic that would not come. The strategy itself did not pay off, but events during 1984 and 1985 began to bring European perceptions around to the American view of the problem: A policewoman was shot by someone from inside Libya's People's Bureau on St. James Square in London; an Air India flight blew up over the Atlantic; a Kuwait Airline flight was hijacked to Iran with several Europeans on board; TWA Flight 847 was hijacked in Athens; the Italian Cruise ship *Achille Lauro* was pirated in the Mediterranean; and the Abu Nidal group pulled off bloody attacks at Rome and Vienna. Suddenly, Europeans, it seemed, far more than Americans, were the preferred targets. But the need for concerted action suggested by that fact penetrated only slowly, and Americans continued to wonder when the Europeans would come around and "pull more of their own weight in the alliance."[2]

Events in the 1986 brought a faster change in perceptions in Europe. The sabotage of TWA Flight 840 on its approach to Athens, in which four passengers died, the near-miss bomb attack on El Al by Nazer Hindawi at London's Heathrow Airport, and the bombing of West Berlin's Belle Disco brought home a point that Americans had been stressing: the governments of Iran, Syria, and Libya were deeply involved in sponsoring terrorist attacks inside Europe. The evidence was substantial: the number of terrorist attacks of Middle Eastern origin in Western Europe had risen to more than one every week, and with hardly an exception the groups involved were sponsored by one or more of those three states.

In the wake of the Belle Disco bombing, which killed a U.S. serviceman, U.S. F-111 and carrier-based aircraft carried out raids on Libya. There was little European help or enthusiasm for the attack. French leadership was opposed and unwilling to let U.S. aircraft overfly French territory, but the French people were strongly supportive. British Prime Minister Margaret Thatcher approved the launch of F-111s from Britain, but she was not supported by the British public. In that ambiguous climate, the United States delivered a message to terrorism-sponsoring states: it had to stop.

Sanctions Once Again

In the meantime, the United States, looking at the mounting intelligence file on Muammar Qaddafi's terrorist plans and activities, went back to Europe to try, once again, for sanctions. The prospects were not visibly good, but as one analyst observed, "There aren't very many arrows in the quiver of statecraft."[3] Sanctions appeared to be as good a tool as any available. Success was not immediate, but in 1986 Britain, France, Germany, and Italy all experienced terrorist incidents that underscored their vulnerability to imported terrorism. In France, Germany, and Italy, moreover, domestic terrorist groups displayed increasing signs of cross-border communications and cooperation. Those countries and others reached independent decisions to curb the size and the freedom of movement of Qaddafi's agents in the Libyan People's Bureaus, expelling more than one hundred "diplomats," while Italy and France acted to restrict their traditionally open travel relations with North African states.

It would be tempting as well as satisfying to say that these decisions were the fruit of persistent American pressure, but the main factor compelling action was a clear and present danger that appeared far more evident and serious to European leaders in 1986 than it had appeared to be in 1983.

The great bulk of the terrorism experienced by Europe in this period was indigenous to the individual countries, even though foreigners were often the victims. Through the mid-1980s, however, the frequency of imported, particularly Middle Eastern, attacks in Western Europe grew rapidly. In 1985–86 the number of terrorist attacks in Western Europe reached nearly three hundred each year, about a quarter of them Middle Eastern in origin. This pattern of attacks, already visible in early 1985, was very disturbing.[4] This trend, rather than the frequency of terrorist attacks in general, brought the Europeans to the realization that they had to deal with terrorirsm as an international problem while coping with it as a domestic one.

The Iran-Contra Impact

The situation had reached that point when the Iran/contra scandal broke, and the immediate reaction of administration critics, armchair counterterrorists, and the media was that the long campaign of U.S. policymakers to get the Europeans on-board had been derailed. That reaction failed utterly to take into account the kind of analysis of European reaction I have just described. It assumed a linkage between U.S. pressure and European behavior that is in significant measure false; and it also presumed that the Europeans are a good deal less focused on their own national interests than indeed they have been. This says, in turn, that Americans still have a good deal less clear picture than they should have, either of how the Europeans interpret the pattern of terrorism in the 1980s or of how they may intend to approach it.

Europe's Terrorism Challenge

Terrorism in one form or another has become a commonplace challenge to democratic governments. The United States, Japan, and every major country of Western Europe have one or more domestic terrorist groups. In many cases, the groups represent themselves as insurgents with long-term goals of separation. Examples include the IRA in Northern Ireland, the Basques in Spain, the Corsicans in France, the Kurds in Turkey, and the Machetero Puerto Rican following in the United States.

Western European countries also have terrorist groups who represent a so-called armed struggle. Their stated objective is to overthrow existing authority, but they express no definite plans for its replacement. In that category are West Germany's Red Army Faction and the Revolutionary Communist Cells, Italy's Red Brigades, Belgium's Fighting Communist Cells, and France's Direct Action. All of these groups represent essentially domestic challenges to the authority of the state. Some, like the IRA, are known to receive sympathy and support from abroad.

Terrorism in most of these countries involves some order of insurgency. Moreover, each of these governments must contend with communities within their own countries that variously sympathize with the insurgents. As was discussed in chapter 9, in West Germany, the Red Army Faction is known to have sources of sympathy and support in the Greens party, which now has 10 percent of the seats in the Bundestag.

The interesting aspect of this situation is that a number of European critics of U.S. counterterrorism policy have said that the Americans take terrorism too seriously, give it too high a policy profile, and perhaps give the terrorists more credit than they deserve. That may in some degree be true. It is not, however, the reason why European governments are nervous about U.S. approaches. There are essentially two problems.

First, the pattern of domestic insurgent and terrorist activity in several Western European countries makes those governments quite rationally seek to avoid agreements with other governments which will interfere in dealing with situations they consider entirely domestic. A significant nationalistic element, even some who would not willingly support those insurgents, could well be moved to help such groups or hinder a government action against them if it were to appear that the governments concerned might be bending to outside pressure in dealing with an internal affair. Thus the interests of those governments require them to keep a maximum free field of action around their domestic terrorist challenge.

Second, the internal management of terrorist activities in European countries, as inside the United States, is a law enforcement matter, not a military one. Using criminal codes and criminal procedures against terrorists enables those governments to deal with terrorist incidents as crimes, thereby keeping them out of the complex entanglements that go with having to weigh the merits of a political motive. It is best in every case, as those governments define it, to keep terrorism out of domestic politics as much as possible. That means dealing with terrorism as crime and as a routine law enforcement matter if that is possible. Getting into an agreement with another government on how to deal with terrorism automatically starts a process of politicizing the issues.

European governments treat each other in much the same way they treat the United States where this type of issue is concerned. When Britain sought cooperation in isolating Syria for its role in the aborted attempt by Nazer Hindawi to blow up an El Al flight, the twelve-nation European community initially said no, and key countries France and Germany were among those who refused to go along.[5] A few weeks later European governments did approve measures, but Greece continued to refuse.

The issue of possible abridgement of sovereignty is not an unimportant element of national behavior in this instance. That is probably less consequential, however, than the potential a treaty or some other form of external agreement has for agitating the rhythms or interfering in the management of domestic political affairs. In fact, the potential for an agreement with other countries to cloud the management of internal affairs may be the abridgement of sovereignty that is of greatest concern.

Areas of Common Ground

Members of the European community who have worked within the framework of the Trevi group or the Council of Europe to make decisions on cooperative measures against terrorism have tried to mediate such concerns among members and still make some headway on arriving at common approaches to the terrorism issues of deepest concern. Those concerns include:

The export of terrorist activity from one country to another

The safe havening in one country of terrorists who are conducting operations in another

The refusal to extradite a terrorist or letting one go when that person is wanted for a crime in another country

The linkup of groups from one country to another and use of the resultant network to support terrorist operations

The avoidance of significant gaps in procedures of mutual interest—for example, aviation security, enforcement of the rules of diplomatic behavior, and so on

Complicating European efforts, no less than those in the United States, is a complex dispersion of authority across national boundaries and individual country agencies. During a September 1986 meeting of the Council of Europe, Secretary General Marcelino Orejarpt Oreja commented that one of the major problems is the proliferation of organizations engaged in antiterrorist activity, and he called for the creation of a clearinghouse for information, as well as for agreements within member countries to designate one senior person who could "bear full responsibility."[6] By that he meant that government should have someone in charge of both policies and programs.

The Uses of Force

As European countries have grown increasingly vulnerable to imported terrorist activity, the risks have grown that any of those countries could become host to a terrorist incident of such vital concern to another that the offended nation would feel compelled to take direct action. This kind of situation raises the issue of foreign military force in its most nightmarish form. The nature of terrorist incidents is such that a government can find itself in the position of being unable to take forceful or decisive enough action to resolve the problem quickly. Governments do not want to contemplate situations in which external force might be thrust upon them, and they are mostly not prepared, for internal political reasons, to make arrangements in advance to accommodate either the passage of or the use of outside military force in their territories. They cannot get away from the thought that when Americans talk aggressively about using military force in a terrorist incident, in 40 percent or more of the recorded cases they could be talking about an incident in Western Europe, and none of these countries would take kindly to the threat of an outside rescue force's barging into their territory without permission.

The International Environment

Governments so far have not translated their concern into a recognition of the need to close effectively the spaces between countries that are represented by the weaknesses of international law and custom. Yet the trend of thinking is most definitely in that direction. In fact, much of the discussion of practical measures boils down to consideration of steps that assure a better mesh between country activities—for example, respecting border controls, passport and visa requirements, deportation or expulsion procedures, and the identification and circulation of information about known terrorists or their plans. One of the few things European community members—excluding Greece, whose representative would agree to nothing—seemed able to agree on in response to Britain's October 1986 request for sanctions against Syria was a common refusal to accredit Syrian diplomats expelled by Britain.

The political sensitivity of terrorism in most countries tends to force a focus on practical measures, because practical measures usually can be justified on merit without trespassing on any other agenda. The areas of greatest promise are:

Common approaches to the physical security of public transportation, arrival, and departure facilities

Developing and using enhanced procedures or new technologies

Closing gaps in border control procedures that may let a terrorist slip through

Sharing information, mainly on a bilateral basis, about abuses and tightening the enforcement of rules of diplomatic conduct

Developing and sharing data bases on known terrorists and groups

Gathering and sharing information about the terrorism-sponsoring states and their activities

Problems of Getting Together

How do governments deliver a unified and consistent stand on terrorism? Through most chapters of this book, we have found numerous cases in which some individuals and groups are almost bound to take a position at odds with their own government. Representative governments, therefore, have a problem: they do not always have a reliable consensus. Nor is it clear, particularly in the instance of the larger countries, at what level of generality a reliable consensus could be achieved. The situations of the major European countries are similar to that of the United States on this point. That is by no means because Americans have exported their lack of unanimity. Rather, it is because most open, complex states harbor significant differences of opinion on many issues internal to their societies.

This fact of life presents a government with an immense challenge when it sets out to make policy. Few if any issues of national importance are ever simple. Because they are not simple there is seldom any perfect right answer for them. Here, an old bureaucratic adage has real application: "Where you sit is where you stand"—meaning that the position you are likely to take on an issue has something to do with the kind of interest you have in it. On that premise people can be expected to stake out claims all over any big, complex issue, with the result that you have people standing all over the landscape and trampling all over the issue. The prospects for solid consensus in those circumstances are bleak, and the chances that a consensus would mean anything, even if one could be obtained, are more so.

Making Policy on Terrorism

Trying to make policy about terrorism engages a large, convoluted piece of public policy. The reasons for that, as we have seen in numerous instances in this book, lie with the fact that the motives for terrorism or for support of terrorist activity are often deeply imbedded in the history and the personal and group goals of the people who support it. That is looking at the problem only from the perspective of people who carry out acts of terrorism or who are directly supportive of them. An even larger community of groups and individuals around the world have views and take positions on the processes of political, economic, and social change, not only in their own countries but in others as well. Those people bring to the problem of terrorism and what to do about it a very complex agenda for managing improvements in the human condition. One of the attitudes that many of those people harbor is a sense of sympathy for anyone who rises up in rebellion against adverse circumstance. In that framework, terrorism is often viewed only as a measure of the severity of the adverse circumstance the individual seeks to conquer.

What this analysis basically suggests is that governments cannot make policy about terrorism alone, and if they try they will only get into varying orders of trouble depending on which of the competing agendas respecting the uses of violence their policy happens to rub up against. A new terrorism policy per se might make a fair amount of sense, but the particular attitudes and interests it impinges upon could make it extremely difficult to attain or to carry out.

Getting Countries Together

The things I've said so far may not describe the most promising possible environment in which to get international cooperation to deal with terrorism. The task set for the foreign policymaker is to develop agreements with other governments regarding issues on which the people of those countries don't necessarily agree and in many instances are not likely to. Once that is understood, some progress can be made toward cooperative effort. Before it is understood, policymakers are likely to make many mistakes.

The picture that I have just painted suggests some things that the policymaker definitely should not do in trying to get other people to cooperate. One is not to state the problem of combating terrorism as if inventing a new ideology. Such an approach either immediately antagonizes adherents of other ideologies or looks as if this is just another one. This dissipates energy in pointless heat and friction. The national debate over Reagan administration policies is proof enough of what can happen. Second, the policymaker should not pose lavish goals but should try to work out specific problems. Rule number three is not to treat terrorism out of context. The problem in the past is that U.S. policymakers have tended to deal with terrorism in the abstract so far as other people's issue sets were concerned. Because they have tried to get other governments to buy the U.S. version of the problem, they have, in effect, tried to get them to cope with it out of context, something governments generally are not prepared to do. The realization that terrorism has to be approached in context in dealing with other governments has slowly moved U.S. authorities away from sweeping rhetorical statements of intent over to a search for specific and practical measures on which governments can agree and which, if implemented, will have some impact. No government appears prepared to deal with terrorism in a way that splashes over everything else it does. Many governments seem prepared to take specific measures in a number of different fields, and each one of those measures attacks some element of terrorism in context.

The Broad Strategies

What are the main choices? The broad strategies available to the United States or any other government span at least a dozen fields. Those strategies, to name a few, include physical security, personnel training, intelligence collection and sharing, cooperative measures such as political and economic sanctions, development and sharing of counterterrorism technologies, passage of effective laws within countries, and adoption of effective extraditions treaties between countries. As Neil Livingstone and I discussed in the final chapter of *Fighting Back*, an effective attack on terrorism requires coordinated effort in all of those fields.[7] In approaching these strategies, of course, it is helpful to recognize that each one reaches into a different area of society or engages different institutions.

There are many issues on which prospects for cooperation are slim. A definition of terrorism, for example, is not something on which governments at any specific level are likely to agree. This suggests that U.S. officials have made a basic mistake for a long time in the way they have tried to define the subject of mutual interests. They have assumed that the subject is "international terrorism." In fact, the topic of international terrorism per se does not seize a head of state with any immediate need for decisive action. International terrorism, if carried out against foreigners, in remote locations, by people for whom you have no responsibility, is likely to attract no attention at all. In the policy terms we're talking about, the terrorist activity may as well be on another planet. If you think that is not true, look carefully at the way most countries in the Third World deal with international terrorism. You find by and large that they don't do anything about it, because by and large it doesn't mean anything to them. That an occasional diplomat or traveling citizen gets caught in an act of terrorism doesn't really stir up much excitement. Even if the victim is someone famous the excitement lasts only a few days.

In any case it's all very far away, and no one insists that you do anything about it except possibly to put the heat on some other government to fix it.

The Problem Is Domestic

Domestic terrorism is another matter. By definition, domestic terrorism occurs entirely within and among elements of a single country. Many governments have some version of that problem. CIA estimates at times have placed the number of so-called domestic terrorist incidents at about ten times the number of international incidents each year. On that basis, in 1985 to 1986, there were close to eight thousand such incidents each year. That is only a crude estimate because even a tiny country like Sri Lanka may have one or more incidents every day.

I have said a number of times in speeches that the distinction that U.S. officials try to maintain between "domestic" and "international" terrorism, both in global statistics and in U.S. policy formation, is in point of fact unreal. The unreality of that distinction is most sharply pointed up when you approach another government. The authorities you seek attention from are more than likely to be preoccupied with internal terrorism, and they will tend to understand what you are saying in terms of the version of a problem they have, not in terms of some distant, "international" problem. Given limited time and resources, it is a fair question as to why a leader should take on a version of a problem that, even if it gets solved, won't help that leader deal with the home problem.

In the intelligence field, for example, the most important sharing that one government can do is the kind that helps another government deal with its own internal terrorism problem. Whether that problem is created merely by indigenous groups or results from the acts of traveling terrorists, every government needs intelligence about activities that are occurring or may occur within its own borders or within countries of interest to it. If governments are not prepared to share specific information then no country has gotten very far on the matter of intelligence sharing. Professionals in the field say that this is still a delicate matter, meaning there is a good deal of hesitancy on all sides about sharing hard information that might reveal sources, methods, operations, or specific intelligence interests.

The Foreign Connection

Domestic terrorism, and the degree to which that problem involves the outside world, becomes the version of the terrorist problem most governments will think about most seriously. Take the example of Sri Lanka that I mentioned earlier. This is a small country with an insurgency by members of its Tamil minority population which bedevils the stability of Sri Lankan society. There are hundreds of casualties every year among government officials, military, police, and private citizens. Incidents occur at a frequency of several every week, and casualties in April 1987 exceeded four hundred in a single day.[8]

Sri Lankan authorities would view the Tamil insurgency as an entirely domestic affair except for a pattern of intervention from India. On the one hand, Indian authorities act as a kind of unsolicited human rights watchdog over the way the Sinhalese government of Sri Lanka deals with the Tamils. On the other hand, in the largely Tamil south Indian state of Madras, Indian authorities have permitted the existence of training camps and safe havens for rebels from Sri Lanka. What the Tamils do rarely gets counted in the statistics of international terrorism because it occurs entirely within Sri Lanka, against Sri Lankans. The very significant element of sympathy and support from India makes you wonder, however, whether such definitions are all that sound.

In late July 1987, following a period of intense clashes between Sinhalese and Tamil communities, India and Sri Lanka signed an agreement aimed at achieving a cease-fire. Under this agreement, India agreed to station a peacekeeping force in the largely Tamil northern region of Jaffna and to get the Tamil insurgents to lay down their arms in exchange for the creation of an autonomous, Tamil-run territory and the release of Tamil prisoners held by Sinhalese authorities mostly on terrorism charges. This action should facilitate an immediate pause in the conflict, but unless India also dismantles the safe havens and training facilities, this lull could be only temporary, because the willingness of the Tamils either to compromise or to take risks is affected by their freedom to retreat into Indian territory.

The True Program of Work

If domestic terrorism is the subject that interests and preoccupies other governments, how do you engage their energy in the task of combating international terrorism? The way to be most persuasive is to demonstrate the ability or willingness to do something about sources of support for terrorism across international boundaries.[9] The United States, for example, would carry a great deal more weight in dialogue with the British on international terrorism if it showed some willingness to do something about the continuing pattern of support by some American citizens for IRA, PIRA, and INLA terrorism in

Northern Ireland. As long as it does not do this, the United States does not have real credibility because it is not helping the British solve the version of the terrorism problem they face most frequently. The United States is choosing rather to be a continuing part of the problem.

Where domestic terrorism is the issue, the thing that most clearly demands fixing is often the involvement of outsiders. The source is an endemic kind of meddling by governments and private groups in the internal affairs of other countries. If anything, that problem is getting worse. As you recall, in chapter 6 I noted that there were as many as twenty-five terrorist groups represented in the United States. Half or more of those groups make it a business to get involved with other countries, in order to acquire assistance for themselves, to support the activities of those countries, or to support groups in those countries. If you could observe the flows of trainees and terrorist group leaders across the borders of the Soviet Union, Cuba, Libya, Syria, and other nations, you would see just how much a part of the pattern of so-called domestic terrorism such traffic has become. Claire Sterling described this in depth in her book *The Terror Network;*[10] Yonah Alexander and Ray Cline added further depth to the picture in their more recent work, *Terrorism: The Soviet Connection.*[11] James Adams adds yet greater understanding in his 1986 work, *The Financing of Terror.*[12] As you look at the patterns they describe, the distinctions that have been so carefully erected in U.S. practice between domestic and international terrorism break down completely, because so many of the domestic groups get funds, training, weapons, ideas, or sympathy and encouragement from abroad.

It is hard to say that the matter is purely domestic when a terrorist goes to the Soviet Union, is trained, and then returns home to disrupt the government of his own country. Clearly it is not merely a domestic affair. In fact, these cases, which are quite numerous, represent international terrorism by proxy. This pattern of support from abroad for domestic violence has been the most common one of the past, and it is definitely the most likely one in the future.

Taking Terrorism Too Seriously

The problem partly is one of communications. In its approach to international terrorism, the United States doesn't appear to take seriously enough the domestic terrorism problems facing other governments. For their part, other governments have not appeared to take the international terrorism problem as seriously as the United States does, because the internal problem is the more serious one for them. In their view, the United States takes an exaggerated posture toward international terrorism but it does not seem to understand the severity of their domestic terrorism problem.

We thus are forced to come to grips with the problem: what does the United States do about domestic terrorism? Step one obviously is to shift its sights toward cooperating with other governments whose version of the problem is essentially a domestic one, whose losses from international terrorism per se are relatively small, and whose political challenges from international terrorists are infrequent. Specifically, this means that the U.S. and other governments, as well as private groups within these countries, must start looking critically at the effects of sympathy and support patterns on the level and targeting of violence in other countries. This is where the next generation of policy efforts toward international cooperation to combat terrorism must be focused, because it is here that genuine progress can be made. It is also here that U.S. policymakers need to communicate most candidly with others about the nature, the sources, and the remedies for such violence. The United States and other cooperating governments cannot progress much beyond where they are unless they are prepared to deal with the terrorism problem in this context.

The solutions that governments will accept are practical ones that will help them deal with their own problems. Therefore, what governments should seek in the way of solutions to international terrorism are really "dual use" solutions, things that will help a government deal with its own domestic problem but that will have the benefit of also helping that government deal with the problem of the international community. In a pragmatic world, where there is a shortage of everything but problems to be solved, we probably cannot get any better fix than this on the true nature of the terrorism problem. Governments just won't agree to answers that do not meet their own needs. To get more done through international cooperation, it is essential to get onto this course.

12

The Violence Formula

A SCIENTIFIC understanding of our behavior, leading to its control, may well be the most urgent task that faces mankind today." So stated N. Tinbergen, looking at a pattern of violence that already was well developed in the 1960s.[1] Throughout this book we have looked at many different sources of that violence and at the kinds of sympathy and support that people lend to it. This final chapter looks at the pattern as a whole, considers some of the mechanisms that lead us into it, and outlines some ways out.

In a number of chapters I have talked about protest activities. In several ways I have made the point that these activities are taking on the characteristics of an alternative mode of governance that confronts and contends with established authority for control of major decisions. Contention with the government for control of national policy is not unique to groups in the United States; one of the objectives of so-called peace research in Western Europe is "to break the monopoly of governments on the making of foreign policy."[2] This approach is a natural outgrowth of the great emphasis we have placed in recent times on the concept of participatory democracy. The basic notion is a bit like treating all public policy issues as matters to be decided in a town meeting in which all citizens are participants.

It is easy to be captivated by this idea and to be deeply satisfied by participating, by "fixing something." It is easy to get caught in the heady atmosphere of forcing decisions or promoting change, and to fail to take the time to assess the real value of benefits gained from it or to count the costs of this procedure. Over a period of more than two decades, this is the way protest strategies have come to work, and they are now seen by many activists as a panacea for all public ills. It is time to look closely at the accumulating by-products of this decision-making style.

The Impact of Protest

The great wave of popular protest activity that developed in the early 1960s, mainly in the United States, proved to be a remarkable incubator for patterns of protest that developed throughout the world, even penetrating the closed societies. Attention-getting devices, approaches to the media, slogans, marches, and banners, all those trappings of modern dissent spread rapidly across the United States and the rest of the world. The pattern had such commonality of aspect that by the early 1970s, as a diplomat experienced in observing protest activities in the United States, Egypt, India, Sri Lanka, and the Philippines, I found that street demonstrations all looked pretty much alike. Their rhetoric also sounded much alike, except for obvious differences of language and the specific issues of protest.

That sameness of aspect has become so common that, on New Year's Day, 1987, when students took to the streets of Beijing, the chants and the V-for-victory hand signs all seemed too familiar. The rhetoric of China's new protestant young, whether provided in interviews with English-speaking protesters or translated for U.S. electronic media,[3] evoked a feeling of déjà vu. Even in a society as opaque to Western influences as China had tried to be under Mao Zedong, the idiom of protest had permeated young minds as completely as a rise in humidity fills a dry room.

A liberal United States, proud of its habits and traditions of political protest, would say that the worldwide spread of popular dissent is altogether a good thing. But is it? Open protest is only one strategy for influencing behavior or policy. But is it the best strategy for all times, targets, and places? Does it achieve durable improvements in the human condition? Does it achieve those benefits faster than other strategies? Do the changes wrought by protest get perpetuated through successive renewals of consensus? Should we be concerned about side effects? Under conditions of severe political protest and related stress do societies move toward the center or toward the extremes? When societies move toward the political extremes, are stability conditions—meaning the capacities of our institutions effectively to support us—enhanced or eroded? Are human rights and civil liberties advanced or undercut? If protest evokes a backlash, does that work itself off in a reasonable time and manner? For example, will a frail, renewed democracy like that of Argentina be able to recover from half a generation of repressive reaction to the insurgent protest of the Montaneros? Will Chinese leadership under Deng Xiaoping continue to open China's decision procedures in the incremental and cautious way of the past decade, or will that promising window be closed in response to student protest? Is there more immediate and personal satisfaction to this pattern of protest than there is durable political achievement?

None of those questions can be given hard, clear, yes-or-no answers. That fact alone should give us some pause. There are major positive achievements, such as the advancement of blacks in the 1960s, but in a society in which political protest has become a frontal competitor with electoral procedure for control of national decisions, the track record for protest ought to be more consistently positive. If it is indeed a panacea, its outcomes ought to be a good deal more predictable. Its overall results should be unequivocally affirmative to make us comfortable with it as a way to make important decisions. The way political protest works on other participants in the decision process, however, makes it unlikely to deliver clear-cut satisfaction on such questions of cause and effect.

The Protest Strategies

A more or less continuous range of protest strategies—really coercive bargaining strategies—extends from peaceful to violent methods for achieving satisfaction or change. Political protest is at one end of this range of coercive bargaining. At the other end, the extreme coercive strategies are revolution or repression. All of these strategies share a common quality: they are outside the normal legal or institutional channels for decision making, even though their goal is usually to change or to influence institutional or legal behavior.

Some people refer to protest decision making as the "tyranny of minorities," and it is true that this procedure increasingly has emerged as a means perceived by minority groups to force their will on the majority. This is another way of saying that protest is increasingly a means chosen by groups with singular, or at least specific, goals. The aim of protest is to force favorable decisions on issues from other parties to bargaining who may be inattentive, unwilling, or unresponsive, or who simply disagree. It is not a consensus procedure, but an adversary one, a way of getting concessions from people who do not want to give them. A satisfactory outcome for the protester is a favorable decision, even if the decision is made against the will of the other party.

This procedure achieves inherently unstable results. Where resources are forcibly reallocated by protest procedures, the protesting group usually gets resources, or gets them bestowed on a targeted group, at someone else's expense. In the process, the rights and interests of other individuals or groups may be deliberately ignored or rejected. If the focus of protest is a policy decision, say, disposal of toxic wastes, an environmental group may seek to avoid the selection of particular sites or to load the costs of disposal on chemical industries. In either case, the group adversely affected by any decision is not likely to be fully consenting; the decisions are likely to be coercive and non-voluntary; and even when such decisions have the force of law, the parties who were coerced, or whose interests were peremptorily affected, lobby to have changes made to reflect their interests. Decisions, to be sure, are achieved by protest, but the decisions are not based on consensus; they thus are flawed in the manner of their achievement, and the decisions lack stability. We keep coming back to them, over and over again.

The possibility that the behavior of the parties coerced may be morally, legally, or practically wrong does not much improve the chances for the stability of the changes wrought through any of the coercive bargaining strategies. Rather, individuals or groups forced to make concessions often feel that their rights have been violated, and their objections, their grievances, often look and sound as righteous as any others. The losers in protest strategies view themselves as victims.

It is easy to be a victim of something in the late twentieth century. As I discussed more fully in chapter 9, we live in a world where nearly everything is scarce, where decisions on resource allocations usually mean that somebody wins and somebody loses. Democracies cannot be arbitrary about such decisions and survive, or expect the decisions themselves to endure. But protest strategies usually result in some manner of arbitrary decision. Repressive governments seem able to enforce arbitrary decisions, but only at some cost in human rights. It is doubtful that such decisions can be sustained when they are forced by minorities within a democratic society without similar penalties. Yet the list of decisions various minority groups would like to impose on the rest of us has grown quite long: it includes adherence to extreme ideologies, either left or right; it includes support for or opposition to abortion, right to life, humane treatment of animals, creationism in school textbooks, prayer in the schools, and a ban on nuclear power, to name only a few such issues. The list of protest agendas is made up largely of matters on which significant elements of American society do not agree.

Some By-products

The by-products of protest decision strategies must concern us. First, a residue of grievance and frustration remains if you happen to be the party who is forced into doing something you would not willingly do. Some people deal with such grievances and frustrations without disagreeable side effects; a number of people do not, and they harbor grudges or they bide their time to redress an actual or merely perceived injury. Such feelings of injury, coupled with real effects on personal or financial interests that often result from coercive bargaining, are the primary sources of instability in the decisions obtained by protest.

Second, there is an erosion of confidence and trust between parties to a coercive bargaining procedure. The procedure automatically places the parties in confrontational or adversarial relation to each other. In that frame of mind they are not likely to be interested in talking. In this respect a protest situation is much like the strike of a labor union in that as long as the parties are talking a chance exists that progress can be made; however, once the issue is taken to the street the situation becomes confrontational, and normal bargaining for some period is ruled out.

Third, there is distilling down of hard-core protest activists, often a small minority, into users of violence, including terrorist organizations. In West Germany, the Baader-Meinhof gang grew out of the generation of Vietnam protest and evolved into the Red Army Faction. In the United States, black protest in the 1960s produced the Black Panthers, who used terrorist methods. Some members of the Students for a Democratic Society became the Weather Underground, and other students of the Vietnam protest era became the United Freedom Front.

Fourth, the procedure both uses and creates its own victims. Numerous ethnic, religious, national, or other groups find the protest strategies to be natural vehicles for expressing their grievances, some of which are ancient and insoluble. In those cases, the protest strategies have the virtue of providing an outlet for emotional energy but also the vice of perpetuating and even reinforcing an old hurt. That process develops one of the common sources of recruits for terrorist organizations. At the same time, as the profiles of terrorists and groups clearly show, people with no established grievance or visible basis for one—for example, young, middle-class, or wealthy people with educational and other opportunties—become terrorists. These are the children of protest, people who work their way through activism to increasing levels of anger and frustration until they become a class of victims themselves.

The Consequences

Obviously we must deal with the commonplace frictions that arise among groups that variously compete for resources or other advantages. In a society made up almost entirely of minorities, dealing with those frictions is an increasingly important mediation requirement, because several minorities have problems that should be heard. Hearing in this case means recognizing and trying where possible to assuage the grievances of ethnic and other minority communities. However, minorities should not expect to be accommodated on everything—not everything can be fixed, even by people who try—and in any case, at some point the sum of minority interests must add up to some sort of working majority or the system won't work. I sense that many groups are forgetting that point, and particularly they seem blissfully unaware that everybody can play the game of protest, thereby turning a rising number of resource allocative decisions or points of friction between groups into a continuing tug-of-war.

There is a confluence of frictions at this point, some of them real, some of them merely perceived, but all of them capable of forming a stream of discontent. If you are a student of the loose science called "victimology," you can think of a dozen groups that harbor some historic complaint that has never been worked off or redressed. It does not matter whether the complaint is objectively real; it matters only that the complaint is widely believed within a group to be based in reality and perceived to be unresolved. Cases in point include the Armenian genocide, the Croatian dispossession, the Irish Catholic denial of control over their own destiny, the denial of Tamil rights to self-determination. You can go through a long list, but remember that each one represents a grievance with potentially explosive manifestations, depending on how deprived or determined the person who feels he or she is a victim may feel.[4]

What these phenomena imply to me is that we must find ways to moderate the protest agendas or to find alternatives to the coercive bargaining tactics increasingly adopted to achieve them. If we do not, they pose an immense potential danger to the stability of American society, and here again I emphasize that when I use the term *stability* I am talking about effective, continuing functioning of institutions, not about some steady state or fixed position. In the first two hundred years of the United States, the combination of inmigration and geographic dispersion created a diverse society, really a coalition of regional, ethnic, cultural, religious, and other minorities. At the present time, it has been said that the United States takes in more new immigrants every year than all the other countries of the world combined.[5] Changes within the past two decades alone have yielded an exploding diversity of groups, backgrounds, and interests. According to a recent estimate made to me by a social worker, there are 120 such groupings in one sector of Chicago alone.

Here an obvious distinction should be made between public demonstrations that are mere lobbying for attention and protest activities that are designed to coerce or intimidate. The latter category has the capacity for inflicting severe damage on American institutions and on the rights of individuals. The former is usually harmless.

In this context, we must weigh the impact that protest decision making is having on the cohesiveness of American democratic society: it tends to identify, isolate, and set interest groups apart in contentious rather than cooperative relationships. If those new groups as well as the myriad of already established ones see their interests as best served by protest and other coercive bargaining tactics, then American society is in for very unstable times.

The Violence Formula

This prospect of instability's growing out of mostly peaceful political protest causes me to look with some concern on patterns of spreading resort to political violence. Much has been said and written in the post–World War II era about the growing patterns of violence in society and about the motivational/causative factors contributing to violent responses in human communities.[6] Precious little has been written, however, about the impact of violence as a coercive bargaining strategy on societal decision processes or on the content of decisions. Moreover, the factors likely to move an individual from peaceful protest to violence have been addressed by few recent writers in this field.[7] Yet we must become interested in those factors, because they contain a formula for violence.

That violence formula really involves an escalation of the intensity of protest strategies in search of one that will work. The chemistry of the violence formula begins with a decision to abandon or to work outside usual institutional or bureaucratic decision channels. This choice is not necessarily made because the individual or group has tried normal channels and failed. Rather, going outside usual channels can be prompted by poor experience with established channels, by ignorance or suspicion of them, by a belief that a decision cannot be gotten through normal channels either quickly enough or favorably enough, or by a preference of the decision seeker for active participatory approaches over mere appeals to administrative or other authority. More often than not, however, members of a group will choose a protest strategy because they do not believe their petition will be treated favorably unless they apply some order of confrontation and coercion. By this I mean that the choice of a protest strategy, at least initially, appears to be based on a judgment that other approaches will not work. It is usually rational but often uncompromising, because it boils down to trying to get without giving.

If the targeted authorities respond favorably to low-order confrontation and coercion, for a specific cause that may be the end of the story. If not, however, what happens next depends on a complex chemistry of commitment, encouragement, frustration, anger, and hope. The degree of commitment to the cause and of frustration among members of the group will determine how quickly peaceful protest moves up toward civil disobedience. Ted Robert Gurr's concept of relative deprivation, defined as the gap between expectations and the capacity to achieve them, is a good way of thinking about the order of frustration that might arise in some cases.[8]

I hesitated to use Gurr's concept here when I first read about it because in many instances of civil disobedience in the United States the actual deprivation of the participants is not really relevant. What is relevant, perhaps even central, however, is the fact that the frustration of protesters at their inability to make the system do what they want done is a cumulative kind of pressure that builds, even though the protesters are not personally disadvantaged by their lack of progress with regard to the cause at hand. As was noted earlier, this type of frustration creates its own class of victims. In any case, encouragement of two sorts, either the approval and support of other groups or active promotion of the effort through the media, will help the pace along.

How far civil disobedience moves toward actual challenges to authority and breaches of the law will depend in part on the frustration and anger of the group members, on their psychological makeup, and on such factors as degree of commitment. It will depend also on how hopeful they are that a little more pressure will get results and on how forcefully and sensibly authorities react to challenge.

A protester gets easily trapped in a matrix at this stage, because as he or she meets resistance frustration builds. If that pressure continues to grow, the anxiety, frustration, and anger components of judgment take over, moving the protester ever closer toward the violent choices. Although the individual personally may not go for violence at this point, a precondition for recruitment, exploitation, or direct involvement in violent activities is certainly created.

Either deliberate or inadvertent excesses on either side at this point can cause a group engaged in a demonstration of civil disobedience to become aggressive. Those excesses can also cause individuals or subsets of the group to experiment with violence, to seek to provoke authority to excess, to try to make a point with a violent outburst, or to dabble in terrorism through attention-getting violence, such as the bombing of an abortion clinic.

In long, drawn-out protest programs, the trigger to excess may not be street confrontations but a conclusion by group members, based on their experience or perception, that political protest and civil disobedience will not get the desired results. In the words of Bernadine Dohrn, one of the leaders of Students for a Democratic Society and later of the Weathermen, the individual reaches a judgment that "protests and marches are not enough; revolutionary violence is the only way."[9]

The threshold for deliberate choice of violent methodologies is reached about at this point, where perceived obstacles to the advancement of a cause are greater than the perceived opportunities for moving ahead. Some threshold akin to that on Gurr's index of relative deprivation is reached,[10] and at this stage individuals who continue to support a cause not perceived as attainable by means short of violence can choose any of three paths. One choice is to opt out of the struggle because of perceived risks or conflicts of values; in this instance, it is not necessary to quit fighting, but the individual may decide to look for alternative, peaceful ways to realize the goal. A second choice, of course, is to continue the pattern of protest and civil disobedience; this is really a decision to stretch out the process, and it probably means that frustration with the lack of progress has not risen very high.

The third option is to decide to change fundamentally the strategy of the group, to move up the intensity of protest to violence in the forms of ordinary crime, political crimes, let's say terrorism or insurgency, or possibly all three. According to Carl Oglesby, the last president of the Students for a Democratic Society (SDS) and one of its most articulate spokesmen during the 1960s, when SDS faced this set of choices in 1968 it disbanded because most members were not prepared to go the violent route, nor were they comfortable with pressure from extremists in SDS to make common cause with Havana and Hanoi. Those who were prepared to use violent methods coalesced into the Weathermen (now the Weather Underground) and became a terrorist group.[11]

There is a fourth choice, obviously, and that is to become a supporter of the terrorists or of the insurgents, taking no part in their activities but aiding the cause with influence, money, and logistical and other forms of assistance. As discussed in chapter 6, many domestic and foreign groups inside the United States count on those forms of support from ethnic or other friendly communities.

Becoming a Terrorist

Once the step from civil disobedience into violent methods has been taken, the individual and the group undergo radical change. Whereas protest activities up through occasional law breaking during civil disobedience events in no sense made the participant an outlaw, the first pipe bomb, kidnapping, or robbery changes the relationship of the group to the community. With that step, group members become fugitives; they need to hide, to become concerned about arrest, trial, and imprisonment. Group priorities also change. While the main use of time for the group when it was part of a protest movement was promotion of the cause, the main activity of the group after a terrorist attack becomes survival. The cause may remain important, but real attention focuses on keeping alive and staying out of jail.

Difficult and complex choices of style and methods face the group at this point. The choices are in part goal dependent, in the sense that if the objective is only to change the policies of an existing government, then the group might opt for terrorist violence. But if the objective is to overthrow the government, the choice may be insurgency; it may continue to be terrorism, or it may end up as some mixture.

If the choice is to operate as terrorists, the group must usually work covertly to attack largely civilian, noncombatant, and symbolic targets; to operate entirely outside the law; and to surface only at the moment of attack. Their primary strategy becomes use of terrorist incidents as largely indirect, attention-getting means to influence target audiences.

On the other hand, the decision to go insurgent is effectively to declare war against established authority, to operate at times covertly, but in due course to go public and seek a popular basis of support. This is a forceful but still fairly direct step beyond civil disobedience, because it represents an effort to extract concessions from decision makers by engaging them directly and openly. Under current international practice, if a group aspires to legitimacy as an insurgency, there are rules, as indicated in chapter 1, that would rule out resort to terrorism.[12]

Open, direct action to test the will of authority or the force of law looks like an insurgent tactic, but it may be practiced by unlikely looking groups. To give an example, in late 1986 a group that advocates humane treatment of laboratory animals broke into a Bethesda experimental laboratory and stole the animals. In watching media coverage of that incident, I was startled by how far acceptance of such direct action appeared to have advanced when I noted that throughout the media treatment of the story, including interviews with the spokesman for the perpetrators, the word *crime* was never mentioned.

This is the natural regime of the violence formula. People who apply the formula work their way upward through a progressively complex chain of rationalization for attempting to get decisions by means other than voluntary agreement or consensus. The process seems to build quite naturally from peaceful bargaining to peaceful protest; from peaceful protest to aggressive protest and civil disobedience.

If protesters break through the threshold to violence at this point, they move on up through the occasional terrorist act, a pattern of terrorism, the onset of insurgent activity, or warfare. As they move up they become less amenable to dialogue with the target audience. Coercive incidents and propaganda become the preferred instruments for influencing that audience.

Breaking the Pattern

The critical points in this process for interrupting the move upward to violence exist at two places. One is obviously near the boundary of civil disobedience, where the individual is at the point of crossing over into use of primarily violent methods. If the individual or group can be persuaded at that point that alternative strategies exist for achieving their goal, that the objective is not attainable by any acceptable means, or possibly that it is not worthy, then the violent stage can be avoided.

There is no single avenue to that result. Any avenue that exists is likely to depend on the specific characteristics of a group and of the cause it espouses. For example, the Armenian groups, the Armenian Secret Army for the Liberation of Armenia (ASALA) and the Justice Commandos against Genocide (JCAG) both seek unattainable goals. The territory that ASALA would reunite is split between Soviet Armenia and eastern Turkey. The prospect that those areas would ever be recombined and given to the Armenians as an independent homeland is somewhere between remote and zero. For JCAG, the cause is only slightly more manageable in that a possibility still exists that Turkish authorities might make some amends for the deaths of Armenians in 1915, but the prospect that present Turkish leadership could do more is also very remote. The practical solution, that both groups disband and stop practicing terrorism, will remain hard to achieve unless the Armenian communities abroad, in the Middle East, Europe, and the United States, take a concerted stand against terrorism. So far, they have not done that. A lull in activity by these groups in 1985 and 1986 suggested that the Armenian communities might have a good chance to end this type of terrorism, but as was indicated in chapter 6 the prospect that they will use their influence to that end does not appear promising.

The argument is made often that the way to end terrorism is to deal with the root causes that largely reside among the global issues discussed in chapter 9.

In the case of much of the terrorism of the Middle East, as well as Armenian terrorism, root cause theories of the way to end it all do not count for much. The hopes of Druze, Maronite, Shia, Palestinian, or other groups in Lebanon that each might achieve the dominant power position are largely responsible for the present mess. Their continuing practice of terrorism against each other only sustains a standoff that will have to be resolved through achieving workable levels of compromise if they are to live together peacefully. That lesson was learned, however, at least a hundred years ago. Here again, the leadership of those communities must get together and solve the problem. Nothing will happen, except further cycles of chaos, until they do.

Many ethnic communities currently face a problem of what to do about a volatile element, some part of which may be involved in terrorism. As the recent efforts of young militants to take over control of Sikh temples in Vancouver, British Columbia, showed the violence is often directed at members of the ethnic community itself.

Rethinking the Role of Protest

The other influence point for breaking the pattern of escalation toward violence lies with rethinking the role of protest and civil disobedience in the decision processes. This requires us to make decisions and develop discipline about when and in respect to what sorts of issues the protest strategies are appropriate. It leads us toward reassessing the functions of major institutions in society whose roles center on important areas of decisions affecting our lives. It bears on the ways in which we assign authority, responsibility, and legitimacy to those institutions. Finally, it forces us to look in a new way at our own roles and responsibilities for supporting the institutions to which we assign the key management functions of our society.

Undertaking this assignment will bring us squarely into confrontation with some fanciful notions about the way society works. For most of its history as a country the United States has romantically cultivated or tolerated rebellion and revolution as cleansing devices for bringing the system back on track, but Americans have never examined that proposition closely enough to judge precisely when or in what circumstances those extreme actions actually make sense. Americans have allowed protest strategies to evolve in much the same uncritical way, never considering the effects that setting aside institutions to get decisions will have on the overall effectiveness of the system.

Redirecting Participant Energies

Obviously no interest of a democratic society would really be served by shutting off the urges of many people to participate in management of the country. In the United States, we want that; we believe it is essential to proper performance of a democracy. The question that must be answered, however, is what kind of participation is beneficial? So far Americans have tended to the view that some participation is better than none, and the overall view of the democracies has been broadly tolerant, but that approach has growing defects.

Take, for example, the problem of weapons in U.S. society. As I wrote this chapter, the advance billing for the 1987 annual meeting of the National Rifle Association indicated that it would be "a shootout at the O.K. Corral." The prospective debate was to center on whether or not the leadership of the NRA had lost its will by failing to combat two measures passed by the U.S. Congress. One measure was to prevent the manufacture and sale of the so-called cop-killing bullet, the Teflon-coated bullet that penetrates body armor. The other was to restrict the ownership of machine guns. The NRA hard-liners seemed incensed by these "infringements" of their right to bear arms. They never answer the question why any upstanding member of the NRA wants a cop-killing bullet or why private ownership of a machine gun should be a matter of constitutional right.

The strongest argument of the NRA is that private weapons owners constitute protection against a possibly repressive government. NRA members thus see themselves as participants in the maintenance of constitutional freedoms. In the NRA view, the balance of power in society lies between private citizens with weapons in their hands who are prepared to use them, and government with weapons prepared to enforce the law. But what happens when the constitutionally intended right to bear arms, designed to keep citizens from falling under the yoke of tyranny, gets redefined as the right to defend any particular cause you want to defend, no matter what it is and no matter whether there exists a tyrannical government that is restraining your freedom?

For us, this is not a hypothetical question. The right to bear arms now permits people to become armed members of the Aryan Nations, the Order, the KKK White Patriot party, the Weather Underground, the Puerto Rican Macheteros, the Cuban group Omega 7, a subgroup of the Palestine Liberation Organization, or any of at least a dozen other terrorist groups resident in the United States. This right makes no ideological distinctions between people who say they wish to defend human liberty and those who are bent on taking it away. And in all of that, somehow, the basic constitutional motive of assuring always that there will be some counterweight to the possible excesses of government has been completely lost. The ownership of weapons in the United States has reached a stage where the rights of ordinary citizens are jeopardized mainly by the excesses of other "ordinary" citizens.

Participation at this level can destroy the United States, whereas the better way to be helpful is to take an active continuing part in the selection of public officials, especially in the law enforcement area, so that any threat of the abuse of power is controlled or eliminated. In any case, if we are going to have some shadow government to keep leadership honest, it should not be one that is chosen and maintained by only a few for narrow, partisan, and often merely personal reasons.

The same basic philosophy applies to protest strategies in general. The emphasis of citizen efforts has to be on doing what makes democratic institutions work, not on doing what sets the system aside or undermines its effectiveness. We have a mutual stake in assuring the legitimacy of our authorities and the effectiveness of our institutions. Just getting decisions is not good enough. The emphasis cannot be on participation for its own sake, nor do we have the luxury of saying, the system doesn't work this week, let's do something else.

The question in this context is not the conventional one about how to protect constitutional liberties. It is, how do we develop, use, and control freedom within a framework of constitutional guarantees? I think the answers lie with achieving better understandings and disciplines respecting the role of the individual in the creation and management of public policy.

What Do We Mean By Control?

The drafters of the U.S. Constitution used the best ideas of the Age of Enlightenment to define civil liberties, but they could not foresee the effects either of technology or of human numbers on the society they outlined. They understood the future well enough, however, to draft the Constitution so that its principles could guide a process. It was not a once-for-all description of reality; it was a working model. It did not define the limits of freedom.

In the succeeding two hundred years, Americans established that the central idea of the Bill of Rights is correct but have been wary of trying to set any bounds on that idea. Americans have not really wanted to decide in any formal way what the restraints are to be on civil liberties. Quite rightly, this is a subject that people's best instincts have told them should be approached with the greatest of care.

However, Americans have tended to look at any possible limitation on the exercise of freedom as something to be brought about by changing either the language or the interpretation of the Constitution. Considering constitutional liberties to be essentially an environmental quality, Americans have looked at the task of modifying those freedoms in an institutional and legal way rather than in operational or behavioral terms.

I think we must look at the whole subject anew, because in most instances the problems we are having are operational and behavioral in character. The fixes needed are not formal and legal; rather, what is stated in the Constitution has proved to be entirely adequate for setting the framework of freedom.

The problems mostly lie with the way people think about the exercise of freedom. People are not being trained and sensitized to the tough process of influencing decisions through the support and use of institutions; instead, much of what is being taught in a loose "learn by doing" fashion actually centers more on strategies other than making the system work. As a result of talks with people of all ages, but particularly with young people in many parts of the United States, I know that direct action, actually taking part in making decisions or fixing something, has immense appeal. It is much more fun than trying to get institutions to perform. However, that approach, which appears to dominate much of the teaching about the role of the individual in public policy, represents a distortion, both of the needs of the individual and of society at large. To correct that, I think we need a stronger focus in the schools on the institutional framework for decisions, along with an emphasis on learning to work the system.

Overseeing the Protest Decisions

I don't see any prospect that we will go out of the business of making protest decisions. Nor should we, because the protest strategies should continue to serve as a fail-safe mechanism. In some areas of public policy, we probably will go on making a certain number of coercive decisions. When we do, however, the leadership must take into account the unstable character of such decisions and observe the implementation of them closely to assure compliance until time, adjustment, and acceptance stabilize the results. There are indications that the racial integration decisions of the 1960s and 1970s need that kind of careful oversight.

What I am saying is that important decisions reached by coercive means cannot be left to take care of themselves. If they are important enough to make by such means, they deserve the extra continuing attention required to make them stick.

The underlying issues of protest often concern the legitimacy and the responsiveness of institutions. I happen to believe that American institutions respond a great deal better than most. I also believe it can be easily demonstrated that the great majority of officials conform to high standards of legitimacy in public life. The final issue I would raise, however, centers on the way failures are handled in public discourse. In an atmosphere of protest activism, public policy failures tend to be turned by the media and by activitists into the raw material of doubt, suspicion, and denial of legitimacy. That reinforces a natural bias of protest strategies toward treating the relation between protesters and authority as adversarial. In the process, the individual gets pushed up the rungs of protest toward violence, while the authority and legitimacy of public officials is undercut. Nobody wins.

With those prospects before us, do we take the view that it is unwise to tinker with any element of individual liberty? I think not. We must go about any changes from here with the greatest of care, but I don't think we can duck either the task or the responsibility. We must have participation in democracy, but we need a more committed kind of participation, a kind that is dedicated both to promoting the role of the individual and to securing the integrity and the effective function of democratic institutions. Any standard of participation that serves only one of these requirements is not adequate.

I come back to Tinbergen: "A scientific understanding of our behavior, leading to its control, may well be the most urgent task that faces mankind today."[13] Our capacity to get in each other's way is advancing by leaps and bounds. Our ability to moderate our behavior is not. We are at a point where we must experiment with the boundaries of individual liberty to protect society from the individual, while at the same time we must train the individual to exercise personal freedom better. Our task is not alone to protect the individual from government, but to protect the individual from other groups and institutions in society whose activities are increasingly capable of curtailing personal freedom. However we go about this we must find a peaceful formula to balance the interests of individuals and groups in the framework of society. We don't have a lot of time, because the quick-brewing alternative formula is violence.

Notes

1
Terrorism: The War of Definitions

1. See Irving R. Kaufman, "Cold-Blooded Killers, Not Freedom Fighters," *New York Times*, 22 August 1986, p. 23.
2. Christopher Hitchens, "Wanton Acts of Usage," *Harper's*, September 1986, 66–70.
3. See *Webster's New Collegiate Dictionary* (Springfield, Mass.: G. & C. Merriam, 1951).
4. See *Webster's Third New International Dictionary* of the English Language, G. & C. Merriam Co., Springfield, Mass., 1976, p. 2361.
5. See *Legislation to Combat International Terrorism: 98th Congress*, Hearings and Markup before the Committee on Foreign Affairs, House of Representatives, U.S. Government Printing Office, Washington, D.C.: 1984, pp. 59–61. The definition of *international* that I use has appeared in one form or another in several U.S. Government documents.
6. See the *Public Report of the Vice President's Task Force on Combatting Terrorism*, U.S. Government Printing Office, Washington, D.C., February, 1986, p. 1.
7. You will find the House Foreign Affairs Committee discussion in *Legislation to Combat International Terrorism: 98th Congress*, hearings and markup before the Committee on Foreign Affairs (Washington, D.C.: U.S. Government Printing Office, 1984), 50–75.
8. Marshall used this phrase himself in reference to the basic rules of economics, but the thought, it seems to me, is also very apt here.
9. Charles William Maynes, "Testing the US Definition of Terrorism," *Los Angeles Times*, 20 April 1986, p. V-1. Reprinted with permission.
10. Ibid.
11. *Legislation To Combat International Terrorism: 98th Congress*, op cit.
12. Moorhead Kennedy, *The Ayatollah in the Cathedral* (New York: Hill and Wang, 1986).
13. Martha Crenshaw, ed., *Terrorism, Legitimacy and Power; The Consequences of Political Violence* (Middletown, Conn.: Wesleyan University Press, 1983), chap. 1.
14. See the discussion of the political offense in chapter 3.
15. *Proactive* in my view is a made-up term that means forceful response, it is *pro*, meaning *for* action, specifically the use of covert operations or special forces to combat terrorism.
16. The unclassified preamble to NSDD 138 states several important propositions that have not been shared adequately with the public. A more or less exact rendering is as follows:
    1. The U.S. government considers the practice of terrorism by any person or group in any cause a threat to national security and will resist the use of terrorism by all legal means available.

2. State-sponsored terrorist activities or directed threats of such action are considered to be hostile acts, and the United States will hold sponsors accountable. Whenever it has evidence that a state is mounting or intends to conduct an act of terrorism against it, the United States has a responsibility to take measures to protect its citizens, property, and interests.

3. Intelligence collection against groups and states involved in terrorism must be improved in order to better prevent or counter attack, warn citizens, friends, and allies, and, thereby, reduce the risk to them.

4. Terrorism is a common problem for all democratic nations. The United States will work intensively with others to eliminate the threat of terrorism to its way of life. States that practice terrorism or actively support it will not be allowed to do so without consequence. All available channels of communication will be used to persuade those now practicing or supporting terrorism to desist. Assistance and support shall be provided to those democratic nations suffering intimidation because of terrorist threats or activities.

5. Acts of state-sponsored and organized terrorism should be appropriately exposed and condemned in every available forum.

2
Some Place to Hide

1. Walter Cronkite, "War in the Shadows," a CBS Special Report, September 1985. Reprinted with permission.
2. Ibid.
3. *Webster's New Collegiate Dictionary* (Springfiled, Mass.: G. & C. Merriam, 1951).
4. Stanley Meisler, "Court Ruling Spells End to France's Traditional Role as Basque Terrorist Haven," *Los Angeles Times,* 27 September 1984, p. 6.
5. *Insight,* 6 April 1987, p. 43.
6. Marc Duvoisin, "Italy Ponders Question of Who in Rome Aided Terrorists," *Philadelphia Inquirer,* 8 January 1986, p. 12.
7. John Newhouse, "A Freemasonry of Terrorism," *The New Yorker,* 8 July 1985, 46–63.
8. See *Immigration and Naturalization Service* v. *Cardoza-Fonseca,* Supreme Court of the United States, opinion no. 85–782.
9. See Ronald L. Soble, "Palestinian Unit Seeking Help in the U.S., FBI Says," *Los Angeles Times,* 23 March 1987, pp. 1, 18–19.

3
When Is a Crime Not a Crime?

1. This typical formulation of the IRA goal was cited by the Associated Press, 23 December 1986, in reporting a Christmas visit of Prime Minister Thatcher to Northern Ireland.
2. James Tunstead Burtchael, "Moral Response to Terrorism", in Neil C. Livingstone and Terrell E. Arnold (Eds), *Fighting Back: Winning the War Against Terrorism,* D.C. Heath and Company, Lexington Books, Lexington, Mass., 1986. Burtchael provides a very interesting perspective on pp. 194–202.

3. See "U.S.-British Treaty on Extradition at Issue in 2 I.R.A.-Related Cases," *New York Times*, 20 August 1985, p. 15. Copyright © 1985 by the New York Times Company. Reprinted with permission.

4. Harry H. Almond, Jr., "The Legal Regulation of International Terrorism", *Conflict* 3, no. 2/3, (1981): 145.

5. Ibid., 154.

6. See *United States and United Kingdom Supplementary Extradition Treaty*, Hearings before the Committee on Foreign Relations, United States Senate, U.S. Government Printing Office, Washington, D.C. The debate on this treaty amendment is contained in a record of more than 900 pages, and it is recommended that the reader leaf through that record to get the flavor of both congressional and public views.

7. See Patrick Marshall, "New Extradition Treaty Casts a Long Shadow," *Baltimore Sun*, 30 July 1986, p. 15.

8. See "U.S.-Britain Extradition Pact Worth Wait," *Atlanta Constitution*, 22 July 1986, p. A10.

9. William Joseph Quinn's case is a bit unusual, because he was born and raised in San Francisco, and the charges against him relate to a stay in Ireland during the 1970s. Nonetheless, the extradition issues are not basically different from those in the other IRA cases, and the treaty language would apply equally even if he were a national of some third country.

10. These comments on trial procedure are excerpted from responses to Senate Foreign Relations Committee questions provided by the Department of State to Committee Chairman Richard G. Lugar on September 12, 1985.

11. See "U.S.-British Treaty on Extradition," p. 15.

12. Martha Crenshaw, ed., *Terrorism, Legitimacy and Power; The Consequences of Political Violence*, (Middletown, Conn.: Wesleyan University Press, 1983), chap. 5. Copyright © 1983 by Wesleyan University. Reprinted with permission of Wesleyan University Press.

13. Ibid., chap. 1.

14. See "U.S. Is Said to Weigh Abducting Terrorists Abroad for Trials Here," *New York Times*, 19 January 1986, p. 1. Copyright © 1985 by the New York Times Company. Reprinted with permission.

15. Ibid.

16. Associated Press, 12 March 1987.

4

To Deal or Not to Deal with Terrorists

1. Mohammed Salam, "Americans' Kidnappers Urge U.S. to Negotiate for Them," *Philadelphia Inquirer*, 17 September 1986, p. A-11.

2. Lt. Colonel North's remarks are recorded in a videotape titled "The Management of Terrorist Incidents" produced in early 1986 by the Center for the Study of Foreign Affairs, Foreign Service Institute, U.S. Department of State.

3. The occasion was a meeting at the Rayburn House office building with hostage family members and members of the Congress on July 30, 1985.

4. See Roger Fontaine, "White House Faces Credibility Gap on Its Policy," *Washington Times*, 1 July 1985, p. 1.

5. For a recent report on those connections, see Richard M. Weintraub, "Militant Rebels Move to Fore amid Sri Lankan Ethnic Conflict," *Washington Post Foreign Service*, 15 February 1987.

6. See "Terrorists Free Couple, Americans Unhurt in Sri Lanka," *Chicago Tribune*, 16 May 1984, p. 1.

7. Jeane Kirkpatrick, "What Credibility Problem?" *Washington Post*, 16 November 1986, p. K-8.

8. Terrell E. Arnold, "The King Is Hostage," *National Review*, 10 April 1987.

9. Michael Ledeen, "The Iran Affair: An Insider's Account," *Washington Post*, 25 January 1987, pp. B-1–2.

5
The Quality of Mercy

1. In a brochure circulated in the Washington, D.C., area in early 1987, the movement had upped its numbers to three hundred sanctuaries and three thousand participating congregations.

2. For a discussion of this background and the role of dependency theory in Latin American thinking, see Arthur F. McGovern, "Debt, Dependency, and Liberation Theology: II; Latin America and Dependency Theory," *This World* (Spring/Summer 1986): no. 14, 104–23.

3. George S. Weigel, "Central American Lessons: I; How the U.S. Catholic Bishops Missed Their Chance to Be a Force for Peace," *This World* (Winter 1986): no. 13, 8–26.

4. Ibid., 10–11. I have drawn on the source cited, but responsibility for this formulation of the U.S. Catholic Conference positions on Central America is mine.

5. Gary MacEoin, *Sanctuary, A Resource Guide for Understanding and Participating in the Central American Refugees Struggle* (San Francisco: Harper & Row, 1985), 15.

6. Ibid., 104–7.

7. Ibid., 18.

8. Ibid., 19.

9. Ibid., chap. 13.

10. See "Sanctuary and the Sanctuary Movement," *This World* (Spring/Summer 1985): no. 11, 19.

11. Ibid., 20–21.

12. Ibid., 12.

13. See William Sloane Coffin, "The Tasks Ahead," in *Sanctuary*, chap. 19.

14. Ibid., 181.

15. Ibid.

16. Roger Connor, "The Case against an Open Immigration Policy," *The World and I* (January 1987): vol. 2, no. 1, 83–89.

17. Marc Fisher, "Legal Confusion Disrupts Area Salvadorans' Lives," *Washington Post*, 2 March 1987, p. A1.

18. "Sanctuary and the Sanctuary Movement," 15.

19. London, Associated Press, 27 February 1987. Reprinted with permission.

20. See *Congressional Record — House*, 99th Cong., 1st sess. April 16, 1985, pp. 2042–2051.

21. At the time of writing, you could call a number and get "CASA," which is run by the Presbyterian Church of Tacoma Park, Maryland. In case no one was there to answer the

phone, an answering machine identified "CASA" in both Spanish and English and invited the caller to leave a message.

22. *Sanctuary* op cit.

23. Herb Schmidt, *Sanctuary*, Preface, p. 1.

24. Cynthia Arnson, *El Salvador; A Revolution Confronts the United States* (Washington, D.C.: Institute for Policy Studies, 1982).

25. Leon Bouvier and David Simcox, "Many Hands, Few Jobs: Population, Unemployment and Emigration in Mexico and the Caribbean," (Center for Immigration Studies, Washington, D.C., Paper 2), 39–44.

26. See "Sanctuary and the Sanctuary Movement," *This World*, Spring/Summer 1985: No. 11, p. 10.

27. Bryna Brennan, "Salvador-Refugees," Associated Press, 5 March 1987.

28. Sanctuary movement leaders claim the court decision as a great victory, but in fact it was also a victory for the Reagan administration. Cardoza-Fonseca came to the United States from Nicaragua in 1979 and overstayed her visitor's visa. When caught, she petitioned for asylum, saying that she feared because of her brother's political activities she would be persecuted by the Sandanista government. Thus, Sanctuary lost on two points: they have argued regularly that all the problems in Central America flow from Reagan administration policy, however, the case began during the Carter administration; and the victim is a Nicaraguan, whereas Sanctuary has steadfastly supported the Sandinistas, refusing to listen to complaints of human rights violations.

29. See *INS* v. *Cardoza-Fonseca*, Supreme Court of the United States, opinion no. 85–782, 9 March 1987. Public debate managed thoroughly to confuse the issues in the case. Both thresholds of proof are in the Immigration and Naturalization Act of 1980. The "clear probability of persecution" test is contained in section 243(h), which concerns a petition to withhold deportation, while the "well-founded fear of persecution" test is contained in section 208(a), which concerns eligibility for asylum. The Supreme Court reiterated the purposes of these two sections of the law, saying in effect that it was inappropriate to use the determination required under section 243(h) to make decisions in asylum cases. This decision reasserts alignment of U.S. practice with the language of the 1951 Geneva convention on refugees, which contains the "well-founded fear of persecution" test that is used in section 208(a) of the Immigration and Naturalization Act of 1980.

30. Patrick Burns, "Winning the Battle, Losing the War," *The World and I* (January 1987): 71–81.

31. "Sanctuary and the Sanctuary Movement," 20.

32. See Associated Press, "Philippines Church Is Cracking Down on Rebel Priests, Nuns," *Northern Virginia Daily*, 25 April 1987, p. 11.

6
Abuses of the Power of the People

1. "A Rehnquist Watch?" *Washington Post*, 5 December 1986, p. A-26. Reprinted with permission.

2. See FBI documents cited in Uri Ra'anan, *Hydra of Carnage* (Lexington, Mass.: Lexington Books, 1986), 614.

3. See Arnaud de Borchgrave, and Richard Moss, *The Spike* (New York: 1980), Avon Books, 88–144.

4. Patrick Boyle, "Terrorist Incidents Down in 1985; 23 Attacks Foiled, FBI Declares," *New York City Tribune*, 11 July 1986, p. 5.

5. See chapter 9 for a discussion of the global issues and their role in this development. Reprinted with permission.

6. Linda Hunt, "The New KKK," *Common Sense* (November–December 1986): 32–38. Reprinted with permission.

7. This and the immediately following sketches are based on W. Joseph Campbell, "U.S. Is Proving Infertile Ground for Terrorism," *Hartford Courant*, 3 August 1986, p. 1. Reprinted with permission.

8. See "FBI Analysis of Terrorist Incidents in the United States, 1986," a report prepared by the Terrorist Research and Analytical Center, Terrorism Section, Criminal Investigation Division, Federal Bureau of Investigation, Washington, D.C., p. 22.

9. That "Declaration of War," dated November 25, 1984, states in part that "we no longer consider the regime in Washington to be a valid and lawful representative of all Aryans."

10. For example, the rules say that "any member of the Congress of the United States or their counterparts in Canada who introduce legislation which is harmful to us or the people for whom we fight will be regarded as combatants."

11. Campbell, "U.S. Is Proving Infertile Ground."

12. Ibid.

13. See "U.S. Indicts Five in Arms-Theft Plot," *Washington Post*, 9 January 1987, p. A-16.

14. Hunt, "The New KKK," 32.

15. Klanwatch Law Report, November 1986, p. 3.

16. Joseph W. Campbell, "U.S. Officials Say Attack by Terrorists Could Be Matter of Time," *Hartford Courant*, 3 August 1986, p. 10.

17. See " 'Born' in the U.S.," *World Press Review*, September 1985, p. 39.

18. *Christian Science Monitor*, 25 March 1986, p. 2.

19. In fact, the bill titled "The Prohibition against Training and Support for Terrorism Act of 1984" never made it out of committee. In 1986, however, language was added to section twenty-two U.S. Code 2712 by Public Law 99–399 which would give the secretary of state power to "impose controls" over "(1) Serving in or with the security forces of a designated foreign government. (2) Providing training or other technical services having a direct military, law enforcement, or intelligence application, to or for the security forces of a designated foreign government." This provision is aimed at stopping the type of assistance former CIA agent Edwin Wilson was charged with providing to Libya's Muammar Qaddafi.

20. Harold Liden, "U.S. Army Officer Wounded in Ambush in Puerto Rico," *Washington Post*, 7 November 1985, p. 17.

21. John Ward Anderson, "Terrorism Has Local, Federal Authorities Preparing for the Worst," *Washington Post*, 8 December 1985. Reprinted with permission.

22. *Atlanta Constitution*, 30 April 1984, p. 4.

23. *Washington Post*, 19 May 1985, p. 8.

24. *Hartford Courant*, 3 August 1986, p. 10.

25. See Ronald L. Soble, "9 Detainees Face Ouster," *Los Angeles Times*, 30 January 1987, p. 3.

26. *Washington Times*, 11 August 1986, p. B-8. Reprinted with permission.

27. Qaddafi's "Green Book" borrows the idea of Mao Zedong's "Little Red Book" to circulate the sayings of his revolution.

28. David Segal, "Millions for Murder," *Soldier of Fortune*, August 1986, p. 108.

29. See the *Washington Times*, 15 April 1985, p. B-8. A group called Nuke Watch was organized in early 1985 to set up surveillance operations around facilities where the U.S. government

produces, processes, and stores nuclear materials and prepares them for shipment. The group has set up a reporting network that passes the information around among members. The group has publicized its discoveries, including detailed descriptions of the vehicles that carry weapons, through an organization called Friends of the Earth. If it has not already happened, it is only a matter of time until these groups become the hosts for Soviet or other intelligence people who will happily use them as cover for espionage.

7
Getting Too Close to the Story

1. I chose Charles Glass as my model journalist who gets too close to the story and wrote this chapter in January 1987. The manuscript was sent to the publisher on May 4, 1987, and on June 17, Charles Glass was kidnapped by Hezballah near Beirut International Airport, having apparently ignored State Department warnings about travel to that city. He was released two months later.
2. Steve Daley, "Terrorism and the Press," *Chicago Tribune*, 11 May 1986, sec. 6, p. 6. Copyright 1987, Chicago Tribune Company, all rights reserved. Used with permission.
3. Ibid.
4. Katharine Graham, "Safeguarding Our Freedoms As We Cover Terrorist Acts," *Washington Post*, 20 April 1986, p. C-1. Reprinted with permission.
5. Ibid.
6. Teresa R. Colvin, "Terrorism and the Media," *Armed Forces Journal International* (June 1985): 128, 130–31.

8
The Dirty Little Wars

1. The Geneva conventions of 1949 were supplemented by the Geneva protocols of 1977, which included under the coverage of the conventions "armed conflicts in which peoples are fighting against colonial domination and alien occupation and against racist regimes in the exercise of their right of self-determination." That set of cases is too narrow to cover the field of modern insurgency. For example, it leaves out the fight against indigenous repression that is not racist. If we were to substitute *foreign* for *colonial* and *repressive* for *racist*, we would get much closer to defining insurgency.
2. N.C. Livingstone, "Fighting Terrorism and 'Dirty Little Wars' " in *Defense Planning for the 1990s*, ed. William A. Buckingham, Jr. (Washington, D.C.: National Defense University Press, 1984), 165–96.
3. Alistair Horne, *The Savage War of Peace* (New York: Penguin Books, 1979).
4. See Herbert Matthews, *The Cuban Story* (New York: George Braziller, 1961), 15–44, 231–79.
5. "Castro; A Historical Analysis of the Cuban Revolution," in *Revolutionary Thought in the 20th Century*, Ben Turok, ed. (London: Zed Press, 1980), 136–45.
6. For a very useful discussion of the dynamics of this case and several others, see Hans Bennendijk, "Authoritarian Regimes in Transition," *Washington Quarterly*, published by the Center for Strategic and International Studies, Georgetown University, (Spring 1987): 153–64.

7. In fact there were 17.5 tons of documents captured. See "Inside the Sandinista Regime: A Special Investigator's Perspective," U.S. Department of State, 1986.
8. For a thorough review of the Grenada experience, see Gregory Sandford, *The New Jewel Movement,* (Washington, D.C.: Center for the Study of Foreign Affairs, Foreign Service Institute, U.S. Department of State, 1985).

9
Global Issues: The Catalytic Factors

1. I am grateful to Bowman H. Miller for this evidence of linkage between German terrorism and the peace movement. The specific examples are from "Terrorism and Language: A Text-Based Analysis of the German Case," a speech he made at the 1986 International Studies Association annual convention in Anaheim, California. His speech later was published in *Terrorism* 9, no. 4 (Georgetown University Press, 1986): 373–407. Reprinted with permission.
2. Kevin Costelloe, "German Election," Associated Press, 17 January 1987.
3. These comments on peace activities in Italy were made to me by a senior middle-grade officer of the Italian Carabiniere during an interview on March 11, 1987.
4. Both quotations are comments made to me in a January 13, 1987, interview with Bowman H. Miller, an experienced analyst of German affairs and a German linguist in the Bureau of Intelligence and Research, U.S. Department of State. Printed with permission.
5. See the Associated Press review of the results of U.S.A. for Africa, January 6, 1987. Reprinted with permission.
6. I wish to thank Mr. John Sewell, President of the Overseas Development Council, Washington, D.C., and Mr. Thomas W. Wilson, a Washington, D.C.-based writer and consultant on food, the environment, and the quality of life, for contributing through their lectures at the National Defense University to my understanding of these qualities of the global issues.
7. This discussion is based on two lectures I delivered to the students of the National War College as part of their International Studies Program in the academic years 1981–82 and 1982–83.
8. Patrick Burns, "Winning the Battle, Losing the War," *The World and I* (January 1987): 71–72.
9. Ibid.
10. The data used here are contained in an unpublished report by Thomas A. Robertson, "Central America: Land, People, and Economies in Transition." Data used for comparisons are for 1982 and earlier.
11. I am grateful to a very talented and articulate consular officer of the U.S. Department of State, Sandy Voglegesang, who identified many of these quotations for use in her own writing and speaking on human rights issues.
12. Cyrus W. Vance, "Human Rights and Foreign Policy," The Department of State Bulletin, vol. LXXVI, no. 1978, May 23, 1977, p. 505.
13. Frederico Branco, "Terrorism: A Worldwide Trend," *World Press Review* (September 1985): vol. 32, no. 9, 35.
14. Thomas Powers, *Diana: The Making of a Terrorist* (Boston: Houghton Mifflin Company, 1971).

15. Jeffrey Herf, "War, Peace, and the Intellectuals; The West German Peace Movement," *International Security* (Spring 1986): vol. 10, no. 4, 172–200.

10
The Matter of Legitimacy

1. Herbert Matthews, *The Cuban Story* (New York: George Braziller, 1961).
2. Earl T. Smith, *The Fourth Floor* (New York: Random House, 1962).
3. See Associated Press wire service report datelined Manila, Philippines, 6 January 1987.
4. Martha Crenshaw, ed., *Terrorism, Legitimacy and Power; The Consequences of Political Violence,* (Middletown, Conn.: Wesleyan University Press, 1983), chap. 1.

11
Taking Terrorism Too Seriously

1. The United States, Japan, Britain, France, West Germany, Italy, and Canada.
2. Harold Evans, "When Friends Fall Out," *U.S. News & World Report*, 28 April 1986, p. 82.
3. John Boykin, "With a Small Stick Loudly," *Stanford Magazine*, Winter 1986, 43–46.
4. Robin Knight, "A New Kind of Terrorism Rattles Western Europe," *U.S. News & World Report*, 25 February 1985, p. 34.
5. Robert J. McCartney, "Europeans Rebuff Britain on Sanctions against Syria," *Washington Post*, 28 October 1986, p. A-1.
6. Andrew Borowiec, "Europeans Urge New Approaches to Terror," *Washington Times*, 11 September 1986, p. 6-A.
7. Neil C. Livingstone, and Terrell E. Arnold, *Fighting Back: Winning the War against Terrorism* (Lexington, Mass.: Lexington Books, 1986), chap. 16.
8. See the Associated Press, Colombo, Sri Lanka, in *Northern Virginia Daily*, 24 April 1987, p. 3.
9. Third World critics are likely to agree on this point as well. See Frederico Branco, "Terrorism: A Worldwide Trend," *World Press Review* (September 1985): vol. 32, no. 9, 35.
10. Claire Sterling, *The Terror Network* (New York: Holt, Rinehart & Winston, 1981).
11. Ray S. Cline and Yonah Alexander, *Terrorism: The Soviet Connection* (New York: Crane, Russak, 1984).
12. James Adams, *The Financing of Terror* (New York: Simon and Schuster, 1986).

12
The Violence Formula

1. See N. Tinbergen, "On War and Peace in Animals and Man," cited in José M.R. Delgado, "The Psychophysiology of Freedom," *Political Psychology* (June 1983): vol. 4, no. 2, 356.
2. Jeffrey Herf, "War, Peace, and the Intellectuals; The West German Peace Movement," *International Security* (Spring 1986): 180.
3. "CBS Evening News," 1 January 1987.
4. Joseph V. Montville, "Nationalism, Sectarianism and Political Separatist Minorities: Aggression and Defense Behaviors of Threatened and Separatist Minorities," unpublished manuscript.

5. Patrick Burns, "Winning the Battle, Losing the War," *World and I*, Vol. 2, No. 1, January 1987, pp. 71–78.

6. I agree with Dr. David Long, Middle East analyst in the State Department Office of Counterterrorism, that the basic theoretical literature on this subject from the 1960s and 1970s is better than recent writings. The primary reason is that terrorism tends to be viewed by those earlier writers in a broad context of low-level conflict and not as a phenomenon unto itself.

7. See Ted Robert Gurr, *Why Men Rebel* (Princeton: Princeton University Press, 1970), chap. 2, for a discussion of the concept of relative deprivation.

8. Ibid., p. 37.

9. This was her own statement of the conclusion, which she gave on an ABC special, "Protest in the Vietnam Era," March 3.

10. This tendency to escalate both expectations and the intensity of protest is outlined very well in Gurr, *Why Men Rebel*, 49–56.

11. I first heard this description of the demise of SDS from Carl Oglesby when he lectured to a class I attended at the Kennedy School of Government, Harvard University, in July 1981. During the writing of this chapter I talked with Oglesby for about an hour on the telephone.

12. See the definition of *insurgency* used in chap. 1.

13. N. Tinbergen, op. cit.

Index

About the Author

T ERRELL E. ARNOLD is a former senior officer of the U.S. Foreign Service who has studied and worked for the past thirty years on foreign affairs. Specific assignments enabled him to get well acquainted with the people, living conditions, political processes, and leading issues in more than thirty countries of Africa, the Middle East, Latin America, Asia, and Europe. He began to study carefully the conflict issues that led to this book while on assignment in the Philippines during 1971–76, a time of political upheaval which led to martial law in that country. In the succeeding three years he evaluated U.S. diplomatic missions, policies, and programs in twenty-four countries, in the process expanding his understanding of the sources of violence and the consequences of specific responses to it. In Brazil during 1978–80, as U.S. Consul General in Sao Paulo, the author became deeply interested in the extremes of Brazilian society and the responses of its hard line right military and business leaders as well as those of an activist and liberal clergy and the media. Since his return to the United States in late 1980, he has served as Chairman of the Department of International Studies of the National War College; as Deputy Director of the Office of Counterterrorism in the Department of State; and as a consultant to the Vice President's Task Force on Combatting Terrorism. He is now a consultant to the Department of State on counterterrorism, a consultant to private firms on security and crisis management, and a writer and lecturer on terrorism and other forms of political violence. He is coauthor and editor of *Fighting Back: Winning the War Against Terrorism,* and he is coauthor of a high school textbook titled *Terrorism: The New Warfare.*